A Pr

A Princess Remembers

The Memoirs of the Maharani of Jaipur

by Gayatri Devi of Jaipur
and
Santha Rama Rau

TARANG PAPERBACKS

A PRINCESS REMEMBERS — The Memoirs of the Maharani of Jaipur

By Gayatri Devi of Jaipur and Santha Rama Rau

First published by Weidenfeld and Nicolson, 11 St John's Hill, London SWII, simultaneously with J.B. Lippincott Company, Philadelphia and New York.

Photographs on pages 115 and 236: Lenare Ltd.
Photograph on page 140: The Statesman Ltd., India.
Photographs on pages 159 (top) and 222: Kulwant Roy, Delhi.
Photograph on page 272: UPI.
Photograph on page 273: Baldev TIME Magazine, © Time Inc.

TARANG PAPERBACKS
a division of
Vikas Publishing House Pvt Ltd
Regd. Office: 5 Ansari Road, New Delhi 110002
H.O.: **Vikas House, 20/4 Industrial Area, Sahibabad 201010**
Distt. Ghaziabad, U.P. (India)

Fifth Indian Edition, 1984

ISBN 0-7069-2581-5

Printed at Jupiter Offset Press, Shahdara, Delhi (India)

To the people of Cooch Behar and Jai

Contents

List of Illustrations

Part One

Chapter 1

A Visit to Baroda

DURING OUR CHILDHOOD, our family often journeyed the two thousand miles from our home, the palace in Cooch Behar State, tucked into the north-east corner of India, right across the country to my grandparents' palace in the state of Baroda, on the shores of the Arabian Sea. All five of us children had watched with excited anticipation the packing of mountains of luggage. We seemed to be preparing for the most unlikely extremes of heat and cold, not to mention more predictable occasions such as a state visit or a horse show. On the day of our departure the station was a bedlam, what with all the luggage and staff that accompanied us wherever we went. But by the time we arrived everything was checked and on board, thanks to the efforts of our well-trained staff.

Nonetheless, my mother invariably had a deluge of instructions and questions as soon as we arrived. Where was the dressing-case that she wanted in her compartment? she would ask, in her slightly husky, appealing voice. Well, then, unload the baggage and find it. What about her *puja* box, which contained the incenses and powders necessary for the performance of her morning prayers? Ah, there it was. Fortunately, that meant that no one need hurry back to the palace to fetch it.

When she did actually leave, telegrams were sent in all directions: PLEASE SEND MY GOLD TONGUE-SCRAPER, or, HAVE LEFT MY SPOON AND LITTLE ONYX BELL BEHIND, or, IN THE LEFT-HAND CUPBOARD IN THE THIRD DRAWER DOWN YOU'LL FIND MY GREEN SILK DRESSING-GOWN. Then came the supplementaries: NOT THE DARK GREEN, THE LIGHT GREEN, or, IN THAT CASE LOOK IN THE DRESSING-ROOM.

Anyway, once we got started, those week-long journeys were among the most cherished memories of my childhood. As a child it seemed to me that we occupied the whole train. We had at least three four-berth first-class compartments. My mother, elder sister, and a friend or relation occupied one; my younger sister, a governess, and myself were in another; my two brothers and their companion with an aide in another. Then the aides and secretaries would have a couple of second-class compartments, while the maids, valets, and butlers travelled third class.

In the twenties, a train trip by even the most plain-living Indian was reminiscent of a Bedouin migration, for everything in the way of bedding, food, and eating utensils had to be taken along. In those days most Indian trains had no dining-cars and did not provide sheets, blankets, pillows, or towels, although there were proper bathrooms where you could take a shower. We always travelled with our personal servants to cope with the daily necessities of living on the long journey to Baroda.

First there was the overnight trip from Cooch Behar to Calcutta, and we broke our journey for a couple of days in our house there. Then we set off again for the longest part of the trip. The cooks prepared "tiffin-carriers," a number of pans, each holding different curries, rice, lentils, curds, and sweets. The pans fitted into each other, and a metal brace held them all together so that you could carry in one hand a metal tower filled with food. But those tiffin-carriers were intended to supply us with only our first meal on the train. From then on we were in the hands of a chain of railway caterers. You could give your order to the railway man at one stop and know that instructions would be wired ahead to the next stop and that your meal would be served, on the thick railway crockery, as soon as the train came into the station. More often than not we hadn't finished before the train left the station—but that didn't matter. Another waiter would be ready to pick up empty containers, glasses, cutlery, and plates at any further stop that the train made.

For us children the excitement of travelling across India by train was not so much in the ingenious arrangements for meals and serv-

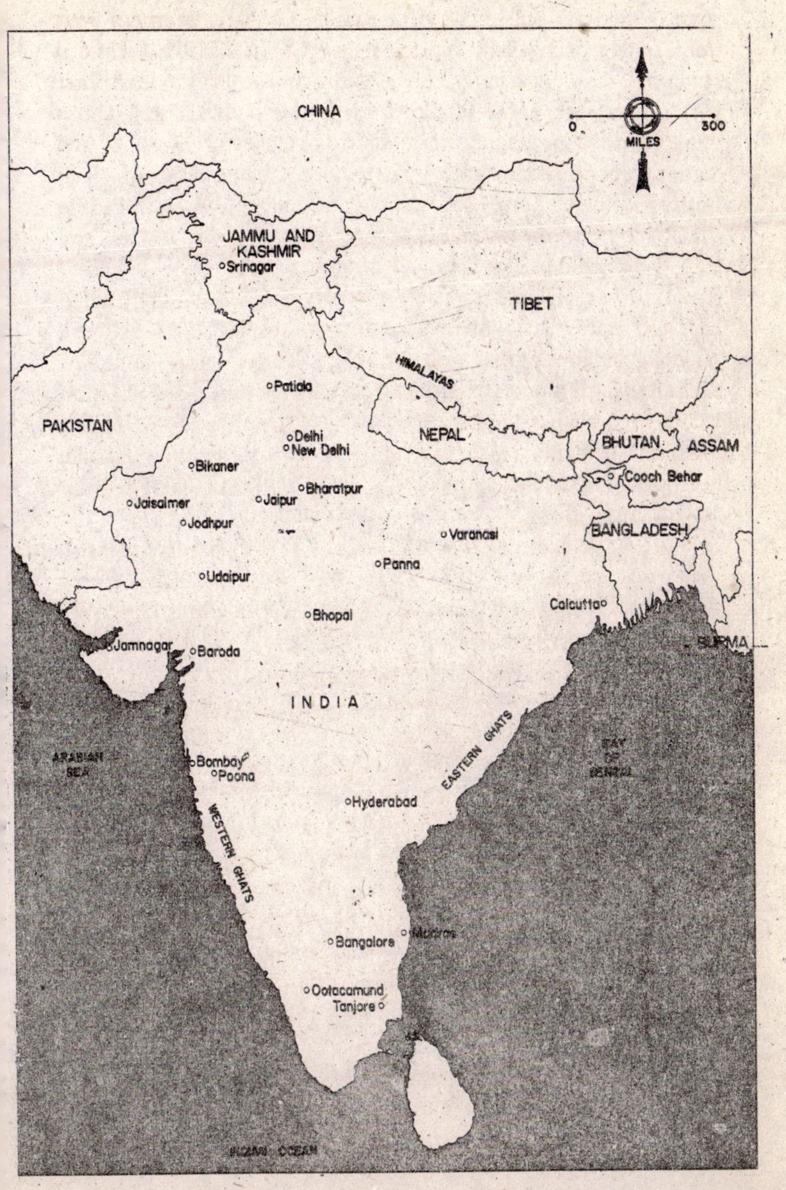
CHINA
0
300
MILES
JAMMU AND
KASHMIR
Srinagar
TIBET
HIMALAYAS
Patiala
PAKISTAN
Delhi
New Delhi
NEPAL
BHUTAN
ASSAM
Bikaner
Cooch Behar
Bharatpur
Jaipur
Jaisalmer
Jodhpur
BANGLADESH
Varanasi
Panna
Udaipur
Calcutta
Bhopal
Jamnagar
Baroda
INDIA
EASTERN GHATS
ARABIAN
SEA
Bombay
Poona
Hyderabad
WESTERN GHATS
Bangalore
Ootacamund
Tanjore

ice as in the atmosphere of the station platforms themselves. As soon as the train pulled in to any station, our carriage windows were immediately besieged by vendors of sweets, fruit, hot tea, and—my favourites—by men selling the charming, funny, painted wooden toys that I have seen nowhere except on Indian station platforms: elephants with their trunks raised to trumpet, lacquered in grey and scarlet, caparisoned in gold with floral designs picked out in contrasting colours; horses decked out as though for a bridegroom; camels, cheetahs, tigers, and dozens of others, all stiff and delightful, with wide, painted eyes and endearing, coquettish smiles. I wanted them all, but my mother said, "Nonsense, nonsense! You children have too many toys as it is." But she could never resist bargaining, so she had a lovely time with the fruit-, flower-, and sweets-vendors, and afterwards our compartment was filled with clinging tropical scents from all her purchases. I don't really know whether she was as good a bargainer as she thought—she was, by nature, very generous—and the vendors always went away looking appropriately bereaved, although with a secret air of satisfaction.

In any case, it didn't matter. All of us had the fun of chasing each other about the platforms, and when the train stayed in a station for an hour or more, we ate in the railway dining-room, ordering what we used to call "railway curry," designed to offend no palate—no beef, forbidden to Hindus; no pork, forbidden to Muslims; so, inevitably, lamb or chicken curries and vegetables. Railway curry therefore pleased nobody. Long before the train was due to leave we were summoned by our aides or governess or tutor, telling us to hurry, not to dawdle over our meal in the station restaurant; the train was leaving in five minutes. Of course it didn't, and we soon learned to trust the railway personnel, who let us loiter till the last possible moment before bustling us back to our compartments.

Finally we would arrive in Baroda to be met at the station by a fleet of Baroda State cars and driven to Laxmi Vilas, the Baroda Palace and my mother's girlhood home. It is an enormous building, the work of the same architect who built our own palace in Cooch Behar in the mid-nineteenth century. In Baroda, he had adopted what

I believe architects describe as the "Indo-Saracenic" style. Whatever one calls it, it is certainly imposing. Marble verandas with scalloped arches supported by groups of slender pillars bordered the building. Impressive façades were topped by onion-shaped domes. Outside the main entrance were palm trees standing like sentries along the edges of perfectly kept lawns that were watered daily. Tall and rather municipal-looking street lights with spherical bulbs illuminated the grand approach. And always on duty were the splendid household guards, dressed in white breeches with dark blue jackets and black top-boots. Because we were the grandchildren of the Maharaja, the ruler of the state, every time we went in or out of the front gate they played the Baroda anthem.

Inside, the palace was a strange blend of styles, partly Victorian, partly traditional Indian, with here and there a touch of antique English or French. There were courtyards with little pools surrounded by ferns and palms. Persian carpets flowed down interminable corridors. The halls were filled with displays of shields, swords, and armouries of spears. The sitting-rooms overflowed with French furniture, with photographs in silver frames, with ornaments and knick-knacks on occasional tables. The palace also contained a gymnasium and a dispensary. Two doctors were permanently in residence, and one of them used to travel with my grandfather wherever he went.

Throughout the palace silent formality reigned, and there always seemed to be a number of anonymous, mysterious figures around—two or three sitting in every room. They must have had some proper place in the design of things, but we children never found out who they were or what they were doing. Waiting for an audience with our grandfather? Visiting from some other princely state? Guarding the many precious objects that were scattered throughout the palace? True to our training, we knew that we must pay our respects to our elders, so we may well have folded our hands in a *namaskar*, the traditional Indian greeting, or obeisance, to maidservants and companions as well as to distinguished guests.

In sharp contrast to our own decorous behaviour and the general standard of proper courtesy in the palace were the huge long-tailed monkeys which roamed everywhere. They were easily aroused to anger and would often follow us down the passages, chattering and baring their teeth in a most terrifying manner.

As with all old Indian palaces and family residences, our grandparents' home was divided into two parts, and each of them had its separate entrance. This tradition of special zenana quarters for the women, and their keeping of purdah, literally "a curtain," to shield them from the eyes of any men other than their husband or the male members of their immediate family, was introduced into India at the time of the Muslim invasions during the twelfth century. At first only Muslims kept these customs, but later, during the rule of the Mogul emperors of India, which lasted from the sixteenth century until the Indian Mutiny of 1857 when the British took over sovereign command, most of the princely states of India as well as the families of the nobles and the upper classes adopted a number of Muslim customs ranging from styles of architecture to a rich and varied cuisine. Among these borrowings was the tradition of keeping their womenfolk carefully segregated from the view of outside eyes.

In Baroda the full tradition of purdah no longer existed; both my grandparents were too liberal to allow it. Strict purdah would have required the women to stay entirely within the zenana quarters and, if they had any occasion to venture outside, to travel well chaperoned, only in curtained or shaded vehicles. But my grandparents treated the custom relatively loosely—women could go about fairly freely as long as they were chaperoned and had nothing to do with men outside their family circle. If, for instance, there was a cheetah hunt or a polo match, the ladies would all go together, separately from the men. They didn't have to be veiled; they just stayed on their side of the grounds and the men stayed on the opposite side. For us children, there were no restrictions at all. We wandered freely all over the palace, even to the billiard-room, which in Edwardian days was considered forbidden territory to any female.

My grandmother, a formidable lady, had grown up totally accepting the idea of purdah. Following the custom of her time and the tradition of her family, she had, through her early years, observed the strictest purdah, never appearing in public, and in private only before women, close male relatives, and her husband. When she was only fourteen, a marriage was arranged for her to the ruler of Baroda. Her family, like his, was Maratha, members of the Kshatriya caste, which included many warriors and rulers. Like other Indian communities, Marathas traditionally married among themselves. She was, besides, of the right noble background, and he, after the untimely death of his first wife, the Princess of Tanjore, wanted to marry again.

My grandfather, well ahead of his time in many of his attitudes and actions, hired tutors for my grandmother, first to teach her to read and write (she was illiterate when she was married), then to expand her education. Later still, he encouraged her to free herself from suffocating Indian traditions and to pursue a role in public life. It was owing to his liberal views that my grandmother emerged as an important leader in the women's movement in India. She became the president of the All-India Women's Conference, the largest women's organization in the world and one which concerns itself with women's rights as well as with the spread of education and the loosening of the constricting ties of orthodox Indian society on its women. She was not just a figure-head in this important office but a very effective spokeswoman for the emancipation of Indian women. Eventually she even wrote a book, now a standard reference work, on the position of Indian women in their society. After all, she could draw amply on her own experience, first as a sheltered, obedient daughter of a conservative family and later as a free and progressive wife.

But it wasn't for her—or for any of us, her three granddaughters or our mother—a total transformation. Within the family in the Baroda Palace she still retained much of the conventional manners and the severe sense of propriety of all upper-class Indian households. All of us always touched her feet as a sign of respect when we first arrived in Baroda, again before we left, and also on all ceremonial occasions. (This custom, still observed in most Hindu families, applied not only to our grandmother but to all close relatives who were our seniors, even brothers, sisters, and cousins who might be just a few months older.)

It was at public functions that my grandparents made it most clear that they had more or less dispensed with the rules of purdah, for they always appeared together. Although they still maintained separate kitchens and separate household staffs, my grandfather came to take his meals with the rest of us, and with whatever visitors happened to be staying in Baroda, in my grandmother's dining-room. There she served the most marvellous food in the Indian way, on *thals*, round silver trays loaded with small matching silver bowls containing quantities of rice pilau, meat, fish and vegetable curries, lentils, pickles, chutneys, and sweets. She was a great gourmet and the food from her kitchen was delicious, whether it was the Indian chef who was presiding or, when she was unsure of the tastes of foreign visitors, the cook for English food who was in charge. She spent endless time and trouble consulting with her cooks, planning menus to suit the different guests she invited. It was dangerous to be even faintly appreciative of any dish, for if you took a second helping, she noticed and thrust a third and a fourth upon you, saying, "Come on, come on, you know you like this." Her kitchen was particularly well known for the marvellous pickles it produced and for the huge, succulent prawns from the estuary. Only when there were a large number of outside guests, and on ceremonial occasions like my grandfather's Diamond Jubilee, were meals served from his kitchen and in the banqueting hall on his side of the palace.

On religious and ceremonial occasions, durbars were held in his great audience hall. These were very elaborate affairs, something like holding court. The nobility and other important families came formally to offer their allegiance to their rulers—usually a token of a single gold coin.

Often we went duck shooting, sometimes we watched the falconing, and then there were the special thrills of elephant fights and, better yet, the tense and gripping cheetah hunts, a speciality of Baroda, when carefully trained cheetahs, hooded and chained, were taken out to the scrub land in shooting-brakes. There they were unhooded and let loose into a herd of black buck. With foot full down on the accelerator, one could just manage to keep pace with the astonishing speed of the animals during the chase.

A family picture taken at Baroda. Ma is on her father's right.

My own favourite entertainment as a child came from the relatively tame performances of my grandfather's trained parrots. They used to ride tiny silver bicycles, drive little silver cars, walk tightropes, and enact a variety of dramatic scenes. I remember one in particular in which a parrot was run over by a car, examined by a parrot doctor, and finally carried off on a stretcher by parrot bearers. The grand climax of their performance was always a salute fired on a tiny silver cannon. It made the most amazing noise for a miniature weapon, and the parrots were the only ones to remain unperturbed.

While my grandmother approved of all these innocent diversions for the children, she wanted us to retain the traditional skills of Indian girls. She wanted us, for instance, to learn how to cook proper Maratha food. My sisters, Ila and Menaka, showed talent and profited by the lessons, while I never seemed able to grasp even the rudiments of cooking.

Because almost every princely Indian family put strong emphasis on sports—and also because we ourselves were sports-mad—we used to get up at daybreak and go riding. By the time we returned, my grandmother's side of the palace was already bustling with activity, with maids preparing for the day, women waiting for an audience, and countless arrangements being made. We used to go in to say our required "Good morning" to her before we went to our rooms to settle down to lessons with our tutors. The floors of her apartments were covered, in the traditional Indian fashion, with vast white cloths. We had to take off our shoes before entering, and everyone except my grandmother sat on the floor.

I remember her from those days as an admirable, remarkable, and somewhat terrifying woman. She must have been beautiful when she was young. Even to my childish eyes, at that time, she was still handsome and immensely dignified. She wasn't tall, though she gave the impression of height partly because her manner was so very regal. But she had a nice sour sense of humour.

My grandfather was an impressive though kindly figure in our lives, and I remember how his eyes were always laughing. We often took our morning ride with him on the four-mile bridle-path around the Baroda Palace grounds. It was difficult to keep up with him because he liked strenuous exercise and had his favourite horse specially trained to trot very fast.

When we returned to the palace he would leave us and spend the rest of the morning dealing with work that he lumped under the comprehensive heading of "matters of state." Though I didn't know the details at the time, the ruler of an Indian princely state had important functions to fulfil and was a real sovereign to his people. The British, as they gradually took over the major role in India during the nineteenth century, made varying agreements with the different princes defining the division of responsibilities, although much was also left to evolving custom. One major point of all the agreements was that the princes could have relations with foreign powers only through the British. Each of the more important states—and Baroda was one of the most important—had a British Resident who was the voice of the British Government of India. But the states had their own laws, their own courts of justice, their own taxes, and in many cases their own military forces, so that the people of each state looked towards the prince, and not towards anyone else, as the real governmental authority in their lives. My grandfather had, therefore, to confer with his ministers (who were responsible only to him) and to decide many things that affected the lives of millions of people.

I knew him, however, not as a statesman but as a man and a grandfather. One conversation with him lives clearly in my memory. I had gone to say good night to him. He was, as always at that time of day, at the billiard table. He stopped his game and said, in a friendly way, "Ah, I see you're off to bed. I hope you have a good sleep."

I explained to him that there was no question of sleep for some time to come as I had to think about all that had happened during the day.

"No, no," he said, gently but emphatically. "If you go to bed, you should sleep. If you are reading, you should read. If you are eating, you should eat. And if you are thinking, then you should think. Never mix the different activities. No good ever comes of it, and what's more, you can't enjoy—neither can you profit from—any of them."

Then, because he was playing billiards, he turned back to the table and gave the game his undivided attention once more. He lived by the clock all his life and did everything in strict order: up at sunrise, walk or ride, work until lunch, brief rest, work until tea, recreation, evening work, supper, reading. It had been the same for fifty years.

My grandfather was known as the Gaekwar of Baroda, Gaekwar being both a family name and a title. Most of the Indian princes had the hereditary titles of Maharaja ("Great King") or Raja (simply, "Ruler," or "King"), depending on the size, importance, and history of their states. I always knew that my grandfather was a special person but it was only years later, when I knew the full range of his background and accomplishments, that I realized what an extraordinary man he was.

He had spent the first twelve years of his life in a village about two hundred miles south of Baroda City. His father, a distant relative of the ruling family, was village headman and earned only a modest living from farming. However, when the previous ruler of Baroda was deposed by the British for misrule, someone from the family had to be chosen as a successor. My grandfather, along with one of his brothers and a cousin, was brought to the capital of the state and presented to the Dowager Maharani of Baroda, the widow of the deposed ruler's father. She was asked by the British to select one of the boys to be the new ruler, and her choice fell upon my grandfather.

Since he had been brought up in a village where a sound practical grasp of farming was considered the only necessary knowledge, he could neither read nor write, so the six years following his arrival at the palace were devoted exclusively to his education, and habits were instilled that lasted all his life. He always rose at six o'clock and went to bed at ten, and with the exception of two hours' riding (considered an essential princely skill), one hour of games of various kinds suitable to his rank, and breaks for meals, the entire day was devoted to work. He learned to read and write in four languages:

Marathi, the language of his princely ancestors; Gujarati, the language of the bulk of the population in Baroda; Urdu, the language of his Muslim subjects, employing the Arabic script; and, of course, English. India was still the "brightest jewel" in the British imperial crown, so he had to study English history as well as Indian; beyond that, he received intensive tuition in arithmetic, geography, chemistry, political economy, philosophy, Sanskrit, and something that his tutor called "conversations on given subjects," which was, I suppose, designed to fill any gaps in the small-talk of royal social life.

It is astonishing, when I think back on it, that these two people, brought up in such a tradition-ridden atmosphere, married in the customary way by an arrangement between their elders, should have become leaders of change and reform, encouraging new and more liberal ideas in an orthodox society. My grandfather devoted his life to modernizing the state of Baroda, building schools, colleges, libraries, and an outstanding museum and providing an admirable and just administration. He took an enthusiastic interest in everything from commissioning a special translation of *Alice in Wonderland* into Marathi to working for Hindu women's emancipation, even to the point of introducing the revolutionary concept of divorce in Baroda. (My mother used to tease my grandmother, undaunted by her rectitude, about having a husband who was so warm an advocate of divorce. My grandmother tried to be dignified and huffy but was soon overcome by that wonderful silent laugh of hers, her face contorted, her body shaking like a jelly, and not a sound out of her mouth.)

My grandfather felt particularly strongly about the inequalities and abuses that had evolved in Indian society and were protected by the caste system. Hindus are born into one of four castes, which are, in descending order, the Brahmins (originally the scholars and priests), the Kshatriyas (warriors and often, as a result of skill in conquest or a reward for success, rulers and large landowners), Vaisyas (usually businessmen, traders, artisans), and Sudras (usually the peasants, though all peasants are not Sudras). In a separate group were those Hindus who were excluded from the ordinary social and religious privileges of Hinduism and were known as Untouchables.

They performed the most menial tasks—sweeping streets, cleaning latrines—and thus were thought to carry pollution to caste Hindus.

Mahatma Gandhi, in the emotional battle for the acceptance of the Untouchables by Hindu society, acted as their champion, changing their name to Harijans (Loved Ones of God) and insisting that they be allowed access to temples from which they had always been excluded. Their legal battles were fought for them by one of the most brilliant men in Indian politics, Dr. Bhimrao Ramji Ambedkar, himself a Harijan. Dr. Ambedkar was one of my grandfather's special protégés, encouraged and educated by him when he was a penniless boy. After his long crusade for the advancement of his community, Dr. Ambedkar was appointed chairman of the committee that drafted the Constitution of free India.

My grandmother played a strong though less conspicuous part in the life of Baroda State. I can see her so plainly in the mornings, coping with her personal affairs—choosing saris, making up her mind about lengths of silk or cloth of gold that her maids held up, listening attentively to the cooks with menus for the day, giving orders to the tailor, asking about domestic details; in short, supervising the running of an enormous household—and still giving her alert attention to the grievances and complaints of any of her women subjects, whether it was the illness of a child or a dispute in a family about the inheritance of land.

This was all part of a maharani's duty, and so were the more ceremonial occasions, as when she presided over formal durbars in the women's apartments of the Baroda Palace. I especially remember the first one I saw, her birthday durbar. All the wives and womenfolk of the nobility and the great landowners were assembled in their richest clothes and jewellery to pay homage to my grandmother. She was seated on a *gaddi*, a cushioned throne, and wore a sari made of rose-pink cloth of gold, draped in the Maratha way with a pleated train between the legs.

Along with her dazzling sari, my grandmother wore all the traditional jewellery for this occasion, including heavy diamond anklets and a wealth of diamond rings on her fingers and toes. The noble ladies paid their respects to her with a formal folding of hands in a *namaskar* and offered her the traditional gold coin to signify their allegiance. At the end of the hall was a troupe of musicians and dancers from Tanjore in south India. Like many Indian princes, my grandfather maintained the troupe as palace retainers, and they always gave a performance of the classical south Indian dancing called *bharata natyam* at any important palace occasion. At such festive times, the family all ate off gold *thals*, while everyone else ate off silver. (This distinction always used to embarrass me.)

My mother, Princess Indira Gaekwar of Baroda, was the only daughter of these two extraordinary people. Because of their advanced views on education, she was one of the first Indian princesses to go to school and to graduate from Baroda College. She also accompanied her parents on their trips to England. One of the earliest stories I know about her tells how she and her four brothers, all quite small and dressed identically in white pyjama trousers and brocade jackets, with gold-embroidered caps, were taken to Buckingham Palace to be presented to Queen Victoria. As they stood before her, the elderly Queen-Empress asked which one was the little girl. Five pairs of dark brown eyes stared back at her, and then, because they all enjoyed fooling grown-ups, one of the boys stepped forward. But they underestimated Queen Victoria, who, sensing that something was wrong, walked around to the back of the row of solemn children, and there a long black pigtail betrayed my mother.

It is difficult to describe my mother without slipping into unconvincing superlatives. She was, quite simply, the most beautiful and exciting woman any of us knew. Even now, when I have travelled widely and have met many famous beauties from all levels of society, she remains in my memory as an unparalleled combination of wit, warmth, and exquisite looks. She was photographed and painted many times, but while those pictures show the physical charm—the enormous eyes, the lovely modelling of her face, the slightly drooping mouth that made you want to make her smile, the tiny fragile figure—none of them captures the electric vitality that made her the focus of attention wherever she went. Her own passionate interest and concern for others made her both special and

Ma with her mother, the Maharani of Baroda.

accessible to anybody. She was always called "Ma," not only by us but by friends and even by the peasants of Cooch Behar. As a child I was fascinated by her—what she said, what she did, what she wore. With her, nothing was ever dull and one felt that at any moment anything might happen.

She herself was oddly unaware of the impression she created, and this, I suppose, was due to her mother's fear, during her childhood, that she might become spoiled—an only daughter, adored by her father, loved and cherished by her brothers. If anyone commented favourably on my mother's looks, my grandmother would immediately counter the admiration with some deprecating comment like, "Her nose is too lumpy at the end—just look," or, "Her hair hasn't a trace of a curl to it."

My mother once told me that she had no idea that she was even passably good-looking until one day when her brothers were discussing some attractive girl they had met. Seeing their sister looking a bit dejected, one of them said, with true brotherly enthusiasm, "You know, you're not all that bad yourself."

For the first time she really *looked* at herself in the mirror and thought, Well, he may be right. I'm *not* all that bad.

Chapter 2

My Parents' Marriage

In 1910, when my mother was eighteen years old, my grandparents informed her that in the usual way they had arranged a marriage for her with the Maharaja Scindia of Gwalior. Gwalior was, like Baroda, one of the most important Maratha states in princely India. It was in central India, and the Maharaja, who was then about forty years old, was a friend of my grandfather's. He already had one wife, but she was childless and he badly wanted an heir. In 1909 he went to London for the season and there met my mother, whose beauty and vivacity were already making a considerable impact on Edwardian society. On his return to India he opened negotiations with my grandfather. Astrologers were consulted, horoscopes compared, auspicious dates discussed, and finally the betrothal was accepted.

My mother, high-spirited as she was, still acquiesced to this ordering of her life by her elders without rebellion or even protest. Arranged marriages were—indeed, still are—so accepted a part of Indian society that the idea of marrying for love is considered a rather dubious and risky Western idea, not to be trusted, especially in the hands of young people. Clearly parents know better what is right for their children, particularly in a matter as important as marriage, which shouldn't be founded on something as ephemeral and giddily unreasonable as romance. Consequently, my grandparents never consulted their daughter about her betrothal, but merely told her of the dynastically suitable match they had arranged for her. And then, as a matter of course, my grandmother started buying the trousseau and the linens and began collecting the wedding jewellery. I still have the linen she bought from Givan's Irish Linen Store, all beautifully embroidered with the initials "I.S." for Indira Scindia. Scindia was the family name of the Gwalior rulers, as Gaekwar was of the rulers of Baroda.

My mother told me that even before she met and fell in love with my father she was unhappy about the marriage to Gwalior. The Maharaja was a charming man, but he was over twenty years her senior and was known to be very conservative. She was afraid that after she had married him she would have to live the rest of her life shut up inside the great palace of Gwalior, in the most rigid and confining form of purdah, associating only with women and seeing no men at all except her husband. So complete would be her seclusion from male company that she would rarely, she was told, be allowed to see even her own brothers, to whom she was devoted. It is hardly surprising that to an educated, travelled girl of eighteen the prospect was uninviting. It was in this uncertain and unhappy frame of mind that she set out to accompany her parents to the great Delhi durbar of 1911, when princes and rulers from all over India came to offer formally their allegiance to the British Crown.

The Delhi durbar was, by all accounts, one of the most glittering and imposing pageants of the British Raj. It was held to crown King George V—the first British monarch to come to India—as King-Emperor, and to mark the transfer of the capital from Calcutta, which had been the choice of the East India Company, to Delhi, the traditional and historic capital of India. A huge amphitheatre had been specially built for the occasion and was filled with over ninety thousand people. Accompanied by their relatives and members of the nobility, all the Indian princes attended and sat in the inner circle wearing their ceremonial attire of brocades and cloth of gold, covered with their finest jewels, and carrying enamelled swords studded with precious stones. Each maharaja wore the most famous gems from his state treasury—the Maharaja of Patiala his diamonds, the Maharaja of Gwalior his pearl sash. Even my grandfather, who was renowned for his austerity, wore around his neck the magnificent Baroda pearls.

At the height of the durbar my grandfather was accused of insulting the King-Emperor by turning his back to the throne. The incident became headline news, with the London papers printing outraged accounts of Baroda's "sedition" and "disloyalty," accusing him of every kind of treason. In fact, all that had happened was that when he went up to the throne to offer his formal allegiance to the King, he did not know the correct procedure. For some reason he had been unable to attend the dress rehearsal the day before and had also failed to watch the prince ahead of him, the Nizam of Hyderabad. So, when it came to his turn, he walked up, bowed once, and then tried to back away from the throne. He could not remember where the exit was and, in looking around for someone to direct him, he appeared to turn his back on the King-Emperor. He should also, apparently, have bowed three times, not just once.

This absurd incident caused much ill feeling with the British, while my grandfather immediately became a hero of the Indian nationalists, whose movement for independence, or at least dominion status for India, was beginning to gain momentum. Years later, as children in Calcutta and Darjeeling, we would bask in reflected glory when our little playmates with political leanings would include the Gaekwar of Baroda among the first Indians to show a desire for Indian independence. But although my grandfather was an advocate of independence, he was far too courteous to have deliberately insulted the King-Emperor.

The durbar lasted several weeks, and during that time Delhi was the scene of constant festivities: polo matches, garden parties, ladies' purdah parties, and all kinds of formal and informal entertainment. New Delhi, apart from the government buildings, had not yet been completed, and everyone from the King-Emperor downwards lived in camps—but incredibly luxurious camps with enormous tents and marquees that were elegantly furnished and surrounded by beautiful gardens, lawns, and perfectly rolled drives. Each princely family had its own camp with its own retinue of courtiers, attendants, and servants, and there was much visiting between them. My mother had, during a brief spell at school in Eastbourne, met the young princesses of Cooch Behar, the sisters of the Maharaja. Now, in the festive atmosphere of the Delhi durbar, she spent more and more time in the Cooch Behar camp with them and their brothers. My grandparents were totally unaware that she and the Maharaja's younger brother were rapidly falling in love.

As the camps in Delhi broke up and the princely families went back to their states, my mother, without telling her parents, wrote a letter to the Maharaja of Gwalior saying that she did not want to marry him. She returned with her parents to Baroda, where preparations for the wedding were well advanced. Arches welcoming the bridegroom spanned the streets; arrangements had been made for accommodating hundreds of the Gwalior family members, friends, and retainers; feasts and entertainments had been planned—after all, my mother was the only Baroda princess, and she was to be given away in marriage in the very grandest style.

In the middle of all this excitement, my grandfather received a telegram from the Maharaja of Gwalior: WHAT DOES THE PRINCESS MEAN BY HER LETTER?

My mother was immediately summoned and confessed what she had done. My grandparents were thunderstruck. In India an engagement cannot be broken easily. It is considered almost as binding as a marriage, and the wedding ceremony itself is only the final stage in forming an alliance that is made at the time of the betrothal ceremony.

The impact of my mother's action was tremendous and widespread. It occasioned baffled speculation in Baroda and Gwalior, but, beyond that, the scandalized gossip throughout all the Indian princely states focused on the astonishing fact that an alliance between the two most important Maratha families was broken by the casual whim of a girl. Such a thing was unheard of. And for some nonsense about love at first sight? Impossible.

In all the uproar, the talk, the confused and conflicting stories, my mother's own feelings seem to have been ignored. In stern and appalled lectures from her mother she was made to feel so small, so despicable, so disloyal for having disgraced her own family and, so to speak, let the whole side down, that only the support and affection of her brothers gave her a sense of proportion about the affair and lent her the courage to stick to her guns. However, after a letter such as she had written, there was certainly no prospect of the marriage's ever taking place.

The Maharaja of Gwalior wrote a most understanding letter to my grandfather, saying that he bore no ill-will for what my mother had done, and I am glad to say that he did, in due course, find a second wife who bore him two children, named George and Mary after the British king and queen who were their godparents.

In Baroda, my mother's request that she be allowed to marry the Prince of Cooch Behar instead of the Maharaja of Gwalior met with stern opposition It was not simply that Cooch Behar was a smaller, less important state than Baroda, or that the Cooch Behar royal family were of a different caste and were not part of the proud Maratha clan. It was not even that the Prince was a younger son and would not, in the normal course of events, inherit the throne. My grandfather, in any case, did not attach much significance to such points. His objection was that the Cooch Behar family was Westernized in a way of which he strongly disapproved. They led a purely "social" life, mixing with Edwardian society and entertaining streams of Western guests, ranking from royalty downwards, at home in Cooch Behar. By 1911 they had a reputation in India for unorthodox and wild behaviour which was certainly not calculated to appeal to my austere Baroda grandfather.

All sorts of pressure was put on my mother to forget her infatuation. She was forbidden ever to see the Prince or to communicate with him, and she was even more carefully chaperoned than usual. But she had inherited my grandmother's independence and strength of character; besides, she was in love. For two years she managed to correspond with the Prince in secret and even eluded the watchfulness of her elders for occasional clandestine meetings, usually in London, where her parents spent most summers and where the Prince would follow her. In 1968, when I was going through my mother's papers after her death, I discovered some letters from this time. My father's are all addressed to a series of noms de plume such as "Mrs. Miele Brooke, Poste Restante, Fernhill, Ootacamund" (a mountain resort where my grandparents had a house) or "Mrs. Sylvia Workman." They are full of descriptions of the enticing life in Cooch

My father.

Behar and of the festivities of the winter in Calcutta, the spring in Darjeeling, the gaiety, the balls, the fancy-dress parties, the visits of polo teams, the cricket matches, and the big-game shoots. They would hardly have reassured my grandfather had he seen them.

The deadlock showed no signs of breaking. My mother continued to insist that she would marry my father or no one, while my grandparents remained equally unyielding in their opposition to any such mésalliance. Finally, in the spring of 1913, when my mother, with her parents, was in Bombay en route to England, the Prince of Cooch Behar was summoned to the palace there and received with rigid formality in the great durbar hall, with my grandfather seated with his Prime Minister on his left and the British Resident on his right, while my grandmother watched unseen from a screened gallery above. The Prince was then told in the firmest possible way that he would never, under any circumstances, be allowed to marry my mother and that he should put the idea out of his head forever. At the end of the interview he left the Bombay Palace feeling that the situation was hopeless.

But, in fact, my grandparents' resistance was nearing its end and the audience in Bombay marked their final stand. When they arrived in England, either my mother's continued defiance, or instinct, or rumours made them suspect that my mother was planning to run away. So, sadly, they decided that rather than face an even greater scandal they should withdraw their opposition. However, they refused, on a point of principle, to have any part in the wedding preparations.

They sent their daughter off to get married from the home of a friend of my grandfather's in London. One of his young sons later described the impact she had on their lives.

> I can well remember the sensation all this caused. Indians were rare in England and the saree was still strange enough to attract considerable attention. Indira Devi,* in any case, attracted more than attention for to describe her beauty as ravishing would by no means be using an overworked *cliché*. Reporters flocked to

* "Devi" literally means "goddess," but is often attached to any girl's name simply as a kind of honorific.

our home, endless photographs were taken and we small boys lived in a haze of reflected glory. The marriage was the big news of the season. Every illustrated paper gave it full-page treatment and for a long time we kept a thick file of cuttings over which we used nostalgically to pore.

Finally, in July 1913, my parents were married in London. My grandmother's English companion, a Miss Tottenham, and a lawyer acted *in loco parentis*. My grandfather sent them a telegram on the day of the wedding wishing them happiness, but from my grandmother there was not a word. My grandfather's only stipulation to my father was that, in the event of his becoming Maharaja of Cooch Behar, my mother should receive a personal allowance of one hundred thousand rupees.

My mother's last tearful appeal to my grandmother for her blessing and forgiveness had met with no response. But according to Miss Tottenham, as soon as my mother left the chamber my grandmother broke down and wept unrestrainedly. Still, she refused to bless my mother or to communicate with her for the next two years. It was not until just before my elder sister, Ila, was born in 1914, when my mother became very ill, that my grandmother relented. She re-established friendly contact in a characteristic way, by sending a Maratha cook to Cooch Behar to provide the special Baroda dishes that she was sure her daughter must be missing.

At almost exactly the same time that my parents' wedding took place, another romance in the Cooch Behar family was ending in tragedy. My father's elder brother, Raj Rajendra Narayan, the Maharaja of Cooch Behar, had fallen in love with the English actress Edna May, but his family had refused to grant him permission to marry her. Two years before, he had sworn that if they persisted in their opposition to his marriage, he would drink himself to death. This he proceeded to do, exclusively on champagne, and by 1913 he was very ill indeed. Three weeks after my parents were married, my Uncle Raj Rajendra Narayan died. My father, as the eldest of three surviving brothers, succeeded him as the Maharaja of Cooch Behar.

Chapter 3

Children of the New Maharaja

AT THE NEWS of my uncle's death, my parents had to cut short their honeymoon in Europe. They returned to India and went to "Woodlands," the Cooch Behar house in Calcutta, the capital of Bengal, the British-Indian province which adjoined their state. Ma used to tell us that when she first arrived at "Woodlands" and heard the eerie, long-drawn-out notes of conch shells being blown by palace retainers, she thought that this strange sound was some kind of dirge being played for my uncle's death. She later discovered that this was the traditional way of greeting a bride in Bengal.

After a brief stay in Calcutta, my parents travelled north to Cooch Behar, almost in the foothills of the Himalayas. The state which my father was destined to rule was once known as Koch Behar, "the abode of the Koch people." The origin of the Koch people is steeped in controversy. In ancient times, the territories of Cooch Behar and Bhutan were part of the great kingdom of Kamrup. When this kingdom broke up, a number of petty principalities were formed by independent rulers, and a fresh kingdom was then established by the Koches. Their kings claimed an ancient and divine parentage. The legend is that the god Shiva fell in love with the wife of the Koch chief, and the result of their intimacy was a boy named Biswa Singh. The more prosaic historical account relates that the kingdom was founded in 1510 by a chief named Chandan and that he was succeeded by his cousin, Biswa Singh. But both stories agree that Biswa Singh was a mighty conqueror, who brought under his rule the whole tract of land from the Karatoya River on the west to the Barnadi on the east.

Later kings continued this warlike tradition, conquered all the neighbouring countries to the east and the south, and even ventured to wage war against the daunting armies of the Mogul emperors who then ruled most of India. It was a splendid gesture but a rash one. In the years that followed, the kingdom of the Koches was gradually shorn of its outlying possessions, by the Moguls to the south and west and by Bhutan to the north, until only the modern state of Cooch Behar remained in the precarious possession of Biswa Singh's descendants.

In the late eighteenth century an event occurred which was to change the status of Cooch Behar entirely: The Bhutanese captured the reigning maharaja. His minister immediately appealed to the Governor of Bengal, Warren Hastings, for help, which was given, but only under stringent and far-reaching conditions.

India was not at this time under the direct authority of the British Crown. Most of the country was controlled by that curious mixture of government, trade, and military presence known as the East India Company. So the price of British help in releasing the Maharaja was the acceptance of a treaty with the East India Company. It bears the date 5 April 1773, and under its terms Cooch Behar acknowledged the protection of the Company and promised to make over half of its annual revenue. This amount was later fixed at 67,700 rupees. The following year, after Warren Hastings had managed, with the intervention of the Dalai Lama of Tibet, to conclude a treaty with Bhutan, the Maharaja was finally released.

The links between Cooch Behar and the British grew stronger and more diverse. Placed as it was geographically, Cooch Behar was constantly involved in the expansionist schemes and political intrigues of Bhutan, Sikkim, and Assam, which in their turn were involved with Nepal and Tibet. It was important for the British to have a foothold in this troubled and strategically important area, and when life in the state was further complicated by constant domestic dissensions, eventually, in 1788, a British Resident was appointed to keep order.

The presence of the British became established in Cooch Behar. Almost a century later, when my Cooch Behar grandfather came to the throne at the age of ten months, a British Commissioner was appointed to undertake direct management of the state during the ruler's minority. The British also took care of my grandfather's education. He showed great promise in his studies in India, and when he was sixteen his guardians wished to send him to England to benefit from what was to them unarguably the best education he could receive.

On this matter, however, they met with fierce opposition from the boy's mother and grandmother. They took it for granted that any young man turned loose in decadent Western society could come to no good. Worse than that, he would have to cross "the Black Waters," which would make him lose caste and defile him in the eyes of orthodox Hindus. After much persuasion, the palace ladies agreed to let him go, but only on condition that he get married before he went abroad. This, they felt, would protect him from the terrible temptations of European life and the designs of foreign women.

The British government officials, reluctantly accepting this ruling, were most anxious that he should marry a cultured girl who would be a help rather than a hindrance when he assumed his full responsibilities as maharaja. Consequently, under their auspices, he married an educated Bengali girl of liberal background, outside of royal descent but beautiful, charming, and in all ways suitable to be a maharani.

I never knew my Cooch Behar grandfather, for he had died long before I was born, but my grandmother, Suniti Devi, was a gentle and affectionate presence all through my childhood. Outside the state she worked diligently to encourage the emancipation of women in Bengal, but for some reason she did not attempt to put an end to purdah in Cooch Behar. Although she moved freely in her visits to Calcutta and other places in India, in Cooch Behar she lived in the zenana quarters, where none of the other women had even seen the front of the palace.

It was only a generation later, when my mother arrived in Cooch Behar in an open car, that purdah suddenly ended—except, of course, for the billiard-room.

After my father's succession to the throne, my parents settled down to a life divided between Cooch Behar, Calcutta, and Darjeeling, in the Himalayan foothills, and began raising a family. My sister Ila was born in Calcutta in 1914. Ila was followed a year later by my elder brother, who was born in Cooch Behar. There was great jubilation at his birth because the state now had an heir apparent. He was named Jagaddipendra Narayan, but my sister called him Bhaiya, which means brother, and the name stuck to him throughout his life. In 1918 my second brother, Indrajitendra Narayan, was born in Poona, the town in the hills of the Western Ghats to which the Bombay State government moved during the hot weather. My Baroda grandparents were also in Poona for the very popular racing season, and this was where the final reconciliation between them and my mother took place.

As soon as the Great War was over, my parents decided to take an extended holiday in Europe and sailed back to England with their three small children. Soon after their arrival in London, I was born, on 23 May 1919, at about eight o'clock in the morning. The time is important, because according to Indian tradition one of the first things that must be done after the birth of a child is to have the horoscope cast. The pundits had to make an adjustment in their calculations to allow for British summer time. I never learned what my horoscope foretold except that the most auspicious initial letter for my name was "G," so I was called Gayatri, which is a religious incantation of the highest order. But in the last days of her pregnancy my mother had been reading Rider Haggard's novel *She* and had already made up her mind that if I was a girl she would call me Ayesha, after the heroine of the book. It was only when some Indian friends came to call on her a few days after I was born that she was reminded in surprised tones that Ayesha was a Muslim name belonging to the Prophet Mohammed's ninth and favourite wife. By that time all my immediate family had got used to the name and fond of it, so, although Gayatri is my correct name, Ayesha remains the one my friends know me by. My parents' English staff further complicated the business by deciding that Gayatri was impossible for them to pronounce so, since I was born in May, they all called me Princess May. A year later my younger sister, Menaka, was born, bringing our number up to seven: my parents, two sons, and three daughters.

My childhood produced the usual crop of silly stories that become part of the shared memories of a family. Few of them are

Father and Ma with their children in Sussex.

Ayesha

Indrajit

Bhaiya

Ila

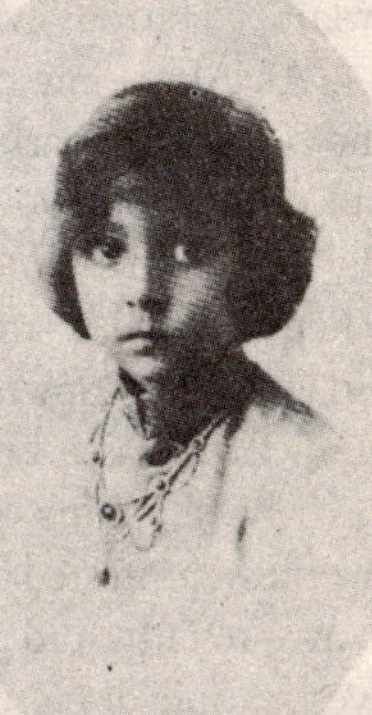

Menaka

worth repeating; anyway, I'm not sure which incidents I actually remember and which seem real and familiar only from constant retelling. My first clear recollections are of a house we rented one summer in the English countryside, and of my father sweeping up the gravel drive in his magnificent Rolls Royce. Later that year, when we moved to London, to a house just across the street from Harrods, I quickly discovered the way to slip out of the house to Harrods' toy department without being detected by our nurses or tutors. This wasn't, in fact, a very difficult feat, for my father had fallen ill with pneumonia and the attention of the whole household was concentrated on him. I was only three, and why the manager of Harrods, Mr. Jefferson, didn't send me straight back home again I shall never understand. On the contrary, standing deferentially in his tail-coat, he would accept my orders and take my instructions, imitated from my mother, to put my purchases down to "the account of Princess Gayatri Devi of Cooch Behar."

On the first occasion I ordered, as well as toys for myself, a colossal version of what the English call a cracker, a long paper cylinder which, when you pull it apart, makes a bang and releases all sorts of little prizes: paper hats, tiny tin charms, miniature cars, and so on. The cracker was for Bhaiya, whom I adored. For Ila, who used to tease me, I bought a package of pins. The whole performance was a child's dream come true, and after my initial success I went to Harrods every afternoon for the next few days.

An ADC, one of the several aides (usually young army officers) who make up part of any princely retinue, used to take us for walks when our governess was off duty and could not understand why I refused to move any farther than the store's front entrance. When he tried to make me walk on the Hyde Park side of Knightsbridge, I lay down on the pavement and screamed, attracting a crowd of passers-by who evidently suspected him of maltreating me. My shopping sprees were not discovered until our English governess protested to my mother that she was giving us far too many presents and that we would all be utterly spoiled. A little investigation disclosed the truth. I can still remember my mother's slightly hoarse, deceptively gentle voice saying into the telephone, "But *surely*, Mr. Jefferson, you didn't take Ayesha's orders seriously?"

Another of my earliest memories is of peering into the dining-room one evening and seeing the table sumptuously laden with gold, silver, crystal, and flowers, all ready for one of my parents' dinner parties. The food, on that occasion, was evidently going to be Indian, for I can never forget how Bhaiya, who had come in with me, handed me a shiny green thing which he said was a sweet and told me to eat it whole. It was my first chili, and when the burning pain seared my mouth, I screamed and screamed. Bhaiya, terrified that he would be scolded, held his hand over my mouth so that no one else would hear.

By this time my father's health was fast deteriorating, and my mother was naturally anxious to keep the house as quiet as possible. Bhaiya and Ila were old enough to be taking daily lessons with our first governesses, Miss Hobart and Miss Oliphant, but Indrajit, who was always very naughty, used to spend his days getting into one of a dozen different sorts of trouble. During our afternoon rests, he would unwind one of our father's turbans through his window at the top of the house and let it hang down into the street below, in the hope, he later explained, that some of the small boys there would climb up and play with him. One afternoon he had succeeded in drawing a small crowd and was trying to persuade someone to risk the ascent when one of the servants caught sight of the yards of brilliant silk billowing and streaming in front of the dining-room window.

Not surprisingly, after a number of such incidents, my mother felt that it was impossible to cope with a sick husband and five small children under the same roof, so arrangements were made for Indrajit, Menaka, and me to be sent back to India with Miss Oliphant, while Ila and Bhaiya stayed in London. But, characteristically, my mother changed her mind at the last moment and kept me with her. She felt that a house without any tiny children at all would be too dreary and depressing. Overhearing a remark of one of the servants, I repeated it importantly to Ma: "It's ridiculous to keep Princess May behind." Ma, who was well aware that I didn't know the meaning of the word "ridiculous," merely asked gently, "Who says it's ridiculous?" She always liked to know, and managed to find out in one way or another, exactly what was going on below stairs or in the nursery, what the mood of the staff was, what criticisms or approval were voiced.

I can hardly remember my father at all. I have a single mental picture of him standing in front of the fire in the drawing-room at Hans Place. He was wearing his dressing-gown and held a glass of whisky in his hand. He was very tall—nearly all the men in the Cooch Behar family are over six foot—and extremely handsome. He used to tease my mother, who was very small, saying that now she had introduced her "stocky Maratha blood" into the family, the Cooch Behar men would never be the same again. In later life, when my brothers had both grown to over six foot, I remember her saying how she wished our father were still alive to see that she had managed to produce two six-footers.

Until my father fell ill he had been a fine cricketer and polo-player as well as a talented musician who could go to concerts and then come back and play quite creditably, by ear, any of the pieces he had heard. Sadly, none of us inherited his musical gifts, though I'm told he did manage to teach me my first song, "K-K-K-Katy," which evidently required such extreme concentration that for a while I developed a stammer.

He was very fond of children, and in Cooch Behar he used to drive about the town in his car picking up boys and girls off the streets and taking them back to the palace. There he would teach them songs, laugh and joke with them, and give them sweets before driving them home again. He must have seemed like some kind of fairy-tale prince, splendid-looking and full of charm, impulsive, generous, and amusing company.

His horoscope had predicted that if he lived for more than thirty-six years he would achieve great things. He died on 20 December 1922, his thirty-sixth birthday. He and my mother had been married nine years, and she was, at that time, only thirty years old.

We left England a few weeks later, taking his ashes with us to be immersed in the Ganges in the correct ceremonial way. I can remember very little about our voyage home. I have a vague recollection of pestering other passengers to write letters for me and then throwing the messages overboard, telling the sea to carry them back to England. I also have confused memories of my mother, dressed entirely in white, crying a lot and shutting herself in her cabin.

Chapter 4

Family Life in Cooch Behar

CIRCUMSTANCES HARDLY PERMITTED my mother to grieve in seclusion for long. She had too much to do. Soon after we arrived in Cooch Behar, Bhaiya, then seven years old, was crowned Maharaja. My mother made all the elaborate arrangements for both the religious and the civil ceremonies of the coronation, and she coached Bhaiya in his quite active part. He had, among other things, to learn by heart a little speech in reply to the address of the British Resident. Ma was very pleased with him for delivering it without a mistake. Soon she was to take on wider responsibilities.

It fell to the Viceroy, Lord Reading, as the King's representative in India, to consult with the British-Indian government of Bengal and the state government of Cooch Behar and then to appoint a regent and a minority council for Bhaiya. Usually a member of the young Maharaja's family was chosen to act as regent, and the Viceroy asked my mother to undertake the task. Although many Indian princesses were living in strict purdah, it was not extraordinary to appoint a woman as regent. Indeed, there are a number of instances throughout the history of India when women have either ruled or acted as regents. The mother of Maharaja Ram Singh in Jaipur and my own Cooch Behar great-grandmother were always consulted about state matters by the British Crown representatives and the minority councils, though they remained in purdah, never being seen by the men they advised. The state of Bhopal, too, was being ruled at that time by the Begum, the Muslim equivalent of maharani, who appeared everywhere veiled, even when she was addressing meetings or presiding over council discussions. Similarly, in the 1890s when the young Maharaja of Gwalior first became a ruler, his mother acted very successfully as regent; the British Resident used to consult her almost daily through a screen in one of the courtyards of the palace.

After all these ceremonies were over, we settled down to family life. I loved the town of Cooch Behar. It was beautifully kept and very charming. The houses were mostly built of bamboo and thatch, as there is no useful local stone. They were perched on stilts to protect them from the monsoon floods, and their roofs were covered with great scarlet plumes of hibiscus. The broad red gravel roads were lined with palm trees, and all over the town little white temples, set in gardens, were reflected in the clear waters of their many tanks, oblong ponds in which worshippers could take a ritual purifying bath before approaching the deity. At the center of town was the largest pool, almost like a lake, bordered by trees, lawns, and benches for the public. All around it stood the white-painted state offices, the treasury, and the council house, with a statue of my grandfather in front of it. These buildings and my Uncle Victor's house nearby were almost the only ones built of brick. There were few cars in the town in those days, just our own and one or two others belonging to the British Resident or the town doctor, but bicycles, which seem to multiply in India almost as fast as the population, were already filling the streets alongside the bullock-carts and the horse-drawn tongas.

Some way out of the town was our palace, a long, thin building constructed of brick, with two great wings stretching out from the central durbar, or audience hall. It was designed in about 1870 by an English architect who had gained a reputation among the princes of India for building spacious and stylish palaces sensibly adapted to the rigours of the Indian climate. The maharajas of Kolhapur, Panna, Mysore, and Baroda had all employed his talent for mixing grandeur with comfort in their palaces.

The Cooch Behar palace, in spite of some destruction in the great earthquake of 1896, is still very extensive and looks from the outside even larger than it is because of its spread-eagle shape. Like most Indian palaces it was built to withstand the scorching heat of the Indian summer, and all the rooms are shielded from the sun by wide verandas on each side furnished with comfortable chairs, sofas, and carpets.

In the days before British influence made itself widely felt in Indian life, the princely palaces were sparsely furnished and decorated mostly with wall hangings, murals, and carpets. There might be a few silver or gold or ivory beds, and perhaps some richly carved chests, but for the most part low wooden platforms, mattresses, and bolsters provided the sitting accommodation. However, by the early nineteenth century the British drawing-rooms of Delhi and Calcutta were being widely copied, however unsuitable they might appear in an Indian context.

Decorating and arranging a house was one of the things at which my mother excelled. She had a flawless eye and was always collecting pieces of furniture, fabrics, and objets d'art wherever she went. Our palace in Cooch Behar and our houses in Calcutta and Darjeeling, the official hill resort of Bengal, were all full of things she had picked up from the different places she had visited—chairs and tables from England and France, fabrics and chandeliers from Italy, rugs from Kashmir, silk hangings, rose quartz, and jade from Calcutta's Chinatown, and so on, until almost the whole palace was a reflection of her taste and personality.

Looking back, though, the two rooms that seem to evoke most clearly our lives in Cooch Behar are the only ones that Ma did not alter: the main dining-room with its huge central table and massive sideboards laden with the gold and silver racing trophies won by my grandfather, father, and uncles, and later by my brother, and the library with its tall white bookcases containing many valuable European editions, where we sometimes had our lessons and where Ma held her council meetings.

Outside, the palace was surrounded on all sides by a large and peaceful park where we used to bicycle and play. There were numerous small lakes which attracted rare species of water birds; one had little white, breezy pavilions dotted round its edge where it was cool even in summer. In the evenings we could watch the fireflies dancing over the water from the palace verandas. Behind the palace, away from the town, was the murky, treacherous river. We used to cycle along the embankment after the monsoon rains to watch the torrent pouring down.

Above: The palace at Cooch Behar.

Opposite: Entrance to the durbar hall at Cooch Behar.

Our palace staff in Cooch Behar probably numbered about four or five hundred. For the parks and grounds there were twenty gardeners, twenty in the stables, twelve in the garages, almost a hundred in the *pilkhanna* (the stables where the elephants were kept), a professional tennis coach and his assistant, twelve ball-boys, two people to look after the guns, ten sweepers to keep the drives and pathways immaculate, and, finally, the guards.

Indoors there were three cooks, one for English, one for Bengali, and one for Maratha food. Each had his separate kitchen, with his own scullery and his own assistants. There were, besides, six women to prepare the vegetables, and two or three bicycle *sowars* whose job it was to fetch provisions from the market every day.

Each of us girls had a maid in addition to our governesses and tutors, while Indrajit had one personal servant and Bhaiya had four. Ma's entourage included a secretary (who, in turn, controlled another secretary and typist), ladies-in-waiting, and a number of personal maids.

Five or six ADCs, from good families and in no way to be considered servants, had the responsibility of managing different departments of the household. They also escorted Ma wherever she was going, helped to entertain guests at the palace—and there were a great many of them—and acted as buffers between Ma and whoever came to see her, sifting out the genuine visitors from the curiosity-seekers and those with manufactured complaints or petitions. Lastly, there was a state band of about forty musicians which played every night before dinner as well as on special ceremonial occasions.

In running this extensive ménage, Ma could and did relegate a good part of the responsibilities to comptrollers, clerks, ADCs, and even relatives who lived with us, but the final decisions always had to be hers. Compared with the rigid formality of other Indian royal families in the 1920s, the almost medieval lives they lived, the domination of their courts by ritual and etiquette and the shutting away of their women in zenanas, or purdah quarters, our life in Cooch Behar had more the atmosphere of a very large and comfortable country house. We children had the run of the whole palace, from the great durbar hall under the dome to the store-rooms and the servants' quarters.

At an early age I discovered how the household was organized and at what hour the store-rooms were opened. I also learned that if I happened to be around at the right time, the catering clerk would give me a piece of chocolate. When my younger sister, Menaka, asked me where I got the chocolate, I explained that a great white owl that lived in the dome found it for me. Just to be safe, I warned her that if she ever went to ask the owl for chocolate for herself, he would fly away for good. Gullible young Menaka believed every word.

Menaka and I shared a bedroom, bathroom, and sitting-room in the part of the palace that my grandmother occupied, the zenana quarters. We had a huge bedroom with the beds and their mosquito curtains placed in the usual Indian way, in the center of the room. It had a sofa and upholstered armchairs, and cupboards and a dressing-table which were mine. Menaka had her own dressing-room, which opened off our bedroom, and it was a good thing that she did. She was exceedingly ladylike and saw that her clothes were always precisely in order; she loved dressing up and wearing jewels. I, on the other hand, was careless and messy, always in a hurry, happiest when I could wear just the pyjamas and loose, comfortable tunic that is the usual informal dress among us, disdaining jewellery, in agony when Ma said that we must wear saris for one of her parties. I would have driven Menaka to distraction if we had been compelled to share a dressing-room.

Our bedroom walls were painted blue with a pattern of white and yellow marguerites. The wooden parts of the furniture were lacquered blue, and to this day I remember the peaceful blend of sky blue and marguerites as I drifted off to sleep under the filmy white cubes of the mosquito curtains.

On either side of our bedroom there was a veranda, reached by three high French doors. There we had our lessons, on the side looking over the tennis-courts, the old skating rink, and beyond these to the fantastic view, on clear days, of the snow-capped Himalayas in the far distance. The veranda on the other side of our bedroom overlooked a courtyard where we used to play badminton and where later the *mandaps*, or marriage pavilions, were erected.

We all had our favourites among the staff. Mine was Jammir, one of the butlers, who used to sing me the most delightful songs. I thought he was the wisest and most understanding person in the whole world. He would listen to my troubles and soothe any injured feelings. When no one else could persuade me to eat, Jammir always succeeded. He took precedence in my affections even over my gentle and protective maid, Boori. Ijahar, Bhaiya's dressing-boy, was popular with all of us. He accompanied Bhaiya to England and stayed with him right through his schooldays at St. Cyprian's and at Harrow and, later still, at Trinity Hall, Cambridge. His brother, Jaffar, was our head butler, immensely grand and renowned throughout Calcutta for the splendour of his cocktails, especially his Alexanders—vermouth and crème de cacao enticingly topped with whipped cream. Jaffar was the kind of P. G. Wodehouse butler who always remembered who everyone was and what kind of drink he liked. And probably a lot more besides.

The ADCs were excellent company and also the objects of both admiration and childish teasing. One of them had been with us in England and had acquired a perfect BBC accent. We used to ask him what the time was at least ten times a day just to hear him say, "It is now two twenty and thirty-five seconds," or whatever it happened to be. Another had a less impressive command of English and often did comic things. Once when we were travelling by train, Ma exclaimed that she had dropped a stitch in her knitting, and he conscientiously got down on all fours in the carriage to hunt for it. Yet another was more serious, and we were always scared that he might "speak" to Ma if he caught us doing anything naughty. Our favourite, though, was Biren Babu, whom we all hero-worshipped because he was a marvellous tennis-player and a superb shot.

As in many large Indian families, various relatives also lived in the palace with us for days or months or the rest of their lives. No one ever dreamt of asking how long they were staying. It wouldn't have been polite. The widow of one of our great-uncles came to help run the household and lived there until her death. Her daughter was one of our playmates, and so were our cousins, Nidhi and Gautam, the sons of our Uncle Victor. He was my father's only surviving brother, and enlivened our days enormously by his immense vitality and love of children. He was a big man, always very jolly, and if you arrived looking downcast, he picked you up, threw you in the air, made you feel special, and somehow overcame your depression. To Bhaiya he was especially important. Uncle Victor in the beginning taught him how to shoot, and how to behave when he went out shooting. But for the rest of us he was almost equally important, teasing us and giving us a sense of proportion, alternating between serious subjects and utter frivolity, and cooking delicious things for us—he was a marvellous cook.

We knew that Ma relied on him for advice because he knew Cooch Behar so well and spoke the dialect perfectly. He had something for everybody. Sadly, Nidhi, his elder son, died very young, and soon afterwards Uncle Victor took Gautam to England. I realize, looking back now, how greatly this affected us because our only close link with our father's family had then gone. In fact, the whole life of the palace lost much of its Cooch Behari character, and the people who now assisted my mother in the ruling of the state all came from other parts of India.

One of the nobles of Hyderabad State, Nawab Khusru Jung, came to look after Cooch Behar's financial affairs. He happened also to be a superb horseman and soon began to supervise the care and training of Ma's string of hunters as well as all our ponies. He gave us riding lessons and inspired the boys to try to reach his own mastery. His young daughter, whom we all called Baby though her real name was Kamala, became so much a part of our family that she lived and travelled with us almost as much as with her father, a widower. Ma's private secretary, several senior members of the household retinue, and even Bhaiya's three young companions all came from outside Cooch Behar.

As a family we were very close and shared the same interests, sense of humour, and jokes. In spite of our closeness we were not demonstrative, but we had our own code of honour—we never sneaked on one another and never let each other down. The triumphs and successes of any one of us were shared by the others, and when any of us were in trouble, the others stood by and sympathized. We were all high-spirited and fun-loving, but we each had our separate personalities. Ila, with huge, lovely eyes and tiny hands and feet, was the witty one. She was specially good at riding and tennis, an excellent mimic, and spoke the local Cooch Behari dialect most fluently. Bhaiya, as a little boy, showed some arrogance and self-importance, but he grew up to be most unassuming in spite of the admiration he received for his looks and his fine tennis and cricketing styles. He was full of fun and a most amusing and well-informed companion but could be serious when the occasion demanded. He loved racing, and years later kept his own racehorses. Indrajit, equally tall and good-looking, was the mischievous one, always getting into the most imaginative kinds of trouble. Menaka seemed quiet and shy because of her gentle manner, but she was really very sociable and had a great sense of humour.

As for me, I was the tomboy—Indrajit used to call me "the broomstick" because I was so skinny and had such straight hair—but I was a daydreamer as well. I hated to be teased about either of these characteristics, and inevitably Ila and Indrajit soon found this out and plagued me unendingly because I reacted with such satisfactory fury and tears and sulks. Bhaiya never teased me. Ila was oldest and consequently the natural leader of our family; when she bossed me around I looked to Bhaiya, who was far kinder, for help. So, close as we all were, certain alliances developed within the family and remained all our lives. Bhaiya was, for me, a natural hero, so handsome, so good at games, so entertaining, and above all so protective, in a most unobtrusive way.

The thing we all shared most deeply was our love of Cooch Behar. It was there that we most enjoyed being, and there that we spent most of our very happy and varied childhood. Cooch Behar didn't offer an exhilarating night-life or fancy shops or parties (other than the ones in the palace), but the time passed quickly and the days seemed very full.

Every morning our horses stood outside the palace waiting for us, and we rode through the town to reach the old polo-ground, now an airport, or beyond it to open country. The townspeople would be getting up and preparing for the day, and the air was tinged with the lovely smell of wood-fires being lit. The people we passed on their way to the fields, the temple, or the river always greeted us affectionately.

After our ride we returned to the palace to have our baths and come down to breakfast, always a hilarious and completely informal meal accompanied by a lot of noise and chatter and gossip about what had happened the previous evening or during the morning ride or about plans for later in the day. Almost nothing was allowed to interfere with our daily routine of lessons. We had two classrooms in the palace, one for the older children, Ila, Bhaiya, and their companions, and one for us younger ones, where our cousins Gautam and Nidhi joined us. But as we grew up some of us went to school outside the palace and some had individual tutoring. At one point Indrajit had an Italian tutor to teach him Latin, which was required for entrance to Harrow, where he was due to join Bhaiya. For the rest, we had an English governess, Miss Hobart, to teach us English, English history and literature, and some French, and two Bengali tutors, one for mathematics and Indian history and the other for Bengali and Sanskrit. The routine was quite strict and couldn't be interrupted. Like an ordinary school, separate periods were marked for different subjects, and like ordinary schoolchildren, we waited impatiently for classes to be over so that we could rush outdoors.

Apart from sports, which we all loved—riding, tennis, and shooting for all of us, and for the boys field hockey, football, cricket, and boxing as well—the palace at Cooch Behar had a huge garden where one could easily and deliciously get lost, and we each had our bicycles on which to roam about as we pleased. While we were still children, much of our lives revolved around a miniature house that my father had originally built for Ila. It was white and had a dome and a porte-cochère into which we drove our toy cars. There were two rooms and a veranda downstairs, and a wooden staircase led to the upper storey, which also had two rooms and a veranda, and a terrace over the porch as well. Here we held tea-parties and cooking parties—Ma's way of introducing us to household skills—and played games. Nearby was a huge banyan tree from which hung a swing big enough to hold four people; this was always very popular. Occasionally we would go to the *pilkhanna* to watch the elephants being bathed, a great thrill, especially after a baby elephant was born when I was about five. Normally elephants do not mate in captivity because the male is tied up as soon as he becomes *masth* (ready to mate), but one of our female elephants escaped into the jungle and, to our wild excitement, came back pregnant. So the baby was born in the Cooch Behar *pilkhanna*, and it seemed to us about the greatest event of our lives.

I suppose that the biggest difference between us and the children of other princely families was that we were allowed to enter much more into the glittering lives of the grown-ups. Naturally, most of our interest centred on Ma's magnetic personality and doings. The time of the day that I loved best was the early evening, when Ma was getting ready for dinner. Night falls very quickly in Cooch Behar, earlier than in other parts of India. The fleeting dusk was accompanied by the sound of temple bells as the evening prayers were chanted and offerings of food, flowers, and incense were made to the gods and goddesses.

Then the palace came to life again after the long, enervating heat of the afternoon. The table in the dining-room was laid with gold, silver, and flowers, the state band tuned up for the evening, and we were allowed to go to Ma's apartments to watch her getting dressed.

The air was filled with the delicious scent of *dhuan*, an incense that the servants carried from room to room in a smoking silver urn, waving it to and fro as they went, to drive away the mosquitoes. But as we approached Ma's rooms the scent of her French perfume started to mingle with the *dhuan*. Her apartments were not on what always used to be the women's side of the palace but on the other side of the durbar hall. Her large dressing-room adjoined her marble bathroom, which had a steam bath specially designed for her as a chaise-longue so that she could lie in it instead of having to sit upright. Her high-ceilinged bedroom was decorated in white and gold, her prayer-room lay beyond, and then came the room where we would all gather—her boudoir, a large, airy room with dark blue walls and gold pillars. There were two alcoves in the boudoir, filled with Chinese jade and rose quartz ornaments, a deep divan, red lacquered furniture, some large silver urns from Hyderabad, and on the floor an enormous round leopard-skin rug made by Schiaparelli from fourteen skins. All the rooms were linked outside by a broad marble veranda rimmed with potted plants. Here Ma sat during the daytime, on a marble divan covered by a thick mattress and scores of cushions.

Dressing for dinner was for us children one of the specially exciting moments of Ma's day. The bedroom was crowded with maids, with female relatives and friends, and with us children, and she held court to us all, switching rapidly from one language to another—English to her friends, Marathi to any visiting relatives from Baroda, French to her Swiss maid, and Bengali to us and to any other Cooch Beharis present. At the same time she arranged her hair, something she liked to do for herself, or made notes on a little pad she always kept in front of her as she planned some future project: a list of guests, perhaps, or a meeting with her ministers, or a twenty-four-hour party in Calcutta. We children were sent in turns to take our baths and dress appropriately for a return to her apartments. Somehow she always managed to emerge from the midst of this hubbub exquisitely dressed, though sometimes she changed her mind about which sari she wanted to wear just as everyone stood up ready for her to leave, and then the maids had to start running in and out of her dressing-room all over again.

Ma was very fussy about her clothes and was considered one of the best-dressed women in India. She was the first person to start wearing saris made of chiffon, which were cooler than the more usual silks and more formal than cottons. She had persuaded a Paris fashion house to order for her chiffons specially woven in the 42-inch width suitable for saris. She also used to go into shops in Delhi and Calcutta and tell the owners to alter the designs of their materials for her—eliminating a flower here, adding a new color there. The next year, after she had worn the new designs, which were invariably more attractive than the familiar patterns, she allowed the shops to copy them for other customers.

Ma's greatest passion was for shoes. She had hundreds of pairs and still went on ordering them compulsively, mostly from Ferragamo in Florence. Although she gave them away by the hundreds, too, her stock was always growing. Her feet were very elegant, narrow and tapering and always beautifully pedicured, just as her hands were beautifully manicured. When, at last, she was dressed and the long wait was over, a message was sent to the men assembled in the billiard-room to come to the drawing-room. The evening never really got under way until Ma appeared.

She was undoubtedly the foremost hostess in India, known internationally for the excellence of her parties and at home because she broke new ground for Indian women. She proved that a woman —a widow, at that—could entertain with confident charm and flair without being in the protective shadow of a husband or father.. She was a great gourmet, and any new gastronomic discovery was greeted with rapture. She encouraged her cooks to experiment and introduced them to all kinds of unfamiliar dishes. On one occasion she took one of our cooks to Alfredo's in Rome because she wanted him to understand what Alfredo's lasagna tasted like. The cook had been a teetotaller, but in Italy she kept insisting, "You must have the wine, it goes with the food."

She always knew the best place to buy anything, and she shopped all over the world. Her hospitality was famous, partly because her expert attention to detail made her friends (and family) so supremely *comfortable*. The palace at Cooch Behar and all our houses had bed linen like gossamer and bath towels so absorbent that you were dry as soon as they touched you. Although she had at her disposal a large staff, perfectly trained to her own high standards, yet, before any guests arrived, she went through their rooms herself, inspecting everything. She even lay on the beds to check that the reading lamps were positioned at the right angle. It was not surprising that everyone wanted to be entertained by "Ma Cooch Behar."

Guests who came to Cooch Behar always arrived on the overnight train from Calcutta, having had to rise in the very early hours of the morning to change to the narrow-gauge line that brought them to the town. When they reached the palace they were given an exuberant welcome. All the family and the household staff came out to the steps of the portico to greet them and garland them with flowers before taking them into the dining-room for breakfast. So many people came and went that I never really knew who most of them were. Once I asked a man who knew Ma well who her friends had been. He replied, "Oh, everyone from the Prince of Wales downwards."

Ma, photographed in the early 1930s.

Whoever they were, for us children Ma's guests ranked high among our many sources of entertainment. We enjoyed all the adult conversations and the constant spectacle of grown-ups playing tennis, billiards, or backgammon or taking part in the various schemes devised by Ma. Although we were encouraged to stay pretty much in the background, to smile politely and to speak only when spoken to, every now and then such restrictions were bound to prove too much for our self-control. On one occasion Ma had decided that all her English guests should dress up for fun in Indian clothes. When I saw them all standing on the veranda, the pale pink arms and legs emerging from saris and dhotis, I exclaimed loudly, "You look indecent!"

To us and to all our guests, the greatest and most thrilling attraction of Cooch Behar was undoubtedly the big-game shooting. It was among the best that India could offer. The jungles of Cooch Behar are linked with the Terai, a great unbroken belt of jungle running across northern India, south of the Himalayas, into Nepal. This was superb terrain for wild animals, which could travel for hundreds of miles without crossing a single man-made path. All kinds of game abounded within a radius of a few miles from our palace: tiger, rhinoceros, panther, bear, wild buffalo, bison, hog, deer, wild boar, and sambar. Once, I remember, we were forbidden to go into the palace vegetable garden because a wild elephant had been seen there.

It was my grandfather who started the tradition of big shoots in Cooch Behar. His game book records the animals killed over a period of thirty-seven years in the jungles of Cooch Behar and Assam: 365 tigers, 311 leopards, 207 rhinos, 438 buffaloes, 318 antelopes, 259 sambars, 133 bears, and 43 bison. In recent years I have become very interested in the organizations that have been formed to protect wild-life, so perhaps I should mention here that although big-game hunting was an important activity of Cooch Behar, the decline of game in India today is not a consequence of reckless slaughter by sportsmen. The decline has, in fact, been caused by the steady destruction of the animals' habitat. Even during my grandfather's youth, jungles were being cleared because of the rapidly growing need for land to cultivate, and since Independence the pace has accelerated. Today only 13 percent of India is covered by forest, while the minimum area needed to sustain our wild-life has been estimated at 30 percent.

My grandfather was a first-class shot and achieved a rather special kind of record by shooting two rhinos with a left and a right. During the beat, he suddenly saw a rhino charging from the left. Just as he was raising his gun—a heavy eight-bore—another rhino appeared on his right. Many hunters think rhinos the most dangerous and treacherous of animals; their horn can rip open an elephant's belly. However, with astonishing presence of mind, my grandfather took two quick shots, first to the left and immediately afterwards to the right, dropping both rhinos, and then finished them off at his leisure. A rhino is an impressive animal, even in death. I have only seen one rhino shot and vividly recall the awesome sight of the blood spurting up in a scarlet fountain. I remember, too, that it was impossible to drag the huge animal to the camp and that a guard had to be mounted over it to prevent the villagers from taking the horn, which is supposed to be a powerful aphrodisiac.

During my childhood, shooting was as much a part of our lives as our lessons, and incomparably more exciting. At that time there were shooting-camps two or three times a year at one of the two reserves in the state, either at Patlakhawa, which was adjacent to the jungles of Assam and the Terai, or at Takuamari in the south. Indian princely shooting-camps in those days were quite unlike anything that an Englishman or an American might understand by the word "camp." There were tents, it is true, but there the similarity ends. Our Indian tents were enormous and had separate drawing-rooms, dining-rooms, bedrooms, and bathrooms. They were fully furnished with carpets, chairs, tables, and everything else necessary for comfort. Our camps consisted of ten or twelve such tents, with smaller ones for the staff, all pitched around a huge open fire that was lit at night to keep the animals away.

I went on my first shoot when I was five. Every morning after breakfast we went to the ADCs' rooms to see if there was any *khubbar*—any "news"—and by that we meant only news of big game that must be destroyed. Villagers came to the palace almost every day with complaints about a panther, or sometimes a tiger, that had

A tiger shoot at Cooch Behar.

killed a goat or a cow. If, after cross-examination by an ADC, the story held together, the villager was given lunch while all of us excitedly joined in the preparations for a shoot. These were the only times we were allowed to break our routine of lessons, and then only if we had finished our homework. If the tiger had been sighted a long way from the palace, we usually drove part of the way to a prearranged meeting-point where elephants waited to carry us for the next few miles. Then, at a second prearranged meeting-point, the howdah elephants with their mahouts stood ready. The howdah elephants acted as "stops" towards which the pad elephants, serving the same function as teams of beaters, drove the game. The howdahs were equipped with racks on either side to hold the guns, and whoever was to shoot sat in front; there was room behind for another couple of people. We soon learned that the seats could be lifted up, and underneath we always found chocolate biscuits and orange squash to keep us going. Ma used to suspect that one of the chief charms of going shooting was to eat the chocolate biscuits.

One spring when Ma was in Delhi and Ila and Bhaiya were both away at school, I had my own moment of glory. Early in the morning, news was brought by some villagers that a panther had to be killed in a nearby area, so after lunch Indrajit, Menaka, and I set off. Each of us was mounted on a howdah elephant with an ADC behind us, and Indrajit was specifically instructed to let me have the first shot.

Naturally, we had all been taught from the time we were very young how to shoot, how to be careful, how to make sure that we got a clear shot without the chance of wounding any of the hunting elephants through overexcitement, and so on. We were in a very small jungle that afternoon, near a village, and we could hear the elephants trumpeting as they usually did when there was a wild or dangerous animal in the vicinity. Then the breathless moment came when the beat began.

By the standards of more experienced hunters, my first triumph might well seem rather tame. When the panther was finally forced out of cover, it snarled once and simply stood still, staring at my elephant. The ADC behind me told me to fire, and the only thing I can say to my credit is that I didn't lose my nerve. I picked up my gun—I used a twenty-bore shotgun—and got him in the face with my first shot.

There was great joy and jubilation; even the mahouts and the professional hunters with us joined in. I was deluged with congratulations, and when we got back to the palace everybody made a big fuss over me. We sent a telegram to Ma in Delhi telling her that I had shot my first panther. I was twelve years old and speechless with pride and excitement.

A wounded tiger is perhaps the most dangerous creature in the jungle and in its death charge can leap to astonishing heights. So can panthers. I remember on one shoot in Cooch Behar, when we were still quite small, a wounded panther leapt up onto an elephant that was carrying my two brothers. Bhaiya, without time to think of the danger, butted it with his gun and, helped by the mahout, managed to push it off. Luckily neither of the boys was hurt, but I noticed that Ma took care from then on never to let them be together on the same elephant.

Cooch Behar was renowned for its *pilkhanna,* and all our sixty elephants were splendidly trained. They were used for all kinds of purposes besides big-game shooting. In fact, the best way—often the only way—of getting about in Cooch Behar is by elephant. The land is nearly all flat, although in the north you can see the snow-capped peaks of the Himalayas, but it is covered with tall grasses that grow up to ten feet high, and much of it is swampy, crossed by broad, slow-running rivers whose course varies from year to year. As children we were always riding elephants and would often race each other home on them after a shoot.

Driving an elephant is not really difficult once it has been trained. We all knew the special words of command to which an elephant responds; we had learned them from the mahouts, each of whom might easily spend the whole of his adult life with the same elephant, developing a curiously intimate relationship of trust, affection, and mutual protectiveness. There were the ordinary commands, "*beht*" for "sit down," "*oot*" for "get up," and then the more special words, said in a kind of chant, when a mahout was steering an elephant through the jungle and came across a tree that had to be knocked down, or tough elephant grass that had to be trampled to make a pathway. Then he said in a singsong lilt, "Dalai, dalai, *dab*. Dalai, dalai, *dab*." At each "*dab*" the elephant made a renewed effort to flatten the obstacle in his way.

Elephants are extremely intelligent animals, and sensitive to insults or harshness. Their mahouts change the intonation of the commands according to whether they are driving a tiger or leopard out of cover or simply guiding the elephant through the jungle, but their tone of voice is always gentle. There are some occasions when you have to kick an elephant behind his ears, and sometimes goad him with an iron spike that can be felt through his thick skin, but this is rare. The only time a male elephant is dangerous is when he is ready to mate. Then the most even-tempered beast can go berserk and has to be chained up until the mating period is over. Usually, however, sufficient warning is given by two tiny holes in the elephant's temple which start to secrete just before the dangerous time begins. Only once in our *pilkhanna* did an elephant break loose and kill his mahout. This was lamented by everybody but recognized as an extraordinary occurrence.

My Cooch Behar grandfather was said to have had a remarkable, almost telepathic understanding with elephants. On one occasion, when one of his best elephants got stuck in a swamp, the mahouts threw in a tree-trunk for the animal to cling to, but no one seemed able to keep him from threshing about and sinking deeper and deeper into the mud. Then my grandfather was sent for. Within a few minutes of talking he had calmed the elephant and then slowly coaxed him out of the swamp. When my grandfather died and his ashes were brought back to Cooch Behar, all his elephants were lined up at the station to salute him. The story is that with tears in their eyes they all lifted their trunks and trumpeted in unison as the train drew in. All the tusks of his favourite elephants are still in the hall at Cooch Behar, with their names on them.

For me, elephants were the most important and beloved creatures in the world. I used to spend hours with the mahouts and their wives, learning elephant-lore and listening to the songs that the wives sang when their husbands were setting off on a tour of duty, for elephants were used not only for shooting but also to collect rents and taxes and to round up wild elephants to be tamed by the fully trained ones in the *pilkhanna.*

A mahout's wife would sing to *sunar bandhu re,* "my golden friend" (meaning her husband), describing him sitting on the noble beast, his elephant, and how small he looked in contrast, but how the elephant had a chain around his neck, and so the mahout was really the master. Another song was about a new elephant that has been caught and how each of his four legs is chained so that he can't stretch too far. And then the song described how he must get used to the presence of people, how the mahouts stroke him with bamboo leaves to get him accustomed to the touch and feel of human hands, and how they wave flames before his eyes so that he is not frightened by fires in the jungle on shoots. And all the time they chant to him, "You are not in the jungle any more. Now you have a master and an owner who will love you and cherish you and look after you, and in exchange you will obey, in love and gratitude."

Even now, when I go back to Cooch Behar, I ask the mahouts to sing for me, and I remember the days, when Bhaiya returned from school in England before he went off to Cambridge, when the mahouts made up a song for his departure: "Our Maharaja is going, our ruler is going, our friend is going. But we hope he'll come back soon. And when he comes back, we hope he brings us a lot of knowledge of the things that will be useful to us here. And we hope that the poisons of the West don't infiltrate him." (By "poisons" they meant liquor and loose women.)

Our elephants had a variety of names, some called after gods and goddesses, some named for family members. I remember that the one called Ayesha was excessively slow and old-looking, and my sisters and brothers used to tease me about it: "That elephant of yours is just like you!" Menaka didn't fare much better, but she seemed to mind it less, and our various aunts and uncles for whom other elephants were named seemed not to care at all.

When Ma had guests for a shoot, I remember that often we would go ahead to the meeting-place on elephants. While we were waiting, I always pleaded with the mahout to let me take his place, sitting on the neck of the elephant. There I used to lie down, my head between the elephant's ears, feeling the faint breeze as he flapped his ears, listening to the buzz of the bees, saturated with the peculiar smell of the elephant, the sense of the jungle all around. I felt completely out of the palace's restricted life. Alone. Just me and the elephant in the jungle.

From the mahouts we picked up a certain amount of the local dialect, enough to converse with the palace staff and their families. I used, at that time, to be known as "*pagly rajkumari*"—meaning "the mad princess"—because I took such an intense interest in the lives of the mahouts and all the rest of the palace servants. I used to draw up plans for new houses that should be built for them. "Here," I would explain, capturing some puzzled retainer and pointing to my drawing, "here will be your bathroom."

"But we haven't a bathroom of our own," he would protest.

"Maybe not *now*," I would carefully explain, "but you *will* have when I build your new houses. And there'll be another separate room for your children."

Usually he would say, unbelievingly, "Yes, Princess, as you wish it."

I used to question the mahouts about how much money they earned, inquire into the conditions in which they lived, and insist that they should get more money and better houses. Bhaiya used to try to shut me up, saying, "There'll be a strike in the *pilkhanna* if you keep this up."

One of the most haunting memories of my childhood in Cooch Behar is of coming home on an elephant just before dusk, tired after the excitement of the day's shooting. The air is full of the smell of mustard flowers, and from a distance comes the lovely and lonely sound of flutes. Far to the north, still visible through the twilight after a very clear day, stands the white half-circle of the Himalayas. This remembered moment immediately takes me back to the happiness and security of my childhood, to a time when my life was untouched by change and the loss of the people dearest to me. Sometimes, as I fall asleep at night during the moist heat of the monsoon rains, it seems that we are all back there still, Ma and Bhaiya, Ila and Indrajit, my husband, Jai, and I, and that Menaka and I are not the only ones left alive.

Chapter 5

The Duties and Delights of Royalty

ALTHOUGH WE WERE, as a family, both close and for the most part casual with each other, and although our home in Cooch Behar had a happy atmosphere of relaxed informality, still it was a palace and, to some extent, a court. We were all aware of Bhaiya's special position and were taught very early to show him respect; for instance, in public, whenever he came into a room, we all had to stand up for him. Bhaiya's birthday was one of the great state festivals of the year. Prisoners were pardoned, the poor were fed at the state temples, and everyone took a holiday. In the evening there was a durbar at the palace attended by the nobles and officials. But the entertainment, with its fireworks, great processions of elephants, and all the pageantry, was for the villagers who came into town for this great occasion.

We had, as well, daily reminders that our home was also the centre of government of the state. Ma's training for her administrative responsibilities had been remarkably good. She had often been taken into the confidence of her father, the Gaekwar of Baroda, who had discussed many state matters with her and used to say that he wished she had been his eldest son because she had such a good head for government. On his one visit to Cooch Behar he expressed himself as very pleased with the way Ma was running things. From a very early age, I can remember her walking around the palace garden in Cooch Behar with some government officials on one side and Bhaiya on the other, discussing the budget or the plans for a new hospital or school and at the same time peering at the shrubs and flower-beds, making a mental note of things that needed the gardeners' attention. She was very serious when people came to advise, consult, or inform her. And she was also amused and rather proud that Bhaiya, unasked, would always follow her and listen carefully to whatever discussion was going on.

The rest of us, too, realized that we occupied a special place in the state. We had many companions who came up to the palace to play with us, but because they were all from Cooch Behar families, even in our rowdiest games there was always a slight difference between us. They wouldn't tease us and push us around as we did each other, and even though we tried to bridge the gap they always held us a little apart. It was understandable, I suppose. After all, we had this huge palace—a fantastic place for a child to be brought up in—as our home, and that must have subdued the ordinary rough-and-tumble of the other children's play. And then, although we had a great deal of contact with the townspeople and the villagers and they addressed us with familiarity and affection, still there was no question in their minds that we were their princesses and had to behave accordingly. As soon as we could be trusted to conduct ourselves properly we had to attend public functions. If there was a prize-giving at a school, or the opening of a new building, we had to be there, sitting quietly and decorously in a row, unable to run about and play with the other children. So from the very beginning a sense of the duties and drawbacks of royalty was instilled in us.

Ma, too, in little ways had begun the process of training us, and as usual she managed to make it all fun. ADCs and secretaries handled much of the routine of the palace and the correspondence and messages involved in state affairs, but often Ma by-passed them and asked us to take or answer messages instead, calling us in from the garden or wherever we happened to be. We were like her page-boys, and each of us longed to be the one chosen to take a message or send off a telegram. By the time we were ten we were all absolutely reliable and proficient at these minor tasks.

For the girls, training included learning how to entertain in a princely style. She would call on Ila and Menaka and me in turn to do such things as decorate the dining-table for a party of twenty, choosing the flowers, the silver and gold bowls, and the trophies to add splendour to the table. Ila and Menaka were rather good at this, while I was absolutely hopeless. I learned a lot more from simply listening to Ma conducting the palace affairs, making up menus, arranging seating, choosing linen and decorations. She trained us early in the handling of money, too. Unlike other princesses who had everything bought for them, we were first given pocket-money to buy our own camera film or comic books and other childish indulgences and later we received allowances from which we had to buy our clothes and pay for our entertainments.

When we were out of Cooch Behar—in Calcutta or Darjeeling—things were easier, and it was possible for us to be part of a group of children on an equal basis. The only slight difference was that we were not quite as free as they were. Other children could, for instance, go out together to a movie by themselves, while we could never go anywhere without governesses or ADCs or some palace retainer to watch over us.

Our whole childhood was a patchwork of the responsibilities and the privileges, the restrictions and the fun of being part of the ruling family in a princely state. There were serious occasions when the ordinary people of Cooch Behar came directly to the palace to express a grievance or ask for help in hard times, but fortunately Cooch Behar was a comparatively rich state with fertile, well-irrigated land and a high annual rainfall. The villagers could grow both the basic staple of the Bengali diet, rice, and cash crops like jute, mustard, and tobacco for export as well. So, although most of the people lived very simply, we rarely had to suffer the appalling famines that periodically ravaged other Indian states.

A splendid succession of festivals punctuates the Indian lunar calendar, and our family played an important and enthusiastic part in them. In India we love festivals and enjoy indulging our unrivalled sense of pageantry. Even the poorest make the most of any occasion which provides a chance to dress up, to garland their oxen, to decorate their houses, temples, and bullock-carts. They find nothing incongruous in the juxtaposition of such extravagant display with their drab daily lives. Looking back at our Cooch Behar childhood, we always seem to have been busy getting ready for some special holiday. The prettiest was Diwali, the festival of lights that marks the Hindu New Year, when the town and the palace were hung with little lamps which were reflected in all the many ponds and tanks. The most fun was Holi, an exuberant celebration of spring, when all of us got a chance to pelt grown-ups and other children with red powder.

Perhaps the most impressive festival was Durgapuja, which celebrates the ten days of fighting between Rama, the hero of the great Indian epic, the *Ramayana*, and Ravana, the demon king of Lanka. During this period the goddess Durga, in her aspect of Kali the goddess of destruction, is worshipped with offerings of flowers, fruit, and food. Most princely families belong to the Kshatriya, or warrior caste, so Durgapuja holds a special importance for them. Bhaiya had to lead the prayer ceremonies which were performed to honour the trappings of war—horses, weapons, chariots. There was one Durga temple, however, in the old ruined capital called Gosanimare, where none of us could worship or even enter. Legend has it that one of my ancestors mortally offended the goddess Durga. He had heard that at night she took on human form and secretly danced in the temple. He hid there one night to spy on her and see this magical performance, but, of course, she discovered him and flew into a rage. As a punishment for his temerity, she cursed him and all his descendants, forbidding them to set foot in her temple again and leaving him a silver anklet as a reminder and a warning.

The Puniya durbar was very formal but, in its own dignified way, even more colourful than the other special occasions. It usually came at the end of April, just as the temperature was starting to become uncomfortably hot, and it celebrated the gathering of the Maharaja's revenue after the spring harvest. The land of Cooch Behar, as in most Indian states, was organized on a feudal basis and divided into crown lands, or *khalsa*, and fiefs held from the crown, some of which were sublet a second, third, or fourth time. The revenue from the *khalsa* came directly to the Maharaja, while the taxes from all the other lands were held separately, but the money from both sources was gathered by officials on elephants, setting out from the five district headquarters.

After they were all collected, the revenues were formally offered to the Maharaja at the Puniya durbar. From early morning the air was filled with excitement, with everybody preparing for the great day. I remember loving all the rushing about, watching the elephants coming in from the *pilkhanna*, one by one, into the back courtyards.

There they sat with their faces and trunks painted in fanciful designs in different colours by their mahouts. Then the great storerooms of the palace were opened and the cloths to cover the elephants were brought out. First plain ones were spread over the great docile backs, then brocaded ones, and then the elephant jewellery was put on, consisting of gold and silver anklets and plaques for their foreheads. Then the mahouts dressed up, received their gold and silver rods, and placed the carved and painted silver-decorated howdahs on their elephants. Even now I recall my childish wonder at the performance and the thrilling trumpeting of the elephants. All through the preparations we children were bubbling over with talk and questions to the mahouts. Then finally everything was ready and the great procession set out, leaving us to the bustle of getting ourselves dressed and ready for their return.

Eventually the elephants, still ceremonially arrayed, came back to the palace carrying the state revenue in brightly coloured clay pots. At one end of the marble durbar hall Bhaiya was seated on his silver throne under a domed silver umbrella, while the Revenue Minister sat cross-legged on the floor in front of him. The rest of the hall was lined with palace guards and officials of the court, all in their uniforms and ceremonial turbans banded with gold. The elephants carried the revenue pots as far as the door of the hall. There the pots were lifted down and taken into the durbar hall to be offered to Bhaiya. The Revenue Minister then performed a prayer ceremony over the offerings, and at the end of the durbar the procession of elephants carried the revenue in a stately line from the palace to the treasury building. My sisters and I, dressed in our finest jewels and our silk and gold saris from Benares, watched the ceremony with my mother and the other palace ladies from a gallery above the hall.

Shortly after the Puniya durbar each year, when the temperature in Cooch Behar became unbearably hot and the air uncomfortably humid, we used to leave to spend the summer in the hills. The signal for our departure was the breaking of the monsoon in May. The rain would suddenly burst from the sky and hurl itself against the earth, spluttering and dancing for a couple of hours on end. I would lie in bed at night, listening to the different sounds as the downpour hit brick, tin, or slate, while the maids rushed about the palace shutting all the windows and fetching us hot drinks. Then, in the morning, we would all run to the comptroller of the household to find out how many windows had been shattered during the night. Outside, the rivers would be swollen with swirling muddy water, and after only a few days the countryside would become a brilliant, almost unnatural green.

With the storms came the insects and the snakes which often took shelter in the palace. Almost every sort of snake and insect known in India is found in Cooch Behar, and my grandmother, Suniti Devi, catalogued over a hundred varieties of flying insects alone. Huge beetles, three inches long, in shiny black armour, crawled across carpets like miniature tanks or butted against walls and ceilings with a sinister clicking sound. Others, known as "stink bombs," made a foul smell if you trod on them, while small unobtrusive flies, deceptively unimpressive-looking, left huge blisters if you squashed them on a bare leg or arm. Scorpions and aquatic insects invaded the bathrooms, and everywhere, of course, there were mosquitoes. My grandfather, during the monsoon, used to live under an immense mesh tent the size of a room, with an ingenious arrangement of double doors, to protect himself from the mosquitoes. Throughout the rainy season all his meals would be served inside it. For myself, I loved the rains. To us children, hazards like snakes and scorpions seemed only to lend extra excitement to our daily lives. However, once the monsoon had set in we would start for the hills and wouldn't return to Cooch Behar until the autumn, after the rains and the dense, steamy post-monsoon heat were over.

For the first few years after my father's death we spent our summers at Ootacamund, a hill-station in the south of India where my Baroda grandparents had a house. It was over a thousand miles from Cooch Behar, and the journey there used to take us more than a week, but our departure for the hills was always such an upheaval that the distance made little difference. On our trips to Ootacamund our party would include over a hundred people, as well as thirty horses and luggage filling several trucks.

The list of people usually ran more or less like this: Ma and her five children, a maid for each of the girls and a valet for each of the boys, assorted relatives and companions, two ADCs and their families, six butlers, four *jamedars,* or footmen, eight guards, an English governess, two Indian tutors, our English chauffeur and his wife and daughter, four Indian drivers, two dressmakers, one medical assistant, one Indian cook, one English cook, four kitchen staff, a clerk of the kitchen, the comptroller of the household, his clerk, an accountant and his clerk, and thirty grooms for the horses. It took four or more lorries to carry all the personal belongings we needed—the saddles and bridles, the cooking utensils, the linen, cutlery, and glass—and once we had arrived it took at least four days to settle into the house.

The journey started with the overnight train from Cooch Behar to Calcutta. In those days a first-class railway compartment was large and completely self-contained, with its own little bathroom and a separate room at one end for the traveller's personal servant. Many of the maharajas had their own state railway carriages with their coats of arms painted on the outside. They had special fittings and furniture of the maharaja's personal choice, and their owners would never travel in anything else. We, however, always used public transport.

From Cooch Behar to Parbatipur, now in Bangladesh, the railway ran on narrow-gauge lines, and we had to change to the broad-gauge Calcutta train in the middle of the night. Half asleep, we were carried across the platform in our dressing-gowns to our new compartments. Next morning we woke up in Calcutta. There we usually spent the next couple of nights in our house, "Woodlands," before travelling on to Madras, where we stayed at the Connemara Hotel for a few days. Another night in the train took us to the foothills of the Nilgiris. The last lap was a three-hour drive by car, climbing and twisting up into the mountains, which rise about 7,000 feet above the scorching tableland below. And then suddenly we had arrived, wondering, like everyone else who came to Ootacamund, or Ooty, as everyone called it, if this pleasant and verdant countryside could possibly be part of India, or if it was a piece of England transported intact, with its little English houses with names like "Cedarhurst" and "Glen View," sprouting Victorian gables or whimsical little terracotta turrets, their gardens filled with hollyhocks, Canterbury bells, and stock, and their orchards with English apples and pears.

I have one rather less than sentimental memory of Ooty. It was there that my future husband, the Maharaja of Jaipur, first visited us. I was five years old and totally uninterested in the pudgy youngster of thirteen who had written to Ma inviting himself to lunch, adding an earnest plea that he be served Indian and not English food. He was far more interested in getting a decent and appetizing meal—his tutors had been trying to make him diet by eating simple English food—than in any small girl in the family. (Ma later received a letter from the Maharaja's guardian asking her never to serve him Indian food again.)

In spite of the charm of the countryside around Ooty and the matchless purity of the mountain air on our early morning rides, I far preferred Darjeeling, the hill resort in the Himalayas where we began to spend our summers from the time I was about twelve or thirteen. That enchanting town, perched over 7,000 feet high, was outside the boundaries of Cooch Behar State, but for centuries much of it had been part of the personal property of the maharajas of Cooch Behar. When the British Government in Calcutta had started to move up there for the summer months, my grandfather had given them some of his land on which to build Government House. Our own house in Darjeeling was called "Colinton" and had been built by him in the middle of the nineteenth century. Set much higher than the rest of the town, at the end of an avenue of magnolias, with a large garden merging into the forest in the north, "Colinton" was magnificently situated and had a superb view of the Himalayas.

It was country that offered the most marvellous scenic walks and picnic places. Sometimes in the early mornings we rode up to Tiger Hill, a vantage-point above Darjeeling, to watch the sun rise over Mount Everest. Sometimes, too, we visited the Buddhist monasteries or the little shrines that were scattered all over the foothills and were covered with tiny fluttering flags. The market-place in the centre of Darjeeling was always full of Tibetans and Bhutanese in great fur-lapped hats and embroidered boots, selling their beadwork or fruits and vegetables.

I loved to walk in Darjeeling watching the village people and getting into conversation with them, though I was saddened by their poverty and the miserable, torn, and patched clothes their

Above: Ma at Bangalore in 1926, with the cups won by her hunters at the Horse Show.

Opposite: Ma and children on horseback at Ooty

children wore. I once thrust our expensive woollens imported from Fortnum and Mason in London on them, delighted to be rid of the nasty, prickly things myself. But Menaka, who was always much more dignified than I was, said, "You can't do that sort of thing. Remember who we are. You can't gossip with coolies and just anybody on the street."

My memories of Darjeeling are full of small family dramas mixed with the vividly recalled freedom and pleasures of our days. For instance, one of the few religious observances that Ma insisted Ila, Menaka, and I should perform regularly was Shiv Puja. This involved giving prayers and offerings to the god Shiv in order to obtain good husbands, which was easy enough. But it also meant fasting all day on Mondays, from sunrise to sunset, without anything to eat or drink, and this was considerably more difficult since we were still expected to go riding, do our lessons, and generally behave as though it was a normal day. I can vividly remember coming into the dining-room at "Colinton" one Monday and seeing the table laid for tea; there, presiding enticingly over the rest of the food, was a splendid chocolate cake. The temptation was too much for me and I quickly stole a slice. What I hadn't realized was that Indrajit had quietly followed me into the dining-room and had watched the whole furtive performance without attempting to stop me. He didn't tell, but for several days he was able to get me to do anything he wanted. None of the rest of the family could understand why I ran about fetching and carrying for him.

This incident was not entirely out of character for Indrajit. I remember that when we were staying in London we had comics like *Tiger Tim* and *Puck* delivered to the house. In those days they cost tuppence each, and Indrajit, who always managed to get hold of them first, used to charge Menaka and me a penny each for the privilege of reading them. His argument was that in this arrangement we all gained: Menaka and I were getting tuppence worth of comics for only a penny, while he was making a profit of tuppence. We were unable to find a flaw in this logic. Even Ma had once been brought to a similar baffled halt by Indrajit's tricky reasoning. He had written to her from school, "You'll be happy to hear that I came second in my maths exam." When his report card, and with it his place in the class, arrived, Ma saw that he was last but one. Indrajit blithely replied to her recriminations, "But I didn't say second from which end of the list."

In Darjeeling we all led a vigorous outdoor life which suited me perfectly. At that time the roads were considered too steep and treacherous for cars. Nowadays, of course, everyone travels by jeep, but when I was a child, motor transport was prohibited and we went about on foot, or on horseback, or by rickshaw. We, and all the other princely houses that summered there, had our own state rickshaws, with our crest painted on the sides. They would be pulled by three or four rickshaw-coolies while a couple of ADCs on horseback rode ahead. We children rode or walked for miles every day. On our bi-weekly expeditions to roller-skate at the Gymkhana Club, for instance, we always walked the five miles each way.

To Ma's distress, true to my tomboy reputation I used to spend most of my days climbing the grim-faced hills, occasionally dragging a reluctant Menaka or a Baroda cousin along. But I had more bravery than talent. Quite often I got stuck and managed to extricate myself only after prolonged manoeuvring, returning home soaking wet and with leeches in my socks. The only blot on this athletic and untrammelled life, as far as I was concerned, was that Ma insisted on our wearing solar topees when we went riding. I hated my cumbersome pith helmet and even threw one into the Darjeeling waterfall, but the supply seemed to be depressingly unlimited.

As a family, we all loved animals and acquired a considerable menagerie. Ma had an uncontrollable Dalmatian, Indrajit had a heron from which he was maddeningly inseparable, while I had a series of dogs and two baby panthers. We all owned monkeys, and Ma had two marmosets. Ila, who had a remarkable talent with animals, collected all sorts of maimed or abandoned creatures. She had a deer with a broken leg; when everyone else thought the deer would die, Ila insisted that it could be saved and brought it to live in the house while she nursed it back to health. Later on, when Ila went to school in Paris, the deer was put in the zoo in Calcutta. When she returned, the first place she stopped, even before coming to "Woodlands," was the zoo. She had been away for two and a half years, but the deer immediately recognized her and came up to the fence to nuzzle her hand. Once, when one of Ma's English hunters gashed his head and was given up for lost, Ila would not allow him to be destroyed and sat up in the stable all night calming him down, which even the grooms had been unable to do. To everyone's amazement, the horse pulled round by morning.

Apart from our trips to hill-stations, as we got older we would often visit other princely states, chiefly our grandparents' palace in Baroda. I remember, as well, going to Bhopal in central India, where Bhaiya and Ila played hockey and other games with the Nawab's three daughters, and once I went with Ma to Bikaner on an imperial grouse shoot.

But our summers in Darjeeling stand out in my memory as the most wonderful times, and all sorts of trivial but endearing details of our life there come back to me now. Going to my first "talkie" film, for instance, and not being able to hear a word of it because of the noise of the rain splattering on the tin roof. Going to the Gymkhana Club, of which my grandfather had been the first president, and skating with our friends to the music of the band, and how Indrajit was especially good and was always chosen to waltz with the teacher. How Ila wickedly mimicked the atrocious Hindi the English visitors spoke to their servants; how Ma, as usual, was the center of a large and permanent house-party. I remember being cold—the only times we ever were, in India—and fussing about wearing silk tunics for dancing lessons and having to take baths. At "Colinton," as always in India, we never had Western-style baths but sat on a wooden bench with a silver jug full of water in front of us. We had to soap ourselves and rinse off before getting into the tub. Ma maintained that this was much cleaner than soaking in a bath, but in Darjeeling it was certainly much chillier, too.

I haven't been back to Ooty or Darjeeling for years, and I don't much want to go back. I imagine they are rather depressing, drab little towns now that neither the state governments nor the princely families move to the hills for the summer any longer. But nothing can change the splendour of the Himalayas, and nothing can erase my memory of those daybreak rides with my brothers and sisters to watch the sun rise over the eternal snows.

Chapter 6

England, the Continent, and Calcutta

WHEN I WAS NINE, we returned to England for the first time since my father's death. Ma had been very worried that if Bhaiya remained in Cooch Behar he would become spoilt. Even before our father died, Bhaiya had shown himself conscious of his position and, much to our parents' amusement, liked to be addressed as Yuvraj, or "Crown Prince." After he became Maharaja, at the age of seven, no one dared to cross him and he got his own way in just about everything.

In the palace grounds there was a playing field where the public used to come to play cricket, football, and hockey with members of our family. Bhaiya often played cricket there with the boys from the town, and Ma noticed that when he was batting, and was clearly out, none of the players called "How's that?" in the usual way, and the umpire remained silent.

For Ma, that was the final straw. She felt that such deferential treatment could only ruin Bhaiya's character and that he should not remain in Cooch Behar. But she was very perturbed about what she should do, because our father, who had been to Eton, had told her that an English education was not suitable for an Indian and that in his own case it had left him ignorant of the country he had to rule. He had always said that he wanted his sons to be educated in India.

Eventually, Ma consulted the Viceroy, whose own sons were at an English prep school called St. Cyprian's in Eastbourne. She must have been impressed with his advice, for shortly afterwards Bhaiya too was enrolled at the school and sailed off to England, to be joined a little later by the rest of us because Ma, characteristically, didn't want to split up the family.

Ila was sent to Ravenscroft, another boarding-school in Eastbourne, Indrajit went to Gibbs School in London, while Menaka and I and Baby, the daughter of Nawab Khusru Jung who lived most of the time with us, all went to a day-school, Glendower, in London. Our first day there was most alarming. We felt ill at ease in our strange new purple uniforms, and as we were, I think, the first Indian pupils the school had ever had, we were the objects of great curiosity. Quite unversed in the ways of English classrooms, we had considerable trouble in understanding the routine and discovering what was expected of us. I puzzled for weeks over a mysterious word that every girl repeated each morning at roll-call in answer to her name; I eventually discovered that it was "Here Miss Heath." But awkward as we were in everything else, we managed to redeem ourselves by being good at games.

Far more interesting than school, though, was life outside it. Ma's social life in London was soon very active. We had a house in South Audley Street and would often meet her in the entrance hall in the morning, coming home from a party just as we were leaving for school. During the winter holidays we took a house at Melton Mowbray, where Ma used to hunt with the Quorn and Cottesmore. She bought a hunter from the Prince of Wales and ruefully recounted how she had fallen off when trying him out. At Easter we went to hunt in the New Forest, but the weather was so cold and miserable when we got there that Ma soon announced that it was impossible and we had better go to France instead. We left at once in a chartered plane for Le Touquet.

Ma was determined that we should all have an unprejudiced but discriminating palate, and the first thing she did after we arrived in France was to persuade us to eat frogs' legs by telling us they were baby chickens. Theoretically our life in Le Touquet was to centre on the beach, with a lot of healthy outdoor activity, while Ma concentrated on the gaming-tables, where she cut a dazzling and exotic figure. Mrs. Evelyn Walsh of Philadelphia, a friend of hers, described her as "the embodiment of charm and grace, the Princess of the One Thousand and One Nights." She wrote to me about seeing for the first time, at the casino in Le Touquet,

> the most fabulously beautiful young Indian lady, holding the longest cigarette holder I had ever seen, wearing a brilliant silk sari and covered with pearls, emeralds, and rubies. She was quite poker-faced but had a pile of chips in front of her to testify to her success and to top it all she had a little live turtle, whose back was laden with three strips of emeralds, diamonds, and rubies and which she was apparently using as a talisman. Every now and then the creature would crawl away across the table but every time she caught it back. The crowd was totally mesmerized by her.

As usual, we were all immensely intrigued by Ma's social life, which seemed so much more amusing than our own. In the afternoons she tried out on us her various newly invented systems for winning at chemin-de-fer, and after she had gone off to the casino in the evenings we sat up, continuing the game, ante-ing up chocolates, long after we were supposed to be in bed. Even Ma's maid followed her fortunes with avid interest. They had an arrangement by which, after a good evening, Ma left her shoes upside down outside her door as a signal of her success.

Alas, Ma's luck was short-lived, and all too soon this delightful and surprising new life came to an end. One evening she lost an enormous amount of money and decided that we could no longer afford to stay at Le Touquet. We took off on one of those overcast April days with strong, gusty winds that I shall always associate with the seaside in England and northern France, and it seemed impossible that our little plane could become airborne. When at last it did, we were tossed about for several hours in terrifying uncertainty before we managed to land at Croydon. Even the pilot was shaken. Ma was the only one who remained quite untroubled and faintly annoyed at the delay.

Early the following year, Menaka had some kind of glandular infection which the doctors feared might be a prelude to tuberculosis, so she was sent to a sanatorium at Leysin, in Switzerland. Baby and I accompanied her and attended a school called Les Noisetiers nearby, while Ila and the boys remained at school in England. Ma sent us off with numerous instructions about studying hard and learning French and being good, and we were to insist on a bath every day. Above all, we were not to let the school serve us any beef, which is forbidden to all Hindus.

As it turned out, baths and beef were no problem; the other students were. At that time we spoke only English and Bengali, and our only interpreter was a tough little redheaded Irish boy. On our very first day he pinned me against a wall and, to cries of "*Demande-lui ça!*" from the other children, conducted a fierce interrogation. Was I really an Indian princess? If so, why hadn't I arrived on an elephant? How many elephants did I have? How many jewels? And so on. The only thing that made them believe my answers was that we were given chicken for lunch instead of beef stew; they assumed that this was because we were royal.

Amusing or exasperating or interesting as our sampling of various schools and various countries was, I still longed to go back to India. It wasn't so much that I was homesick—home was wherever Ma was—but I felt in an amorphous sort of way that my "real" life was in India and would start again, after this European interlude, only when I returned.

To my great joy, the following year, when I was eleven, Ma decided to take me back to India. She herself wanted to get back in time for a *keddah*, a round-up of elephants, which was to be held in Mysore, so she flew home ahead of me, leaving me to travel by ship in the charge of my Baroda grandmother, who was vacationing in Europe at the time. In those days flying was undertaken only by the adventurous, not to say the reckless, and Ma set off without telling her mother, leaving instructions with an ADC to break the news once she was safely airborne. My grandmother was of course horrified when she heard and with tears in her eyes accused the poor Cooch Behar ADC of not taking proper care of Ma. The very next morning the front pages of all the English newspapers carried the news that Ma's plane had crashed into the sea just north of Libya. All the passengers had been forced to climb out and sit on top of the fuselage until they were rescued. The whole experience didn't seem to make any appreciable difference in Ma's attitude towards flying.

My own voyage home may have seemed much more staid to an outsider, as I was on a ship, under the chaperonage of my Baroda grandmother, but to me it was a taste of the wildest freedom I had ever had. Until then I had always been either at school or in the care of a governess to see that I was properly dressed and ate my meals and so on. But on the ship I had a first-class cabin and bath to myself, wandered everywhere unsupervised, and spent my pocket-money on lemonade for the other children. The only person who really took any charge of me was Bhaiya's faithful old valet Ijahar, who was also returning to India for the holidays.

After we got to Bombay the restrictions that were then reimposed on me seemed almost unbearable, but soon we left for Calcutta. It was that winter that I really came to appreciate our house there and the life it contained. "Woodlands" was very much the "third" house in Calcutta, surpassed in status only by "Belvedere," as the Viceregal Lodge was called, and Government House. It was a large white stucco building constructed by the colonial British in the classical East India Company style, with Ionic columns flanking the deep verandas that encircled the house, airy sash-windows, and gracious well-proportioned rooms. At one time the sons of Tipu Sultan, the ruler of Mysore who rebelled against the British and was killed in 1799, were imprisoned there, and they were still said to haunt the rooms. One summer we kept hearing strange sounds on the roof at night, and when no one in the family or on the staff could account for the noises, Ma summoned an exorcist. He turned out to be a most improbable little man wearing a solar topee and bustling efficiently about, but whatever his counter-magic was, it worked, and we heard nothing more of the ghosts.

My Cooch Behar grandfather had bought "Woodlands" from the British about a hundred years after the time of Tipu Sultan and had quickly transformed it into one of the social centres of Calcutta, a tradition that Ma, needless to say, continued magnificently. "Woodlands" was in a residential area of Calcutta, set in such a large garden that no other buildings were visible from the house. As soon as you drove through the great iron gates with the Cooch Behar crest emblazoned on them, and up the red gravel drive, you were surrounded by tall spreading trees and thickets of ornamental shrubs and bushes. There were beautifully kept flower-beds, too, with every kind of tropical flower: jasmine, frangipani, roses, poinsettias, and *baku*, a white star-shaped blossom with a strong scent. Within the grounds there were also a cricket pitch, a riding track, and two tennis-courts.

Behind the main house were the staff quarters and the stables. We kept about six ponies for us children, three or four horses for Ma, and a dozen more for any guests and the ADCs. In the garages Mr. Davidson, our English chauffeur, presided over a collection of motorcars ranging from Ma's latest sedan to some elderly sports-cars that had belonged to my father. Mr. Davidson was reputed to have been the first man to drive a car in Calcutta, and I spent entrancing days talking to him in the garages. His daughter was a great friend of mine and, also, his house was a gathering-place for jockeys, so his advice about horses during the racing season was marvellously sound. I became a very knowledgeable purveyor of Mr. Davidson's racing tips to Ma's guests. The first of them to listen to me on the subject was the Viceroy's son, Lord Rattendon, who excused himself from lunch one day, telling Ma that he was off to place a bet on a horse called Royal Air Force that I had assured him would win the Viceroy's Cup that afternoon. Ma protested that I couldn't possibly know anything about the matter, but Lord Rattendon very sensibly followed my advice. Sure enough, that afternoon Royal Air Force came in first, and Ma was most impressed.

Inside "Woodlands," Ma had given her imagination full rein and had decorated each room in a different style. The scheme for the drawing-room was dictated by a beautiful Chinese screen made of wood and encrusted with jade and rose quartz, while others were French or English or Italian. Her own room was the most oriental in the house, filled with divans and Persian rugs and dominated by the fabulous carved ivory bed, with its great elephant tusks sticking dangerously out of the legs, which is now in the family museum in Baroda. However, the centre of the social life at "Woodlands" was the wide veranda overlooking the lawn where Ma liked to gather her guests and family around her. I think it was the first place in Calcutta ever to be furnished in the new style of the 1930s. At the time it was considered very up-to-date and unusual, with modern glass-topped tables and all the furniture very square and chunky-looking (though comfortable). We were very proud of it. Oddly enough, it seemed to blend perfectly with the formal drawing-room next door.

"Woodlands" was always full of people. Whenever we were in India we spent the Christmas season there, an especially important time because the Viceroy always came down from Delhi for a couple of weeks. As there usually wasn't enough room in the house for all our guests, some were accommodated in tents set up in the garden. In my childhood, Lord Willingdon was the Viceroy, and there was a constant coming and going between "Woodlands" and "Belvedere" when he was in residence. One of my most uncomfortable memories is of a garden-party at "Woodlands" held in a huge marquee on the lawn, when Menaka and I had to dance for Lady Willingdon. Dancing by itself was bad enough, but, worse, at the end of our performance we had to present her with flowers. She had a well-known fondness for the colour mauve, but, as a result of some muddle, the servants gave me a bunch of red roses to present to her, while Menaka got the mauve sweet-peas to give to the Governor's wife. I shall never forget my agony of embarrassment when I heard Lady Willingdon's voice above me, saying firmly, "No, dear, I don't think these can be for me."

Theoretically, viceregal entertaining demanded perfection, but in practice attempting to reach such an unattainable standard invited disaster, and at "Woodlands" there always seemed to be some minor mishap. The most inexplicable and infuriating to Ma was a menu for a special dinner-party. After she had spent days planning it, the menu was finally printed in French, on handsome cards with the Cooch Behar crest at the top. But on the night of the dinner, Ma's Russian chef, who had earlier been a lieutenant in the czar's army, produced a sumptuous meal, not a single course of which corresponded to the printed menu. I don't think anyone minded except Ma, but she was certainly most put out.

Of all the many people who came to "Woodlands," a few stand out in my memory: the Maharaja of Kashmir, who always came for the races and sometimes stabled his horses there; Prince Aly Khan, who, like Ma's other Muslim friends, was intrigued by my Muslim name; and the specially thrilling Douglas Fairbanks, Sr., the great swashbuckling film star. I remember that he was expected at "Woodlands" in the early evening, and for two days beforehand I was in a silent turmoil dreading that he would be late and I should be sent to bed before he arrived. When the evening came, this dismal prospect seemed increasingly likely as the minutes passed, but mercifully I was reprieved. He had, it turned out, been caught by fans at the Howrah Bridge, then—as now—the only bridge over the Hooghly River, which flows through Calcutta. When he finally got to "Woodlands" at eleven o'clock, all his buttons had been torn off as souvenirs. I did meet him, and he was immensely charming. He gave each of us a signed photograph of himself. Mine was inscribed, "Remember the 23rd of May," and I could hardly believe the wonderful coincidence that he and I shared a birthday. I still have the photograph. Later he came to Cooch Behar on a shoot and I had an even more unexpected bit of luck. My nose had started to bleed—probably from overexcitement—and Douglas Fairbanks looked after me and put a key down my back to stop the bleeding.

But in the eyes of Ila, Menaka, and me, the most glamorous visitor of all was the Maharaja of Jaipur, who came to stay with us during the Christmas holidays of 1931, when I was twelve.

Chapter 7

The Maharaja of Jaipur

THE WEEK BEFORE the Maharaja of Jaipur arrived for the Calcutta polo season Ma said that Menaka and I would have to give up our rooms to him because "Woodlands" was, as usual, very full. This seemed the most trivial inconvenience, considering the prospect of a visit from such a hero.

An English writer, Rosita Forbes, describing him at about this time, wrote:

> Because of his appearance and his charm, his possessions and his feats on horseback, this exceedingly good-looking young man, famous as a sportsman in three continents, occupies in the imagination of the Indian general public much the same position as the Prince of Wales did in the minds of workingmen [in England]. In no other way can I suggest the universal popularity, combined with a rather breathless wonder as to what he will do next, which surrounds this best-known of India's young Rulers.

Naturally, we were the envy of all our friends, and our own excitement grew to a feverish pitch when sixty of his beautiful polo ponies with their grooms wearing flamboyant Rajput turbans arrived from Jaipur. Then finally, late one afternoon he came, a dashing figure driving a green Rolls Royce.

Jai, as he was known to his friends, must have been twenty-one at the time and had just completed his training at Woolwich Military Academy in England. He was very slim and handsome, and impeccably dressed, though usually in a casual, informal style. His ADCs, by contrast, were always formally attired, and his grooms wore the state uniform with brilliant orange turbans. Everyone in

Calcutta found him charming and relaxed, and yet he generated an air of graceful confidence that was most compelling. He laughed and joked with everyone in his low, drawling voice, and was very flirtatious, which made him all the more attractive. It was his humour and the sympathy he added to it that drew me so forcefully to him, although throughout my childhood I always referred to him as the Maharaja of Jaipur and addressed him as Your Highness, while my brothers called him Jai Dada, "Brother Jai."

I was still too young to appreciate the significance of his being the Maharaja of Jaipur; besides, we had been surrounded by princely families all our lives, so the title seemed less impressive. In my sports-loving eyes, his special glamour was that he was India's leading polo-player. He had started the Jaipur team soon after he returned from Woolwich, with the famous polo-player Rao Raja Hanut Singh, his brother Rao Raja Abhey Singh, and Prithi Singh of Baria. They were just starting on the glittering career that was to make the team world-famous. From 1933 to 1939 the team was to win the India Polo Association Championship Cup each year without a break. And in 1933, when Jai led his players to England, they won all the tournaments they entered, and his own handicap went up to nine.

Polo in India occupied a place not unlike football in England and America today, so all through the thirties Jai was a popular hero. Whenever he drove to a match, the police had to clear a path through the crowds, and when the Jaipur team won, his fans poured onto the polo-grounds in thousands to touch his feet in homage. Many members of the business community in Calcutta came from Rajputana (now Rajasthan), and quite apart from their local loyalty, they considered the large bets they placed on the Jaipur team to be a sound and profitable investment.

As for me, from the time in 1931 when Jai first stayed with us in Calcutta, I started to daydream—the reverse of the usual fairy-tale—that I would somehow, miraculously, be transformed from a princess into a groom so that I could hold his horse for him and hand him his stick, and he might, inadvertently, touch my hand. From the beginning he took far more notice of Menaka and me than did most of the guests at "Woodlands." Usually in Ma's world we were onlookers, not confined to the nursery yet not encouraged to join in the conversations or make nuisances of ourselves. But Jai didn't treat us like children who were of no interest to grown-ups.

On the afternoons when he wasn't on the polo-grounds, he came and played tennis with us, roping in an ADC or some member of his entourage to make up a fourth. I didn't realize that he was playing a game easy enough for Menaka and me to join in. I learned rather harshly about his gentleness in his games with us when he challenged Ma to a set of tennis. Ma was quite a good player in those days, and I reassured her about the match. "You'll easily win, Ma. He's not very good."

Ma said, "Are you sure? He's a young man and very athletic."

"Oh," I replied airily, "his polo and riding may be marvellous, but he really isn't all that good at tennis."

Jai played normally with Ma and beat her hopelessly; she didn't win a single game. Ma was furious with me. She said, "How *could* you tell me he didn't play well? Didn't you realize that he wasn't trying his hardest when he played with you?"

Later on, Jai decided that I shouldn't be allowed to win all the time. Menaka, Baby, and I had formed a Dare Club, in which we dared each other to do dangerous things like climbing out onto the roof. We had formed the club in the billiard-room, and I had put some blue cue-chalk on the end of my nose to show that I was the president. When Jai saw me, he asked me what on earth I was doing with blue chalk on my nose. I explained to him about the Dare Club, and he immediately challenged me to a bicycle race. He beat me with no trouble at all, even though I rather fancied myself as a swift and reckless rider. Chastened, I realized that however kind Jai might be to me, I still belonged with the other children and Jai was quite outside my orbit.

The next year he came back to Calcutta for the winter season and once again won the India Polo Association Championship. In the midst of all the enthusiastic congratulations, Ma rashly told him that he could have "anything you want." To my dazzled amazement, he immediately said he wanted me to come to a celebration dinner at Firpo's, Calcutta's most fashionable restaurant. Even more astonishing, Ma agreed. A sari was found for me—I still wore the tunics and pyjamas that are the usual children's dress in our part of India—

but evening slippers proved more difficult. Ma's maid and I walked round New Market for hours before we found anything the right size.

At Firpo's Jai insisted that I should sit beside him and asked me to choose my other neighbour. I picked one of his ADCs who was only seventeen, often talked to us and joined in our games, and so was less intimidating to me than Jai's smart polo friends. We were served partridges, which I didn't know how to cut up, so Jai helped me with them. Then after dinner I was driven home by the chauffeur, still dizzy and unbelieving.

Shortly after this extraordinary evening, Ma made another unheard-of concession. Jai had developed water on the knee and was confined to the house. He asked Ma if Menaka and I could have supper with him one evening when the rest of the house-party were dining out. She said we could. We were having a lovely, laughing time when, promptly at nine o'clock, our governess came to take us off to bed. I suppose Jai must have seen our disappointment, because he skilfully persuaded her to let us stay a little longer by telling her, quite untruthfully, that Ma had given us permission to stay up late. He rose still farther in our estimation when he threw a piece of toast at her departing back and then offered us sips of champagne from his glass to celebrate the success of the Jaipur team. I said primly that I never drank out of someone else's glass and, to Menaka's suppressed fury, was given a full glass of my own. After that, I began to have more ambitious daydreams—that the floor of his room, which was immediately above the one that Menaka and I shared, would fall through in the middle of the night, landing him (miraculously uninjured) in our room to spend the rest of the night with us. I even began wishing for something that seemed to me even more unlikely—that I would grow up to be beautiful and that Jai would actually kiss me.

Everything about Jai fascinated us, and little by little we began to learn something of his life. Jai had not been born a maharaja, but the second son of a Jaipur princeling. When he was two, the story goes, Jai's mother had watched him playing with tears in her eyes. She was asked why she was weeping and replied that she had a premonition that her son would be taken from her, as he was destined for higher things.

It happened that the then Maharaja of Jaipur, Sawai Madho

Singh II, had no heir, and as he grew older he decided that it was time to choose his successor. Without explaining the reason, he summoned Jai and his older brother, sons of his cousin, the Thakur of Isarda, to come to Jaipur City to pay their respects to the ruler. They were given an audience in the City Palace, and each boy held out in his cupped hands, in the ceremonial way, a gold coin to be accepted by the ruler in acknowledgement of their allegiance. The Jaipur legend is that while Jai's brother stood there properly waiting, Jai, who was only ten, grew impatient at the Maharaja's slowness in accepting the tribute, dropped his hands to his sides, and pocketed the gold coin. This so struck the Maharaja as a sign of independence and character appropriate to a prince that he took the unusual step of adopting the younger boy.

Four months after his fateful visit to the capital, Jai was awakened in the middle of the night and told only that he was being taken on a journey. It was all very mysterious, and the poor boy was quite bewildered and miserable. Only when he reached Jaipur did he discover that he was to be adopted by the Maharaja as his heir and would then become the Maharaj Kumar, or heir apparent, of Jaipur. All this meant very little to a small boy who had suddenly been taken away from his family, friends, and companions and installed in the vast City Palace in Jaipur in the care of the first wife of the Maharaja. It was explained to him that he had to be guarded very carefully, as there was another family which claimed the right to succeed to the throne, but this did nothing to alleviate his homesickness. So great was the fear that some resentful person might try to harm him that he was rarely allowed out of the palace gates.

He often asked that his own family be permitted to visit him, and they did, but these were uneasy meetings. They would be shown into a room where Jai was sitting. Of course he would get up and embrace his mother and greet his sisters and brother, but then they would all sit down again and the atmosphere would become formal. There was a great difference between a semi-official reception in a drawing-room and a real family gathering, with the children playing around. He was, after all, still a child himself, and he was made uncomfortable by the slight deference that his family had to show him as the prospective heir apparent to their Maharaja. His sisters would sit still, unnaturally restrained. There couldn't be any of the familiar gossip and chat and fun because zenana ladies would be present, sometimes the maharanis, and none of this was conducive to the kind of free and easy exchange with his family that he was longing for, the exuberant mischief that he and his cousins used to get into, the games and the practicing of polo shots on make-believe ponies, the general rough-and-tumble of an easy, happy family life. The Jaipur court was surrounded by so much ceremony that any such occasion was impossible. He told me, years later, that this was the most miserable period of his life, even though the zenana ladies spoiled him, fed him too many sweets, petted him, watched over him, and tried to be kind to him. But for a young, athletic, fun-loving boy, it was naturally lonely and disagreeable, and he got fatter and fatter and sadder and sadder.

A month after his arrival in the zenana, his formal adoption took place and there was great jubilation throughout the state when Kumar Mormukut Singh of Isarda became Maharaj Kumar Man Singh of Jaipur. Gradually, in the months that followed, the security measures were relaxed and Jai was taken shooting and on other outings. He also undertook his other princely duties, attended state functions, and at times even stood in for the Maharaja.

In 1922, one year after Jai had been brought to the City Palace, the Maharaja fell ill. A brave and realistic man, he knew he was going to die and made all the necessary arrangements for the government of the state during Jai's long minority that was to follow. Maharaja Sawai Madho Singh's reign came to an end on 7 September 1922. He had ruled since the beginning of the century, had achieved widespread popularity, and had done a great deal towards modernizing Jaipur State. He had remained, however, a strict observer of all the traditional Hindu customs and beliefs. Not long after his accession to the throne he had been invited to attend the coronation of Edward VII in London. For him this was an awkward predicament, for while he had no wish to offend the King-Emperor, he adhered to the old Hindu belief that a journey across the seas might pollute him in the eyes of the gods—and also of his own subjects.

After consultations with the pundits, a workable compromise was reached. The Maharaja did go to England, and to the coro-

Left: Jai at the age of ten, photographed on the occasion of his formal adoption in 1921.

Below: Jai a year later, with his first tiger.

nation in Westminster Abbey, but only after the most elaborate precautions had been taken. Before he boarded his ship at Bombay, gifts of gold, silver, and silk were thrown into the harbour to propitiate the sea. The ship itself was a brand-new P. and O. liner which he had specially chartered and which had then been redesigned to meet his particular requirements. These included a room consecrated as a temple for his deity. The ship was loaded with specially prepared foods, all cooked in the prescribed way, and water from the Ganges was carried on board in huge silver pots taller than a man and specially made for the occasion. The Maharaja and his retinue were away in England for six months and occupied three houses in Kensington. During this time, Ganges water was regularly sent to them from India; the great silver water containers still stand in the City Palace today.

Five days after the death of his adoptive father, Jai ascended the throne of Jaipur. The British consulted with the ministers of the old Maharaja and with the nobles of Jaipur State, and together they made up a minority council to rule the state until Jai came of age. The British Resident, who became one of his guardians, and a Rajput noble, Donkal Singh, his Indian guardian, arranged for him to move as soon as possible into Rambagh, a palace outside the city walls. A school was started there, and sons of the Jaipur nobility, including Jai's own brother, Bahadur Singh, came to share lessons with him. His life began to take on a much more congenial pattern.

From there, both boys went on to Mayo College in Ajmer, in north India, one of the five schools that had been founded in the late nineteenth century for the sons of noble families. Named for one of the viceroys, Mayo College had been started by Colonel Walter, the British political agent in the Rajput state of Bharatpur. He had always wished that "the sons of the aristocracy in India" might enjoy the benefits of an "Eton in India." But it was not easy to transplant the idea of an English boarding-school into India, and the early masters there must have found it uphill work. At that time each boy was officially permitted to bring only three personal servants with him, excluding grooms. From the start this rule was usually ignored, and many of the students lived in their own houses with large retinues of servants and with stables of several dozen horses. It was a far cry rom the rigorous dormitory living conditions of English public schools.

Another perennial problem that plagued the Mayo College faculty was that of getting the pupils to come back to school after he holidays, and in several cases boys stayed away for a full academic 'ear. But if, in the early days of the school's history, the authorities ıad been unable to exercise the discipline that seemed desirable in a oarding-school run on the English model, things were quite different by the time Jai went there. Early morning parades and sports were compulsory. Turbans had to be worn in all classes, and *achkans*, the formal, long Indian jackets, had to be buttoned right up to the neck, except during examination week. Still, like all maharajas and their heirs, Jai was allowed to live in a separate house with a staff of several servants as well as his Indian and English guardians. Mayo College had made a name for itself in sports, and it was here that Jai first started to play real polo. His Indian guardian, Donkal Singh, was one of the finest players in India, so Jai was lucky to receive first-class coaching right from the start.

Maharaja Sawai Madho Singh, before he died, had arranged two marriages for Jai, both to princesses from the house of the neighbouring Rajput state of Jodhpur. Rajputana was not unlike Scotland, with its clans, and the ruler of Jaipur was the head of the Kachwaha clan of Rajputs, while the heads of other Rajput clans were the rulers of Jodhpur, Udaipur, Jaisalmer, and so on. Jai's engagement to the Jodhpur princesses was dynastically very correct.

Soon after Jai went to Mayo College he was married to his first wife. That was in 1923, when he was twelve. She was the sister of the Maharaja of Jodhpur and considerably older than Jai, but there had been no Rajput of sufficiently elevated rank for her to marry before, so the alliance had been arranged with the royal house of Jaipur. Jai and his retinue travelled to the great fort of Jodhpur for the wedding, a glittering occasion for which all the nobles appeared in their ceremonial attire, and processions of elephants, horses, and camels paraded the streets. In the middle of all the pageantry, the young boy met his bride for the first time. Watching all this was a most interested spectator, the five-year-old princess, niece of the bride, who had also been betrothed to Jai, to be his second wife. Years later she told me that Jai was pointed out to her as her future husband at the time of his first marriage, and that, although she wasn't very clear about what it all meant, she had been teased unmercifully about it by her cousins.

After the wedding, Jai's first wife accompanied him back to Jaipur and was installed in the zenana apartments in the City Palace. Jai himself continued to live in Rambagh. From time to time over the next few years, when he went to pay his respects to Maharaja Madho Singh's widows in the City Palace, he was also taken to see his own wife. In June 1929, their first child, a daughter, was born, followed two years later, amid tremendous rejoicing, by a son. He was the first male heir to be born to a ruling Maharaja of Jaipur for two generations, and so much champagne was consumed in celebration that the boy was nicknamed "Bubbles" by his English nurse. Family and friends still call him Bubbles, and he uses his real name, Bhawani Singh, only on official occasions. His sister, Prem Kumari, was also given a nickname by her nurse, and "Mickey" she remained to most people.

Jai's second wedding took place in 1932, soon after his visit to "Woodlands" for the Calcutta polo season. All of us in Cooch Behar were most curious to know what his new bride was like. It was just at this time that I shot my first panther. When we telegraphed Ma in Delhi telling her my great tidings, she must have passed on the news to Jai, because almost as thrilling as the kill itself was receiving his congratulatory telegram. I seized the opportunity, while thanking him, to ask him to send photographs of his wedding and of his new wife. Of course he never did, but Ma met her soon afterwards and told us how pretty and petite she was, and how bright and lively. I listened to the description with intense interest.

Later that winter, when Jai had returned to India after a triumphant tour of England with his polo team, we in Cooch Behar were due to make one of our periodic visits to Baroda, and on the way, Ma was going to see Indrajit at Mayo College. Since Ajmer was near Jaipur, she decided that we might also pay a short visit to Jai. We were all delighted at the prospect, even though Indrajit wrote an urgent letter to Ma begging her not to bring Ila, Menaka, and me to Mayo since most of the other boys' sisters were in purdah and never came.

We arrived at Jaipur in the early morning and Jai was at the station to meet us, looking very handsome in his military uniform and surrounded by immaculately turned-out ADCs, his military secretary, and a fleet of gleaming cars. We drove slowly through Jaipur on the way to his palace. At that hour of the day it had an extraordinary pastel, fairy-tale quality, something quite different from anything I had ever seen before.

The city lies on a plain, encircled by brown desert hills with fortifications and walls snaking over their contours. The capital itself was the prettiest I had ever seen—an intricacy of domes and towers, lattices and verandas, with all the buildings coloured a deep oleander pink. In the wide well-planned streets the women wore skirts, bodices, and shawls instead of saris, and all the men wore gloriously coloured turbans—red, magenta, daffodil yellow, and an indescribable pink that was both pale and piercing. It was an incredible effect, this pink against the background of desert and blue sky. But I think what struck me most was how astonishingly different it all was from Cooch Behar—language, climate, scenery, everything. In Jaipur the people spoke Jharshahi (a local Rajasthani dialect), while the courtiers spoke Urdu, strongly laced with Persian words. The air was crisp and dry, while in Cooch Behar it was hot and steamy. In all directions there were endless beautiful vistas and an almost stupefying wealth of buildings, constructed of the local sandstone. In Cooch Behar, with its earthquakes and floods, people built in thatch and bamboo only to meet their most basic needs, but in Jaipur were some of the most magnificent stone palaces and temples in all India.

Jai's own palace, Rambagh, was about a five-minute drive from the city and beyond the old walls. It had once been merely a series of pleasure pavilions surrounded by gardens and reflecting pools where the zenana ladies, attended by their maids, would come to picnic, to walk about in the cool of the evening, and to escape, however briefly, from the confines of the City Palace. Later Jai's adoptive grandfather had used it as a shooting-lodge and then had added on to the pavilions the bedrooms, drawing-rooms, and other quarters needed to house visiting maharajas and other important guests. When Jai was at Woolwich, he had Rambagh enlarged, retaining the same style as the buildings of Jaipur City, with scalloped arches

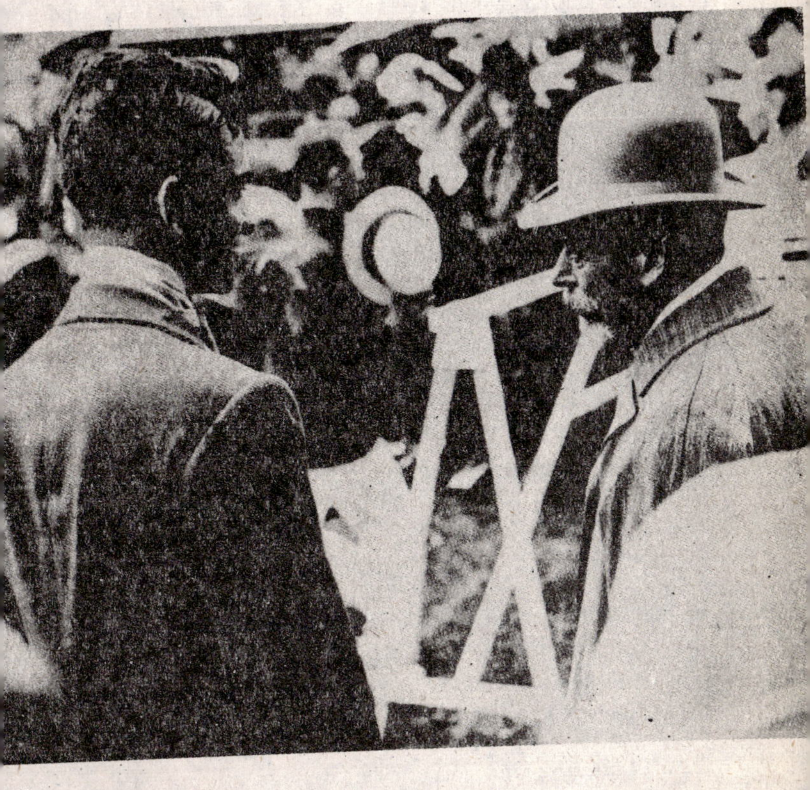

Above: King George V speaks to Jai at the Hurlingham polo, 1933.

Opposite: Jai at twenty-one.

and verandas and cupolas, all arranged around courtyards and all painted white instead of the city's pink. He intended to make Rambagh his official residence, rather than live in the City Palace. Everything inside was modernized and very up-to-date. All the servants wore gold cummerbunds and beautifully tied turbans with dashing great fans of starched cloth on one side, while the ADCs wore jodhpurs and buttoned-up jackets or military uniforms. The nine entrances to the palace grounds were manned by Jai's personal guard.

Later in the day, Jai took us to see the old capital at Amber, set in a gorge seven miles away in the hills dominating the pass to the north. We wandered all over the deserted palace, which had been built to house an enormous court and was completely self-contained within the fortress walls. It was very old, a reminder of the Rajputs' warlike past, and Jai told us that when his ancestors had first come to Jaipur they had captured the fort from a local tribe. You could see, in the vast complex of buildings, how the extreme simplicity of the earliest parts gave way, as the kings of Amber established greater security, to the luxury of the parts constructed in the Mogul period, elaborately decorated with wall painting and mirror-work.

In the afternoon, Ila, Menaka, and I went with Ma to visit the zenana, where the dowager maharanis and Jai's wives and sisters lived in purdah, and I met Jai's wives for the first time. We entered the zenana quarters in the Rambagh Palace and were received in the junior Maharani's drawing-room. Ma's description of her had been absolutely accurate—she *was* very petite and pretty. But somehow I hadn't expected that she would wear make-up and have her hair fashionably bobbed and speak excellent English. Nor had I expected that the furnishings of her apartments would be so modern and have such an air of sophistication; they could have been anywhere, in England or Europe or Calcutta, and only the view from the latticed windows into the enclosed courtyards and the screens of trees in the zenana gardens reminded us of where we were.

However, it was the senior Maharani who came forward to greet Ma first and then be introduced to the rest of us. She was small and dignified and much older. She didn't wear any make-up or make any pretence to modernity, but her manners were regal and impeccable. She sat with Ma and talked almost exclusively to her. It was the junior Maharani who was alive and gay and full of chatter—ordering tea, cold drinks, or whatever else we wanted and more or less acting as hostess. It all made me feel very young and awkward, and as groups formed on chairs and sofas, I was relieved that the two Maharanis occupied themselves mostly with Ma and Ila and left Menaka and me to the company of the young Princesses of Panna, Jai's nieces, who were more our age.

The next afternoon in the zenana there was a garden-party for us which was much bigger and grander. A number of officials' wives, both Indian and English, had been invited, as well as the wives of many of the Jaipur nobles. Refreshments were served and a band played for our entertainment. There was a badminton court, and I remember enjoying playing with the younger girls. Jai came in for a few minutes, and his children were brought in by their English nannies. I will always carry in my mind the picture of Jai playing with Bubbles, throwing him up in the air, taking off his hat—one of those typical round hats with an elastic to hold it under the chin which children wore in those days—and bouncing it up and down just out of Bubbles's reach. He spoke to a few of the guests but soon left, and although it was a charming and beautifully organized party, the pleasure of it dimmed for me as soon as he departed.

On the second day, Jai asked Ma if he could take me out riding, and Ma allowed me to go. Outside the city there were no buildings of any kind except for the palaces, and it was wonderful riding country where one could gallop for miles. Everywhere there were black buck and peacocks, for the land around the city was the Maharaja's reserve and no one was allowed to shoot on it. I was very much in awe of Jai and painfully self-conscious in his presence. He was, as always, perfectly at ease. He was curious to see how well I rode, and several times corrected my seat and hands. When we got home he told Ma that I was quite a good rider, but that when he had told me of certain improvements I could make, I had paid no attention. Afterwards Ma asked me why I didn't take his expert advice, and I answered reluctantly, "I'll do what he tells me, but not in his presence."

I was fourteen at this time, and befuddled as I was with daydreams, one thing was becoming clear even to me. I was in love with Jai. And I hadn't a hope that anything could come of it.

Chapter 8

I Become Engaged

SOON AFTER our visit to Jaipur, Ma told me that Jai had said he wanted to marry me when I was grown up, and that she had replied, "I never heard such sentimental rubbish!"

I couldn't bring myself to believe that someone so far out of my orbit, a hero with a full and fascinating life of his own, could possibly be serious about me. But why would he have said it if he didn't mean it? The more I puzzled about this, the more incredible the whole idea seemed. I fed my own feelings by reading anything I could find about him—and he was much in the news. If anyone talked about him, I listened with extreme interest. Whatever he wore was correct, in my eyes. Whatever he said had to be copied. I liked the way he talked. I liked everything about him.

I did silly, infatuated things. For example, Jai always wore a bandage around his wrist when he played polo. Once I found one of his discarded bandages. It was the only thing of his I owned. I took a couple of threads from it and enclosed them in a locket which I wore everywhere I went. I still have that locket with its bandage-threads.

All through the following six years we saw quite a lot of Jai. He came to Calcutta every winter for the season, and Ma often met him in Delhi, where the horse shows and polo games were held in February and March, attended by many of our friends from the princely families. Ma reported to us things he had said and done, and her maids, who all adored him because he laughed and joked with them, sometimes told me that he had said things like, "Oh, that princess of yours! How she stamps about the place! Has she no femininity?" But when we actually met he never treated me as anything more than a specially nice friend, and that was quite enough to thrill me.

At that time Bhaiya had come back from Cambridge after having completed only one year. He was bitterly disappointed not to be able to continue, but the Viceroy, Lord Willingdon, was about to retire from India, and before he left he wanted to hand Bhaiya his powers as Maharaja. So our brother returned when he was nineteen to have some years of administrative training before he came of age. For Menaka and me it was wonderful to have him back in Cooch Behar. If Jai was a hero in my eyes, Bhaiya was another; indeed, they had much in common and were very good friends. I used to worship Bhaiya, so good-looking, so good at games, so good at everything. At the same time he was gentle and affectionate, funny and mischievous, and kept us in gales of giggles with the sly nicknames he gave to dignitaries. Fun always seemed to erupt around him. Yet when he wanted he could enthrall us with his astonishing store of odd historical facts and strange, little-known stories.

When I was fifteen, Ma decided that we were not speaking enough Bengali (in Cooch Behar we spoke a dialect), so she sent Ila, Baby, and me to Shantiniketan, the school run by the poet and Nobel Prize winner, Rabindranath Tagore. Shantiniketan was in the country outside Calcutta and was considered both very progressive and a centre for the best of traditional Indian culture. Indira Nehru had recently been a student there. Our classes were held under the trees instead of indoors, and Ila took the arts course, while I, since I had not yet matriculated, continued my ordinary education. We were accompanied to school by an ADC, his wife and children, and also by a maid.

At first we were treated very much as princesses by the other girls, who used the formal Bengali address, *apni*, instead of the familiar *tumi* to us (the distinction is much the same as the French *vous* and *tu*). Fortunately, my living arrangements at Shantiniketan made it impossible to continue this formality for long. Although Ila had her own bedroom, I slept in a dormitory with the other girls.

Rabindranath Tagore, whom we called Gurudev, "Respected Teacher," was an imposing figure in his long saffron robe and long white beard. He had stopped teaching by then, but still we saw him quite often. He lived in a charming hut where he wrote and painted, displaying his work on a tree on the campus. His only regular appearances were at the weekly prayer meetings, but he was always accessible and seemed to know all about the pupils in the greatest detail. I used to bicycle over to see him whenever I felt like it, and once, to my consternation, he asked me if my writing had improved —I couldn't break myself of the habit of writing the Bengali "ঽ" backwards. He also sent a message to Ila and me telling us to stop performing the Shiv Puja, with its prayers and fasting, that Ma had always insisted on. Gurudev did not believe in idol worship. Another time, after a bad thunderstorm, he asked me if I had been frightened. When I replied that I hadn't, he said that it was beautiful when a young girl was frightened by a thunderstorm. He also asked me once why I had given up dancing, and added that it was a pity for a girl not to dance. I wonder how much he knew about Ila's growing affection for a fellow student, the cousin of the Maharaja of Tripura. Certainly he gave no sign of any knowledge, and if he spoke to Ila about it in private, she never told me anything.

We stayed at Shantiniketan for almost a year, during which I didn't see Jai at all, and then, in 1935, I went back to Cooch Behar to take the matriculation examination. I sat for it in the college at Cooch Behar, and Bhaiya kept driving past the windows in his new Bentley, waving at me encouragingly. I was sure that this brotherly solicitude had a good deal to do with my passing with a First Class. After this, Ma was not sure what to do with me. She was determined that I should be kept occupied, with no time to moon about the palace thinking of Jai. Eventually she decided that I should go to a finishing school in Switzerland, while Ila was to take another arts course at the Sorbonne. So, in the early spring of 1936, we once again started to make preparations to leave for Europe. My Baroda grandmother took Ila and Menaka with her by boat, while Ma and I were to fly out a little later.

Just after their departure, someone at a party in Calcutta asked Ma whether it was really true that her eldest daughter had married a cousin of the Maharaja of Tripura. Ma denied the rumour briskly, adding some remark about how there was no knowing what nonsense the gossips would think up next. However, just to be sure and to set her own slightly worried mind at rest, she did a little investigation and found that Ila had indeed married Romendra Kishore Dev Varma, in, of all places, a registry office in Calcutta.

Pandemonium ensued. Ma was very hurt, insisting that it was quite different from her own marriage to our father. She had at least asked her parents for their permission, and her marriage itself was entirely out in the open even if it wasn't approved. But Ila had just gone ahead and got married in a thoroughly underhanded way. There was, of course, not much that Ma could do about it now, but she felt that at least we should get to Paris as quickly as possible to bring Ila back to India for a proper Hindu wedding in Cooch Behar. She simply couldn't get over the unheard-of business of an Indian princess getting married in a registry office. To her the wedding hardly seemed valid.

On our arrival in Paris we were met by Ila, looking cheerful, and my Baroda grandmother, looking grim. Nothing was said until we reached my grandparents' house in the Avenue Van Dyck, overlooking the Parc Monceau, and the three of them were left alone. I waited anxiously in the hall throughout the interview, hoping that Ila wasn't having too bad a time of it. To my surprise, she soon emerged smiling, while from the room behind her came the sound of voices raised in acrimonious argument. In reply to my urgent questions, Ila complacently described how she had manoeuvred the conversation around to Ma's own marriage, and now Ma and my grandmother were angrily reliving the conflict and estrangement, minute by minute, and had forgotten all about Ila.

To my own baffled questions about why she had done this extraordinary thing so furtively, Ila explained, as if it were the most obvious thing in the world, that she was pretty certain Ma wouldn't approve of her marrying Romendra Kishore Dev Varma because he was still a student and living with his family, so she had thought it best that they get married first and ask for permission afterwards. Then if there were fireworks and they were forbidden to marry, they could simply say, "Well, we're already married, so there's no point in making a fuss." After they had taken their unorthodox step at the registry office, Ila calmly went back to Cooch Behar and her husband returned to college in Tripura to take his final exams. They would both have kept quiet about the whole thing, pursuing their separate lives and waiting until they picked up the courage to speak or until Romendra Kishore Dev Varma had established for himself the kind of life that would allow him to ask for Ila's hand formally. But things hadn't worked out that way.

We spent a couple of weeks in Paris in my grandmother's house, elegant as only a French house can be, while Ma started to make arrangements for Ila's wedding and to buy her trousseau. From there we went to London, where Ila and Ma stayed at the Dorchester Hotel and continued their shopping, and Menaka and I were installed in a flat in Pont Street in the charge of a German baroness. We would, in any case, have enjoyed being back in London sampling the shops and going to the cinema, but for me that visit was made very special by the fact that Jai was in England too, playing polo with Sir Harold Wernher's team. Since I couldn't join the Swiss school until September, still four months away, Ma was determined that my time should be occupied doing something useful. Lady Zia Wernher recommended a finishing school called the Monkey Club where she had just sent her own daughter. Ma immediately took me over to be enrolled.

My first glimpse of the girls at the Monkey Club made me feel that I should never be comfortable there. They all seemed so sophisticated and confident and worldly-wise, and I was hardly reassured when the principal greeted me with the remark, "You're the first Indian monkey we've had here." But things soon improved, the girls turned out to be much simpler and friendlier than they appeared at first, and the Wernhers' daughter, Gina, who knew Jai, was someone with whom I could talk quite naturally about him. The girls from the Monkey Club played tennis at Roehampton, where there was also a polo-ground, and every tennis day I went there hoping to catch a glimpse of Jai. They tried to persuade me to invite him for lunch, but I never had the courage to do it.

In May, Ma took Ila back to Cooch Behar for her wedding, leaving Menaka and me in the Pont Street flat in the care of the baroness and my grandmother, who occupied her usual suite at the Dorchester Hotel. Occasionally Jai tried to see me with the permission of my chaperons, but these attempts always failed. My Baroda grandmother was always stern and uncompromising. Once Jai invited Menaka and me to the finals of the Westchester Cup, a polo tournament between England and America, played alternately in each country. We were dying to go and were very disappointed when our grandmother said we couldn't, convinced it was the end of the matter. But Jai, with his usual resourcefulness, persuaded his friend and fellow player, Hanut Singh of Jodhpur, to invite us instead. This time our grandmother, seeing no danger in this invitation, allowed us to accept. When we got there, naturally I went off and watched the match alone with Jai.

When the school term finished at the Monkey Club, Menaka and I were due to go to Dinard for our holidays, after which I was to join a domestic science school called Brillantmont in Lausanne. Shortly before we left for France, I went, on an impulse, to consult a fortune-teller. She told me that my fate was inextricably linked with a young man who was going to fly away in an aeroplane and that I must get in touch with him before I left. The only young man I knew who was likely to be flying anywhere was Jai, so I rang him up on the excuse that Menaka and I were leaving soon and would like to say good-bye to him.

"Do you mind coming by yourself?" he asked. "I have something I want to talk to you about."

He told me to go to the Dorchester; that would seem quite proper to the baroness. Jai picked me up from the lobby and took me for a drive in his car around Hyde Park. With no introduction, and quite as a matter of course, he said, "You know, I told Ma long ago that I'd like to marry you when you grew up."

I said nothing, not daring to imagine what was coming next.

"You are only sixteen now, but I have to plan ahead for an event like that and make all sorts of arrangements, so I'd like to know if you want to marry me." He kept his eyes on the road, skilfully weaving in and out of the traffic. "Before I ask Ma and go through all the proper formalities, I'd like to know what *you* feel. Remember I play polo and ride and fly and I may have a horrible accident; still, will you marry me?"

"Yes," I said straight away, too overcome to elaborate.

For the first time he looked a bit disconcerted. "Don't answer immediately," he said. "Think about it a moment. You still have to finish school. There's plenty of time; you don't have to say 'yes' if you don't mean it."

"Oh, I mean it all right."

"I meant that if something happens and I'm mutilated or anything awful, I wouldn't expect you to stick by what you say now."

"No, no!" I insisted. "I wouldn't care *what* happened to you, I'd still want to marry you."

Jai went on, very practically, to suggest that I should write to Ma and tell her, after which he would talk to her when he got back to India. Meanwhile, for the short time left before Menaka and I went to Dinard, we decided to keep our secret from our elders but to try somehow to meet every day.

Both my grandmother and the baroness were conscientious chaperons, but despite their vigilance Jai and I managed to meet every day, usually at the Berkeley Hotel. Jai's interest in me was now obvious, and the maître d'hôtel took a conspirator's delight in our romance. Even much later, after Jai left London, whenever I dined at the Berkeley with a group of friends before somebody's coming-out dance, he whispered, "It's not the same without His Highness, is it?" Another reminder of that summer with its joys and frustrations is the telephone kiosk in Pont Street where I used to go to call Jai. In the flat the baroness always listened in on the extension, betraying herself by a little click.

On the phone Jai would ask, "Can you come out, say, this afternoon or this evening?"

And I would reply, "Yes, I'll manage it somehow. Pick me up at six." Then I would return to the flat and say casually that I was going to the cinema that evening with one of my girl friends.

Behind Pont Street there is a square called Wilton Crescent. Jai would drive around in his Bentley and park there. I would leave the flat dressed as I might be for a nothing-special evening, walk around to Wilton Crescent, get into the Bentley, and off we would go. Once he forgot the secrecy and dropped me home at the front door in Pont Street. Sharp-eyed Menaka, seeing us arrive from an upstairs window, greeted me (out of the baroness's hearing) with, "Since when have your girl friends acquired great shiny Bentleys?" I begged Jai to be more careful in future.

He had a pretty busy schedule himself in London, playing polo and leading a full social life, so it was almost as hard for him to get away as it was for me. Sometimes we only managed a quick snack at the Berkeley Buttery, and sometimes we met at Harrods' Bank, an easy walk for me from Pont Street. We pretended not to know each other when we met in the bank. He would walk out first and I would follow, and we wouldn't speak until we were in the Bentley. By now I was less shy of Jai though still a little in awe of him, but we laughed a lot, I remember, and had our private jokes, and then being in love takes up an awful lot of conversation. One talks endlessly about oneself and listens enthralled to the tiniest details about the other person's life or opinions.

Sometimes Menaka, Baby, or Indrajit—all of whom were in the conspiracy—and I announced that we were going to the cinema together. Jai met us there, and he and I left to spend time by ourselves, while the others watched the film alone. We picked them up after the showing was over. They were wonderfully good sports about the whole affair and carefully told me the story and any other points I should know about the film on our way home.

Looking back on it all now I see that those times were much more fun than an ordinary approved courtship would have been. There was the challenge of outwitting our elders, of arranging secret meetings, of working out how to have letters posted without the knowledge of the ADCs, governesses, or clerks who usually handled this chore. And every now and again there was the marvellous, unheard-of liberty of going for a drive in the country with Jai, of a stolen dinner at Bray, or of an outing on the river in a boat. Altogether, it was a lovely and intoxicating time. We sealed it for ourselves by buying gold rings for each other with our names engraved inside. I had carefully hoarded my pocket-money to be able to buy his.

It was easy enough to be brave when I was talking to Jai, but when I was alone and faced the task of writing to Ma as I had promised, I simply couldn't make myself write such an appallingly unconventional letter. It meant letting Ma know about all the ruses we had used to be able to meet and be alone together, and all the lies I had told, and, besides, it just wasn't done for a girl to arrange her own engagement. I kept putting off and putting off writing the letter.

When our holiday in Dinard was over and I had arrived in Lausanne to join the school, I was still wondering how to word the letter

Above: Menaka, Ila, and I. I was sixteen and just about to enter the Monkey Club.

Opposite: Jai and I at a nightclub, about 1937.

and what sort of a rocket I would get as an answer. Then, to my horror, I received a cable from Jai saying, CANNOT UNDERSTAND WHY YOU HAVEN'T WRITTEN MA. WHAT IS WRONG? He had spoken to Ma, but she had told him that she had heard nothing from me. I was convinced that he must think I had changed my mind. I was miserable and hadn't the least idea what to do next.

That same day, as I was out walking with the other girls from Brillantmont, a voice suddenly hailed me. There, surprisingly, was the Indian valet of my Baroda grandfather. He told me that my grandfather was staying at the Beau Rivage in Lausanne. Of course I went as soon as I could to see him, and to my delight found in his retinue an old and dear friend, Dr. Chandra Chud. I poured out the whole story to him, my distress and Jai's distress and my greater distress at Jai's distress, an incoherent muddle which, as I remember, went something like this:

"Doc, I'm in a terrible predicament and I don't know what to do and the Maharaja of Jaipur has asked me to marry him and I have said 'yes' and I was supposed to write to my mother and I haven't and simply don't know what to say to her and I'm so worried and now he's sent me a wire and I don't know whether he's upset or annoyed with me and he thinks I don't really want to marry him and, for heaven's sake, don't tell my grandfather."

Dr. Chandra Chud listened with admirable patience, and then, with a few bracing words, he helped me to compose a cable to Jai: YOU HAVE MISUNDERSTOOD ME. AM WRITING. Simple enough, but I could never have been so straightforward on my own. It must be remembered that I was a very unsophisticated just-seventeen, still greatly impressed by Jai's man-of-the-world image, still somewhat incredulous about his proposal. I couldn't even bring myself to call him Jai to other people, but always "the Maharaja of Jaipur" or "His Highness."

Dr. Chandra Chud also helped me to draft a letter to Ma which read in part, "I think the Maharaja of Jaipur must have spoken to you. I hope you don't mind our arranging this without asking you first. When His Highness asked me directly about marrying him, there was nothing I could do, so I agreed."

To Jai I wrote, "I know I should have written to Ma earlier but

I didn't have the courage and I didn't know what to say. But now I've done it, and I hope you're not annoyed with me. I didn't mean to make you think I didn't want to marry you because I do."

Weak with relief, I gave the three messages to Dr. Chandra Chud to send so that they would not have to go through the hands of the school authorities. Ma, maintaining her non-committal attitude, replied that Jai and I would have to wait and see how we felt in a couple of years' time.

I was happy at Brillantmont, loved the skiing and the other sports, wrote countless letters to Jai, and waited impatiently for the mail to bring his replies. That winter he had a polo accident and seriously injured his back. He had gone to Vienna for treatment and, after his two weeks' convalescence, came to Lausanne to see me. I was, of course, overjoyed to be with him again, but I date from that time my terror of his polo-playing, combined with a knowledge of how enormously much the game meant to him.

Pupils at Brillantmont were allowed out of the school only with family members. I told the principal that Jai was my cousin, and trembled with nervousness until he came, in case I was somehow found out and not permitted to go out with him. After an eternity, he drove up to Brillantmont. Half the school were hanging out of the windows to watch. Jai and I spent the day together and, in the evening, dined at the Palace Hotel. We were so absorbed in each other's company that Jai nearly missed his train, and I arrived back at school at ten o'clock instead of eight. Soon afterwards there were pictures of Jai's children in the society columns of the newspapers, with captions explaining who they and their parents were. I was summoned to the headmistress's study and asked about my relationship to these children. Brazenly, I said that they were my cousin's, and felt quite proud of myself for being able to lie without a tremor. The headmistress said nothing at the time, but some clue in my manner—perhaps my unnatural composure itself—must have given me away, for I noticed that all my letters were opened from then on.

It was at Brillantmont that I heard the moving address of Edward VIII when he abdicated the throne of England for "the woman I love." I had tears in my eyes as I listened, because Ma had often spoken of him as a dear friend.

That summer George VI was crowned, and all the Commonwealth pupils at Brillantmont were given twelve days' holiday for the occasion. Many of the Indian princes had gathered in London for the coronation, and I joined Ma, Bhaiya, and Indrajit at the house that she had taken in Connaught Square for all the parties and excitement that would accompany this royal event. Somewhere in the middle of it all, Ma discovered that the seats she and I had been assigned in Westminster Abbey were behind a pillar. Typically, she decided not to go to the coronation at all. We went to the Dorchester and with my Baroda cousins listened to the whole ceremony on the radio and watched the procession from the windows overlooking the park. Afterwards we heard that the arrangements for cars to be called to take the élite home from the Abbey had broken down. Dukes and duchesses, in their ermine and robes, were seen running down Whitehall in the slight drizzle trying to get cabs. My Baroda grandparents were given a lift home by some English dignitary whose car had managed to get through the muddle to the jammed steps of the Abbey. My grandmother couldn't help remarking that in any Indian princely state this sort of confusion would never occur. Everything would have been much more efficiently handled.

For me this might have been an uncomfortable and troubling time. I seldom saw Jai alone. His second wife, as well as his children, were in London with him. She was allowed much more freedom than she had in India and sometimes visited us in Connaught Square in a friendly and easy way. Indrajit became a favourite of hers; they often went to the theatre and the cinema together, and she had, besides, plenty of company from her Jodhpur relatives who were also in London for the coronation. It could have been an awkward situation for me, but Jai, with his usual tact, handled all these relationships perfectly.

Ma's attitude was puzzling, and I realized later that not only did she have rather mixed feelings about us herself but also was under a lot of pressure from friends and relatives who had picked up hints and gossip about the situation. On the one hand, Ma adored Jai and would have been delighted by the idea of having him as a son-in-law. On the other, she didn't like the prospect of my being anyone's third wife or of Jai's second wife, of whom she had grown fond, being hurt.

Few people envisaged a happy partnership between Jai and me, and as the news started to get around, people warned Ma that my life as the third Maharani might be a very difficult one. In the early days, Ma could dismiss the whole thing as a schoolgirl crush, on my part, and the ordinary affection of a good friend of the family on Jai's, But later, as it became clear that we were quite serious about each other, Ma was forced to listen to what people were saying. She was told that I might be kept in purdah for the rest of my life, or that Jai might marry again. Jai reassured Ma that he had no thought of keeping me in purdah and that he wanted me to be a companion and hostess, but even though she trusted him, she inevitably had misgivings about the match. She would, quite simply, have preferred me to marry a bachelor. Her policy was to be non-committal, not encouraging our meetings but not expressly forbidding them, keeping me involved in lots of activities, hoping that time and distance would have their effect and that I would fall in love with somebody else.

Still, when the rest of the school term was over and I joined Ma in Cannes, I found that Jai was also spending a few days there. Every morning we got up early, before Ma was awake, and went for a swim together in the sea. We spent most of the day together, although we were also with other friends. Menaka and I were still considered too young to be included in much of the constant round of parties and visits to the casino that occupied Ma's and Jai's evenings. Usually we stayed home and played *boule* with Ma's maid and Jai's chauffeur.

It was in Cannes that Jai and I had our first quarrel. One day as Jai was going into the sea for a swim he took off the ring I had given him in London and handed it to Menaka to hold for him. I was seized with a fit of jealousy because he had given it to her instead of to me, and grabbed the ring from her and threw it into the sea. Jai took me by the shoulders and walked with me to the end of the pier, explaining very gently as we went that he hadn't meant to hurt my feelings. Just as I had calmed down, my ruffled feelings smoothed into place, he suddenly pushed me into the sea, fully dressed.

I emerged furious and threw his shoes into the water in revenge. I arrived late for lunch, with my hair still wet, wearing shorts, and seething. Menaka, who was very prim at that stage, was most dismayed. But if I had hoped for any satisfactory matching fury from Jai, I was disappointed. His only comment, delivered with the most maddening cheerfulness, was that his shoes now fit him much better after their shrinking; they had been a size too large before. However, our quarrels were rare, and parting from Jai grew worse and worse. When he left Cannes I ran the length of the platform, holding his hand as the train pulled out. He went on to Biarritz and telephoned me every day from there. His calls always came in the evening and, because we didn't want them to be monitored, I spent hours sitting on the floor of the telephone booth in the hotel lobby so that no one would see me waiting for the call to come through.

In the autumn Jai went back to India, and Menaka, the baroness, and I moved into a new flat in Grosvenor Place in London. There I was enrolled in the London College of Secretaries. It was really Jai who was responsible for this. He was afraid that if I went back to India I might suddenly find myself involved in an engagement, arranged by my elders, to someone I had never seen, and that I would find family pressures too strong to resist. Equally, he didn't want me to become a debutante in London in case I went about too much to parties and dances where I might meet other eligible young men.

As it happened, I went to quite a lot of parties. Many of my English friends were "out" that season and had dances and receptions given for them. Indrajit was in town, and so were my Baroda cousins, who frequently came down from Cambridge, where they were at college. Both Uncle Victor and my Uncle Dhairyashil of Baroda included me in their activities. I often went to watch the cricket at Lord's or the Indian Gymkhana on the Great West Road, and in the evenings I was taken out to restaurants, night-clubs, or one of the many cocktail or dinner parties or balls that were being given for my friends.

I found myself leading a sort of double life. During the day, for six hours, I was known as Miss Devi, learning shorthand, typing, accounting, book-keeping, business correspondence, and other such useful skills. It was assumed that I, like all the others, was training for a job, and I can remember my embarrassment when I had an interview with the placement bureau and was asked whether I hoped to be a secretary to a doctor, a politician, or an artist. In keeping with my replies, the school was ready to give me specialized training beyond the usual courses. Thinking as fast as I could to cope with this serious and well-intentioned questioning, I said that I didn't actually need a job in this country at all, and added, "My mother does a lot of social work in India, and that's why I'm taking this course—to be able to help her." Even as I said it, I had a vision of Ma scolding me: "What in hell are you doing, involved with some job all day?"

Everyone else at the school was deadly serious. Most of them came from working-class families, and I was fascinated by them. None of them knew who I was, until one day a photograph of me at some debutante party appeared in the papers. Then they started asking questions, mainly, "Are you really a princess?" But I was pleased that this didn't make much difference to our lunches together, or to our exchange of information about what sort of future we looked forward to. I wore Western clothes, travelled by bus and underground, and could say in all honesty that I liked doing something concrete, liked working regularly and hard in a kind of school, and in company of a sort that I had never known before. I liked the absolutely practical, in-touch-with-ordinary-daily-life atmosphere in which we worked. Occasionally, one or another of them asked me out to tea. I was shy and followed the lead of my companion, watching our pennies and seeing how much we could order at Lyons' Corner House for the least money. I never had the courage to invite any of them home, finding it too difficult to explain away either the flat in Grosvenor Place or my grandmother's suite at the Dorchester.

During classes I had to put in all the effort I could muster to keep up with them, and like the rest I rushed to the newsstand to pick up a copy of *Pitman's Journal*, compulsory reading for secretaries. I often phoned because of some social engagement to make an excuse for skipping the last hour of classes—how to handle taxes—and I wish now that I hadn't. It was a matter of some pride for me that I was good at shorthand—I can do it to this day—and during the war I was competent enough to take down the news from the radio and read it out to Jai later. After we were married, I found, as well, how useful my knowledge of typing and accounting could be. My business correspondence and my accounts were always perfect. Altogether, although I missed Jai it was a happy winter, climaxing in a Christmas spent skiing with my cousins in Engelberg.

The following June Ma and both my brothers were in Europe, and Menaka and I toured with them through countries and cities we had never seen before: Carlsbad, Prague, Vienna, and Budapest. Everywhere we found ourselves involved in anxious discussions with people we met about Hitler and the Nazis, about the Anschluss, the future of Europe, and the threat of war. But in spite of the ominous news stories and the edgy atmosphere we felt at parties, a sense of time running out, I remember it as a golden and enchanted summer. This was because Jai joined us in Budapest.

The city seemed at its most beautiful, with flowers everywhere and the evenings filled with the lovely sound, alternately plaintive and merry, of the zithers. There was a big tennis tournament, and we went to watch the matches. I still have pictures of them, Jai sitting by my side, both of us looking so young and happy. We went swimming. We went to see horses and horse shows, which we all loved. We drove into the country and stopped at inns or restaurants, gay with flowers, wild with gipsy music. We drank the local wines and took long walks in the long, melting, European summer evenings. I remember being distressed only when the boys would ask the band to play "The Merry Widow Waltz" and then tell me as if it were a joke that there would soon be a war and they would all be killed and I would be the "Merry Widow."

It all seems unremarkable as I describe it. I suppose it was so magical to me only because I was surrounded by all the people dearest to me and, most of all, because I was young and in love and Jai was with me constantly. Even through the rosy glow that my happiness spread on everything, it was difficult in the late summer of 1938 to ignore for long the menace of war, and soon Ma fel. it was time for us to return to London. Apprehensive as she was, I don't think she—or, indeed, any of us—foresaw what a new war would mean for us personally. We all had every reason to sense impending tragedy for Europe, and perhaps we realized dimly that our own lives, as far as European visits went, would change permanently. But we never dreamt that the war would become world-wide and that it would bring so many changes to India t o.

When we returned to London in mid-September we found that my Baroda grandfather was very ill. His only demand in his desperate state was to get back to Baroda, regardless of the consequences. Ma and my grandmother flew home with him in a chartered plane. Soon afterwards Menaka and I received the sad news that our beloved, conventional but modern, strict but affectionate, high-principled but indulgent grandfather was dead.

A few weeks later Menaka and I sailed for India. When we docked in Bombay, Ma was on the pier to meet us, and to my inexpressible delight Jai was with her. That very same evening I received my first brisk reminder that I was back in India. I was about to walk over to the staff annex of Jaya Mahal, the Baroda palace in Bombay where we were staying. Ma stopped me and told me that it was not done for a young girl to go out unaccompanied in India. We had been away two years and I had almost forgotten the rules that governed our lives. Though we were freer than most Indian princesses and were not compelled to remain in purdah, still there was to be no more going to cinemas and restaurants unaccompanied, and even on a simple shopping expedition we would have to take our governess or an ADC. On hearing all these restrictions repeated to me, I had a sharp pang of nostalgia for the freedom of life in London—for the buses and the underground and for just being one of the jostling crowd at rush hour.

Later that evening, when I was beginning to feel sorry for myself, Ma told us to get dressed and put on our prettiest saris because we were going to the Willingdon Club and Jai was coming to fetch us. I immediately came to life and hunted through my wardrobe for the most becoming sari I owned. I had never been to the Willingdon Club as a grown-up. My only memories of it were as a child, watching the polo, so to be going now, and with Jai, made me uncharacteristically careful of how I looked.

The Willingdon held a rather special place in Bombay life. It was the first really elegant club that was open to both Indians and English, and where the élite of both societies mingled on equal terms. It had excellent facilities for all manner of sports, and glorious grounds and lawns edged with the blazing colours of tropical flowers, floodlit in the evenings. In the daytime people met in the fashionable Harbour Bar in the Taj Mahal Hotel for drinks before lunch, but in the evenings all of Bombay's smart society went to have drinks at the Willingdon, sitting in wicker chairs out on the lawns, knowing they would meet all their friends there and that tables would be shifted and enlarged as parties merged or new guests arrived. The waiters in their long white tunics with green cummerbunds and turbans flitted between the tables serving drinks and delicious hot, spicy hors d'oeuvres.

Once we got there, Ma's and Jai's many friends came over to greet them or to stay and chat and have a drink. Our table grew bigger and bigger. It was all very glamorous, the women in ravishing saris, the men in *achkans* or dinner jackets, ready to go on to dinner-parties, others still in sports clothes, having come in from a late round of golf or an after-office game of tennis. For me there was an extra touch of secret intrigue, for as more and more people joined us, Jai and I had to keep manoeuvring to manage to sit next to each other all the time.

Our stay in Bombay was short, and Ma soon swept us off to Calcutta where the season was just about to begin. I went quite happily because I knew that Jai would soon be coming. We settled into the familiar luxury of "Woodlands" and prepared for the season to go into full swing when Lord Linlithgow, who had just replaced Lord Willingdon as Viceroy, came with the viceregal family to spend their customary couple of weeks in Calcutta.

For me that winter was the most fabulous Calcutta season I remember. It was the first time at "Woodlands" that I was considered a grown-up, and although I wasn't allowed quite the freedom of other girls my age—which was especially irritating when I saw my brothers setting out for an evening on the town—there were plenty of parties to which I could go with Ma as a chaperon. As usual, the chief factor in my happiness was that Jai was staying with us, and I saw him constantly and for virtually every meal. Mostly we had to be in the company of others, but occasionally we managed to slip out alone and sometimes he would let me drive his car. Of course, early every morning we went riding together.

Jai, Bhaiya, and Indrajit were in great demand socially and went out together a great deal. They looked so wonderful, setting off in their silk jackets, their tight trousers, and their turbans. They were all tall, slim, and good-looking and were often mistaken for brothers.

Between them they made "Woodlands" livelier than ever that year. By now my brothers and sisters, as well as Ma, invited friends to stay. It was a centre for sportsmen. Bhaiya, who played in the East India tennis championships, invited his fellow competitors. He also organized cricket matches on the pitch in our garden, inviting the Viceroy's team and the Middlesex Cricket Club, among others, to come and play. Many of Bhaiya's and Indrajit's friends were cavalry officers from the Indian Army, and they came to Calcutta for the polo and lived in tents in our garden. One of them got the shock of his life when, returning to his tent after a late party, he came face to face with a huge tusker apparently ready to charge him in the dark. Next morning, he didn't know whether he had been hallucinating or whether he had really escaped a frightful danger. We never enlightened him, although we all knew the elephant. It had been brought down from Cooch Behar to be sent to my Baroda grandfather as a gift for his Diamond Jubilee. Its tusks had been studded with diamonds, and it had been renamed Hira Prashad ("Diamond Offering") and taken down to the docks to be loaded on a ship for Baroda. Alas, the crane that was hoisting him broke. He fell to the quay and broke a leg. After that it was impossible for him to travel to Baroda and we kept him on at "Woodlands" in special quarters, in great comfort, while his leg healed.

"Belvedere," the Viceroy's official residence, was just across the road from "Woodlands," and Bhaiya and I were often asked to play tennis with our neighbours. This brought its own ordeals, for no one had thought to warn me that the Viceroy never changed sides when his partner was serving. I remember standing hesitantly on the baseline wondering when he would move and if I had the courage to start serving. Finally he turned around and said, "Come on, Ayesha, what's the matter with you? Aren't you ever going to start?" Bhaiya, who knew about this habit of the Viceroy's, shook with suppressed laughter on the other side of the net.

On one occasion he and I were asked to an informal dinner at "Belvedere" by the Viceroy's daughter, Lady Joan. It was the first time that I had dined at Viceregal Lodge and was quite unprepared for the moment at the end of the dinner when the ladies withdrew. The Vicereine led the procession out of the dining-room, dropping a deep curtsy to her husband on the way. The other ladies followed in pairs, each sinking to the floor with perfect composure, while I wondered in panic what on earth to do. I had never curtsied before, and I was too frightened of making a fool of myself to begin on this occasion. In the end, when I reached the door I merely folded my hands in a *namaskar* and hoped that the Viceroy would consider this sufficiently respectful.

Parties, tennis, riding, watching the polo, exploring what it was like to be a grown-up—those were the things that made up my life in Calcutta, and I enjoyed every moment of it. All the same, when the time came to return to Cooch Behar, I think all of us shared that happy sense of homecoming that Cooch Behar always gave us. As a group, we brothers and sisters were very congenial. We found entertainments and interests wherever we happened to be, in Europe or India. But Cooch Behar was the place we all loved the most, and on that particular return I found it even more absorbing than usual.

Ma was no longer regent because Bhaiya was now of age, so she spent a good deal of time away from the state visiting Delhi, or especially Bombay, to be with my grandmother. In her absence I used to act as Bhaiya's hostess. It was enormous fun entertaining guests with him, planning things that we would do, discussing outings we might arrange. I used to listen to his conversations with officials and advisers, sometimes offering my own suggestions. He always heard me out, though he smiled and teased me about the wilder and more impractical ones.

In the evenings, after I had bathed and dressed, instead of going to Ma's room as I did when I was a child, I went to Bhaiya's, even when Ma was in residence. I waited until he was ready and then went with him to the drawing-room, walking just behind him. In fact I went everywhere I could with Bhaiya, to such a marked degree that Ila nicknamed me "Shadow." I found that, exhilarating as the season in Calcutta had been, I really much preferred the relaxed, informal, outdoor country life of Cooch Behar to the social round of the big cities.

Country life had its formidable moments, however. Once I found myself inadvertently in charge of a shoot. A tiger had been troubling the villagers by killing their cattle, so Bhaiya and an English friend, Sir Robert Throckmorton, decided to go after it. They sat up all night in a *machan*, a platform built high in a tree, but managed only to wound the tiger. Bhaiya had to leave the next day to attend a meeting of the Chamber of Princes, a body of all the rulers of states which assembled in Delhi once a year to discuss their mutual problems and to consult and inform the Viceroy about conditions in their states. He couldn't ignore this important function and had to leave us to cope with the dreadful situation of a tiger that was both a man-eater and wounded. Sir Robert, Baby, and I, along with the ADC in charge of shooting, the chief hunter on the Cooch Behar staff, and another experienced hunter, all set off to track the tiger down. We needed two elephants to ride, Baby and the ADC in one howdah, Sir Robert and I in another, and eight more elephants to accompany us, and we proceeded very cautiously to the small patch of jungle to which the tiger had been tracked.

We approached in a long strung-out line, riding abreast with one of the two guns at each end. Everyone was as quiet as possible, and at every elephant pace the tension mounted. Then suddenly the elephants scented the tiger and started to trumpet. The tiger gave a tremendous roar, charged out of the undergrowth, and attacked the nearest elephant, which happened to be carrying the chief hunter. The elephant swerved around, throwing the rider to the ground, and then bolted into the jungle with the mahout trying desperately to control him. The tiger then retreated to the jungle, leaving us frighteningly uncertain of where our hunter had fallen or whether he had been killed. The ghastly silence lasted for about half an hour with no one daring to move. Then the tiger charged again, this time making for the elephant carrying Baby and the ADC, which lurched off into the jungle with its passengers, leaving me, extremely nervous, in charge of my very first shoot. To my great relief, Sir Robert managed to finish the tiger off on his last charge, the hunter was not badly hurt, and the day ended with all the villagers joyously surrounding the dead tiger which had caused them so much trouble.

In April 1939, Ma had rented a house in Kashmir, and Menaka and I joined her. With her usual vigour she set about completely redecorating it, even though she had taken it for only eight months. She seemed to know by some extra sense exactly where to buy the finest carpets and ornaments, where to find the best craftsmen and shops. She was satisfied with nothing ready-made that she saw and, instead, ordered exquisitely carved walnut furniture, embroidered cushions, and a large white wool rug for her bedroom. For us the summer passed pleasantly, with polo matches, tennis tournaments, riding to remote places in the Himalayas and picnicking there, and visits from friends. Bhaiya, who was attached at that time to the Seventh Light Cavalry Regiment, came on leave to delight us all and to take part in the polo tournaments. Indrajit, then at the Military Academy in Dehra Dun, also joined us for the polo. Ila, now the mother of a little boy and a girl, came to stay in the houseboat rented for her by Ma. My grandmother had also taken a house in Srinagar, the capital of Kashmir, and had brought with her seven of our cousins from Baroda. To add to our social circle, the Nawab of Pataudi, the famous cricketer, came to Kashmir on his honeymoon, after his marriage to the Princess of Bhopal, and would often organize cricket or hockey matches in which we all played with enthusiasm.

Kashmir is unbelievably beautiful, and we often picnicked in the ornamental gardens of Shalimar and Nishat Bagh, going by the charming little gondola-shaped boats (*shikara*) called by silly names like "Sweet Honeymoon" or "Lovers' Nest." And when September came, Jai arrived in Srinagar to pay a formal visit to the Maharaja of Kashmir in his palace and later to stay with us. From then on I was living in the clouds because every morning we rode together, and with Baby and Menaka as chaperons we went on bear hunts or picnics or for *shikara* trips. I remember it all as the last idyll of my girlhood.

Jai stayed only a short time, for with war threatening he had to go back to his military duties in Jaipur, training his troops and preparing the state for war. Soon after, I was sitting on the river embankment outside the Srinagar Club after a game of tennis and heard that war had been declared in Europe. Although we were expecting it, we were all shocked. To us the most immediate impact of the news was that all the officers on leave had to return at once to their regiments. We were left in a Srinagar half deserted, still caught in the habit of a carefree summer.

For me the first really sobering news came one afternoon in November when we came in from golf to find an urgent message. Jai's plane had crashed. He was unconscious and dangerously ill. I thought my heart had stopped beating. I had often read in romantic novels how the heroine's heart missed a beat in any highly charged emotional situation, but I never expected to feel this improbable reaction myself. It was then, for the first time, that I fully realized how deeply I loved him. That night I couldn't sleep; instead, I sat up, miserable, not crying but unable to think of anything but Jai and how much I wanted to be with him. Ma was very sympathetic but made it clear that it was impossible for an unmarried girl to go to Bombay alone. The following day a telegram arrived to say that, although he was still seriously ill, he had been pronounced out of immediate danger.

Faint with relief, I listened to the account of how the accident had happened. As Jai's plane was circling Bombay, a vulture had flown into one of the wings. The pilot failed to allow for the damage this bizarre incident had caused, and on its approach to Bombay airport the plane had dropped like a stone from a height of 500 feet. The pilot had been killed instantly, and Jai had been dragged from the wreckage, unconscious and with both ankles broken. I was further reassured by the news that the Governor of Bombay, Sir Roger Lumley, had insisted that Jai be moved from the public ward to which he had been taken by the ambulance and would spend his convalescence in Government House, attended by a team of doctors and nurses.

I continued to be obsessed by Jai's welfare after we had left Kashmir for New Delhi and even after Jai was well enough to be taken to Jaipur. Ma had gone to see him, and I waited anxiously for a letter or telegram. Instead, Ma telephoned and said that Jai wanted to see me and was sending a car for me to motor from New Delhi to Jaipur. On the drive down I was very nervous, wondering how I would find Jai when I arrived. He was on crutches, but in high spirits. I stayed only two days—it wouldn't have been proper to make a longer visit—but that was enough to show me that Jai was on the mend and as optimistic as ever. As I was leaving, we promised to write to each other every day—and we did—until he came to stay with us in Calcutta for the polo season, although this time he could only be a spectator. For me, his lameness brought its advantages. He had to be helped in getting about, and I was allowed, to my great pride, to drive him around in his new two-seater sports-car.

Before Jai left Calcutta he had to have a serious discussion with Ma about our future. I was permitted to be a silent spectator. Jai maintained that although her prescribed two years were not quite over, the war had brought everything to a head, and he convinced Ma that his marriage to me was inevitable. Ma, I think, had come to the same conclusion herself. She merely said, All right, the marriage would take place within a year. But in my mind I wasn't sure she meant it, and Jai must have shared my uncertainty. He gave me a beautiful diamond ring and told me that I shouldn't let anyone know it was a gift from him, but that I should wear it all the time.

I laughed and said that nobody in his right mind would think that I'd gone out and bought such a ring for myself. He started to laugh, too, and we decided that I should wear it only at night when I went to sleep. I knew that Ma wouldn't have been happy to know that I had accepted such an obviously valuable ring from Jai; I myself didn't much care about jewellery at that time and would have been delighted with any trinket Jai had given me. I even found a special pleasure in keeping it to myself and admiring it on my finger only when I was alone.

Later in the year, when Ma went for her annual visit to Delhi, Jai met her there and persuaded her that the wedding really couldn't wait until next year. He wanted to get married as soon as possible. In March of 1940, just months before my twenty-first birthday, she gave us her final blessings and approval, but it was all still to be kept secret until Jai had informed his family and came to Cooch Behar for the betrothal ceremony. Finally the pundits, Brahmin priests and scholars, were consulted and gave us an auspicious date for our wedding: the seventeenth of April.

Part Two

Chapter 9

Indian Wedding, European Honeymoon

THE NEWS OF MY ENGAGEMENT provoked a great deal of gossip and dire predictions in my family circle, as well as some real concern. There were genuine worries about my being a third wife, mixed with the excitement of my marrying the glamorous Maharaja of Jaipur.

Ila remarked that I was so "spineless" in the presence of Jai that she didn't know how I would deal with his flirtatiousness. Indrajit playfully regretted that Jai, his hero, had stooped to an alliance with the "broomstick." Ma predicted gloomily that I would become simply "the latest addition to the Jaipur nursery."

Bhaiya, the most concerned of them all, called me up to his room for a private talk. After a long, clumsy preamble, he came to the real point of his speech: I should accept the idea that Jai was attractive to women, and they to him, and not mind this or make scenes about it.

He tried to make things clear to me, using himself as an example. "You know I've got a lot of girl friends—nothing serious—but men often do. And Jai also likes girls. Just because he marries you, you can't expect him to give up all his girls."

I remember being indignant. "I certainly will expect it. After all, if he marries me, why does he need all those other girls?"

"Listen," Bhaiya said patiently, "the war's on. Jai or I might be sent anywhere. When I go to a new place and meet new girls, I like to go out with them. Jai isn't going to stop liking girls or taking them out just because he's married to you. And really, you mustn't mind—"

"But I *will* mind."

"But you *mustn't*--he isn't trying to hurt you."

"I can't believe that. If I'm his wife, where's the necessity for outside girl friends?"

"Do *listen*, Ayesha. I'm not a bad man, am I? I wouldn't willingly hurt anybody?"

"No, of course not."

"But do you see that I might continue to have girl friends even if I were married?"

"You're different," I said, knowing in a sisterly way that Bhaiya would never change his habits, but refusing to accept that Jai might be the same.

Bhaiya, in exasperation, almost shouted at me. "But do remember Jai is *also* a man. He has lots of girl friends. It doesn't *mean* anything!"

"Then why shouldn't I be like that, too?" I asked resentfully, knowing that I was so besotted with Jai that I couldn't possibly think of outside flirtations.

"No, no!" Bhaiya seemed almost shocked. "Girls are different."

"They certainly are," I agreed warmly. "When Jai is away, I'll miss him and probably mope about it—"

"But men don't do that. *Please* understand. Jai may love you and want to marry you, but that has nothing to do with his being attracted to other girls. Men are like that. *It doesn't mean anything.*"

I said, "To me it would mean a lot. I'd hate it!"

Bhaiya sighed deeply and started his lecture all over again. Jai, he explained, was naturally warm-hearted and demonstrative. He couldn't help showing this, and—let's face it—he *did* like women, and he *was* attracted by them, as they were by him. I continued to insist that none of this would be true after we were married; he loved me and nothing would persuade him to stray, no matter how many women flung themselves at him. Bhaiya said, in a despairing voice, "Don't say I didn't warn you."

Even then, behind my protests, somewhere I knew Bhaiya was right, and in fact, after we were married, Jai and I used to have flaming rows about his casual habit of saying "Hello, Beautiful" or "How's my Wonder Girl?" to women that we knew, and giving them a kiss on the cheek. These quarrels always ended with my saying huffily, "It's no use. I simply *don't* understand."

Because it was wartime, Jai went back to Jaipur immediately after our betrothal ceremony, while we returned to Calcutta. Early the following morning, when Ma came to wake me for riding—we always rode on the racecourse at dawn, leaving "Woodlands" while it was still dark—she found me with a high temperature and a painful sore throat. A doctor was summoned and diagnosed diphtheria. This was just a month before my wedding day.

All through my convalescence impatient letters arrived from Jai. He couldn't be bothered with the doctor's advice that we should wait for several months before we got married, giving me time for the long convalescence that diphtheria requires. He was determined that the wedding should take place on April 17, as the astrologers had suggested. When Ma explained that I was very weak and should put no strain on my heart but must rest, rest, rest, Jai said he was not a barbarian; he would take good care of me and allow me to do nothing strenuous. As usual, he got his way.

Preparations for our wedding started at once. Ma, with her remarkable foresight, had already bought a good part of my trousseau in Europe, knowing it was unlikely that we would return for some time. She had ordered sheets and towels in Florence and Czechoslovakia, shoes and matching bags at Ferragamo in Florence, nightgowns in mousseline de soie from Paris, and a host of other things. Equally typical of Ma, the trousseau had been left behind and neither she nor anyone else could remember where. Finally, it was located at the Ritz Hotel in Paris and was shipped home to arrive a week or so before my wedding.

The rest of my trousseau had to be bought in Calcutta, and I was at that obstructive age when I refused to take an interest in anything except my sports clothes. The only places to which I consented to go were a couple of British shops where I could order slacks and tennis shirts. Ma did finally persuade me that I really ought to order some saris, but the whole thing was a disaster. I went to a shop whose proprietor I had known all my life. As I rapidly and carelessly made my purchases, his face grew longer and longer. No sooner had I left than he called up Ma, begging her to come down and see what my selection had been. She arrived in a judicious frame of mind, but when she saw my choices she couldn't restrain herself. "Rubbish, rubbish!" she exclaimed over each sari I had chosen. She left the shop imperiously, remarking that the only good thing about my selections was that they might be a success in Rajputana, where the untutored eye of the common people might find some pleasure in the bright and gaudy colours. For herself and her daughter she couldn't stand them. She undertook to shop for me herself, and by the time she had finished I had over two hundred saris of various kinds—in plain and patterned chiffon, with and without borders, some hand-embroidered, others appliquéd, some embroidered in gold, and others of simple, heavy silks. Each one was superb, and over the next few years I felt deeply relieved that my own choice had been superseded. My wedding sari was a heavy red Benares silk, shot through with gold thread. Red is the traditional colour for a Hindu bride.

Other preparations for my wedding went on in Cooch Behar. We were able to invite fewer relatives and friends than we would have liked, because many of the trains had been requisitioned for wartime purposes; it was difficult for guests to travel in the crowded conditions of those that remained for civilians. We expected about two hundred—a small number by Indian princely standards—who would be arriving with their servants. All of them had to be housed and fed for at least a week. Since the palace and the three state guest-houses could not accommodate so many, elaborate tents were pitched and schools and public buildings in the town were converted into dormitories for the members of the various staffs.

Jai was to travel to Cooch Behar with a retinue of about forty nobles, each of whom would be bringing his own servants. Catering preparations had to be made on a huge scale. Besides the wedding party, all the dignitaries in the town had to be invited to meals, and special food had to be sent out to the Brahmins, the poor, and the prisoners, as well as the household guards and our staff.

The entire town of Cooch Behar went into fête. All the public buildings and most of the private houses were hung with illuminations. Triumphal arches were erected across the roads where the bridegroom would pass. To entertain the townsfolk and the villagers who would come for the occasion, a special fireworks display had been arranged, and two days later a hockey match, with Jai and Bhaiya captaining the two sides.

The preparations were complete, and the party of my relatives from Baroda arrived before the rest of the guests. We met them in Calcutta. We were due to travel back to Cooch Behar when a frightful accident happened. Ma's favourite brother, my Uncle Dhairyashil, fell on the stairs and cracked his skull. That night he died in the hospital. All of us, but Ma especially, were shattered. He had been so dearly loved by everyone that his death cast a terrible gloom over the whole household, and we scarcely had the spirit to go on preparing for my wedding. The Baroda party returned home for the cremation and the mourning period. Ma did not accompany them because Hindu women do not go to funerals. The wedding ceremony and all the arrangements were postponed, and the pundits were called in to name the next auspicious day for our marriage. It turned out to be the ninth of May.

Even such a tragedy, so close to home, couldn't entirely dampen my excitement about, at last, being married to Jai. As the date of the wedding drew nearer, I started to receive magnificent presents. My favourite was a beautiful black Bentley from the Nawab of Bhopal. When I first saw it being driven through the town, I assumed that it was for the Nawab's personal use during his stay in Cooch Behar. When he formally presented it to me, he asked very tentatively whether I really liked it or whether, perhaps, I might prefer a piece of jewellery. I told him in no uncertain terms that there was not a fraction of doubt in my mind. I had the added pleasure of being able to gloat over Indrajit, who thought that it was simply too much that a "mere girl" should own a Bentley. Even Jai took an unseemly interest in my Bentley, and weakly I agreed to exchange it for an older blue Bentley that he had in Jaipur. Two other exciting presents were a two-seater Packard from one of the nobles in Jaipur, and a house in Mussoorie, in the foothills of the Himalayas, from my Baroda grandmother. Against these, the rest of the presents, marvellous as they were, seemed less impressive—mostly jewellery. My own family gave me a set of pearls and a set of rubies, both specially ordered from a famous Bombay jeweller and following modern European designs. The jewellery included a clip-on nose-ring, an ingenious compromise because girls were expected to wear a nose-ring after they were married, but my nose wasn't pierced to accommodate an ordinary one. Jai saved his present of a diamond necklace until after we were married.

Three days before the marriage ceremony, I had to make the correct preparations. I had to bathe in perfumed oils and rub my skin with turmeric paste to make it more beautiful. I had to perform the prescribed devotions and prayers, and after that to fast for the last twenty-four hours. Bhaiya, as my senior male relative, was giving me away, and he too had to fast. The night before the wedding, strung up and unable to sleep, I spent the time talking to Menaka and Baby.

Jai was due to arrive in the morning and was to be installed at a guest-house with his party. The first indication that I had of his arrival was when I heard the firing of the nineteen-gun salute from the Cooch Behar military base. Only then did I believe with total conviction that after all the years of waiting I would actually marry my beloved.

Soon after Jai's arrival, the customary presents from the groom to the bride were brought in procession to the palace, where they were ceremoniously laid out in the durbar hall. They consisted of the traditional Rajputani jewellery and ornaments for a bride and, added to that, ten or twelve sets of Rajputani clothes for women, also dictated by custom, and trays and trays of dried fruits, nuts, raisins, and other auspicious food.

Then a number of things were placed in my lap, a peculiarly Cooch Behar tradition (I was supposed to hold them all day until after the marriage ceremony)—a conch shell bound with silver, a small silver mirror with a package of betel and areca nut tied to its handle, a handful of rice mixed with the auspicious red powder that we call *kumkum*, folded in a banana leaf—all symbols of good fortune, all auguring longevity for my husband and many children for myself. Still carrying these, I went to say the special bride's prayers and make offerings to that god of universal beneficence, the elephant-headed Ganesha, and then sat down to what seemed like an interminable wait.

Later I learned that Jai had phoned Ma asking if he could come over and have a drink before lunch, and she had replied, "Certainly not. Have you forgotten this is your wedding day? None of us may see you until the ceremony!"

For days the palace had been buzzing with activity as all the traditional wedding finery was brought out and all the proper things assembled. Under Ma's exacting eye, rehearsals had been held—and I had watched them—so I knew exactly how the slow unfolding of my wedding day would take place. There was music everywhere, starting at daybreak, continuing on into the afternoon, coming to a climax in the evening when the actual marriage was consecrated. The low, penetrating sound of conch shells, the lighter, happier music of the reed instruments we call *shenai*, punctuated by the rhythm of drums, filled the air.

I went through the horrid business of being dressed and decorated with jewels. I hate being fussed over, but I forced myself to stand still while this essential part of the ritual was accomplished. The adornment of a bride is, in India, a ceremony in itself, and I was prepared for my wedding by a shoal of chattering married ladies while my own friends looked on, giving me smiles of encouragement. In the bustle and confusion, somehow my insteps got painted with henna, my sari and my jewels were put on, and one by one the ivory bangles of a Rajputana bride were slipped onto my wrists. Finally, my forehead was decorated with sandalwood paste, and I was ready.

Suddenly the cannons boomed out and the band started to play in welcome to Jai. This meant that the bridegroom's procession was at the gates of the palace, and in a flash all my companions dashed off to see his arrival. With my memories of the rehearsals I could imagine the magnificence of the scene outside. First some "messen-

Opposite: A photograph taken during the wedding festivities at Cooch Behar.

Below: Jai alighting from his elephant as he arrives at our wedding.

gers" would be walking down the long drive, next a troupe of danc ing girls, then a procession of forty elephants and many horses, be hind them the bands, and finally Jai himself, followed by his guests the Jaipur nobles and the rest of his retinue.

As Jai crossed the threshold, he raised his sword to touch the lin tel with it as a sign that he came as a bridegroom. He was then received by the palace ladies, family members and wives of noblemen, courtiers, and visiting friends in the durbar hall. They held silver trays containing the proper offerings: *kumkum*, turmeric, a coconut, chilies and other spices, and a small oil light to signify the sacred fire. They waved the trays slowly back and forth in front of Jai, chanting prayers.

I was left standing in the dressing-room, too nervous to sit down, while everyone else milled around the bridegroom. Eventually a few of the women did come back to put the finishing touches to my clothes and appearance and to escort me to the silver palanquin in which I was to be seated when my male relatives carried it into the courtyard.

Against the pervasive background of the music and of the priest chanting, the ceremony of giving the bride away took place. But before that, as was the custom in Cooch Behar, Jai and I exchanged garlands. The wedding pavilion or *mandap*, as it is traditionally called, had been set up in the main courtyard. At the time of its erection, prayers and suitable offerings were made. My elder brother, Bhaiya, performed the ceremony of giving the bride away. The Hindu wedding takes a very long time and the priest went on and on and on and I heard Jai whisper to Bhaiya, "Can't we ask these jollies when this performance will be over?" He sounded just as tired and impatient as I was.

At last the final responses were made, the last prayers were said, and we left the pavilion in the courtyard to go upstairs where the family was waiting for us. We had to touch everyone's feet—a peculiar moment for Jai because he had to make his obeisance even to Indrajit, whom he had always treated as an insignificant, teasable younger brother. Even as he touched his feet, he muttered, "For the first and last time!"

Then we were offered the traditional *thal* to share, and in the proper way I offered him the first mouthful of rice from my fingers, and he did the same for me. We had a bottle of champagne on ice to accompany this ritual meal. After that, Jai went off to join the other men, while my sisters and Baby stayed with me, and Indrajit popped in and out to check on how I was feeling.

When I was permitted to change my clothes it seemed incredible that I had been decked out in all my finery only a few hours before. I still didn't really feel married; I'd seen so little of Jai. However, intensely relieved that it had all gone all right, I could at last relax and wait for the time when Jai would be finished with his part of the ceremonies and we could finally be alone.

The day after our wedding there was a great banquet for the men at which Jai, Bhaiya, and Indrajit all had to make speeches, and they and their friends were entertained with Indian music and dancing girls. Meanwhile the rest of us had a ladies' dinner. During the day there had been sports events and special tournaments held for the visitors. The celebrations in Cooch Behar continued for another week, but on the third day Jai and I set off for our honeymoon —a European custom that we had decided to adopt.

Leaving Cooch Behar was an awful business. All the maids were weeping, but Menaka and Baby made jokes in an off-hand way about gaining a brother, not losing a sister, and Ma, still shattered by my uncle's death, seemed entirely unconscious of the fact that I was going away from home for good. The combination of tears and indifference left me upset, unsure, and close to tears myself.

Originally, Jai and I had planned to go to Ceylon because neither of us had been there, but in the end, because of the difficulties of wartime travel, we decided on my beloved Ooty, the hill resort in south India. Indrajit, who was going to join his regiment, accompanied us as far as Calcutta.

It was on that journey that I had my first chilling taste of purdah. When we reached the Calcutta station, our coach was surrounded by canvas screens. Then a car, with curtains separating the driver from the passenger seats and covering the windows of the rear compartment, drove up to the platform. I was ushered from the railway coach to the car, entirely protected from the view of any passer-by. Indrajit was accompanying me at Jai's request, and he asked in a whisper if Jai intended to keep me so claustrophobically guarded all the time. With one of the Jaipur retinue sitting in the front seat, I could only put my finger to my lips and shrug my shoulders. We were to stay the night at "Woodlands," and there too, as soon as we arrived, the Jaipur party firmly waved away all the male servants, even though I had known most of them all my life. The next day when Indrajit set off I felt as though my last ally was deserting me and could no longer keep back my tears. Jai merely remarked, with his usual good humour, that he had thought I *wanted* to marry him.

By the day after, when we left for Madras, I had recovered my spirits, even though I remained uneasily aware that my brief experience of purdah was only the first of many intimidating situations that lay ahead. I was still very much in awe of Jai and desperately anxious to do everything right, though often unsure of what etiquette demanded. For instance, when Jai's nephews came to call on us in our railway compartment, I found myself in a quandary, wondering whether speech would be considered improper or silence boorish.

Once we reached Ooty everything became cosy and easy. We stayed in the annex of the big house belonging to the Jodhpurs, the family from which Jai's first and second wives came. Some of the young Jodhpur children were staying in the main house, and they used to come and have tea with us. We played tennis with their staff, and it all seemed very friendly and natural. I went riding less than usual because I was still convalescing from my diphtheria, but occasionally we followed the hunt, and often we went on picnics. Jai loved picnics, and in that month we must have visited just about every beauty spot in the area. Some of our friends were in Ooty and we often entertained and were entertained by them—all informal parties for drinks and dinner. If there was a formal party or a reception at Government House, Jai would go alone. Although I wasn't exactly in purdah, still, on occasions where there might be older and more orthodox princes among the guests, Jai didn't want to put

On our honeymoon in Ooty.

me in the embarrassing position of being the only maharani to show her face in public. He told me that this would also be true in Jaipur in the beginning, because I hadn't yet met the people. But he added, "There's no question of your remaining in purdah all your life. Let's wait for a year or so. When people gradually get used to the idea, you can drop purdah altogether."

My twenty-first birthday came while we were still on our honeymoon, and because there were all kinds of princes and their retinues in Ooty for the season, we invited them—at least the younger ones who wouldn't be shocked by non-observance of purdah—to my birthday party. I was miserably shy, and this was my first experience of being a hostess at a party given by the well-known and much admired Maharaja of Jaipur. I didn't want to seem pushing, and when the guests left I didn't see them to the door. I didn't feel confident enough to usher them out of the house.

Jai wasn't at all shy about communicating his disapproval. "What's the matter with you?" he said. "Your mother has such beautiful manners. Anyone would think you might have picked up some pointers from her. Who the hell do you think you are to stay behind in the drawing-room and not go to the door to see your guests off?"

I had nothing to say in reply except that I would be sure to manage it all better next time. But this was minor compared with the unnerving test of delicate diplomacy that came at the end of our honeymoon.

Jai left me in Ooty while he went to Bangalore for the polo and stayed there with his second wife and all his children. He told me to wait until he wrote to tell me whether I should join him or whether he would return to fetch me. For the next few days I hung about the annex, waiting for the mail and wondering unhappily what was happening in Bangalore. Soon I received a reassuring letter from Jai saying that he missed me and that I should come to Bangalore as soon as possible.

I motored down from Ooty, driving my own car, in a panic of nerves. This was to be my first meeting with Jai's second wife after my marriage. When I arrived, Jai was out playing polo and the only member of the family to be seen was Pat, his five-year-old son, who was riding a tricycle round and round the drive in front of the house, waiting to see what I looked like. Inside, an ADC appeared to take me to the apartments I would share with Jai. I didn't dare leave them, and paced about trying to keep from imagining how the rest of the living arrangements were handled.

After half an hour or so the ADC returned to tell me that the second Maharani was in the drawing-room and would be very pleased if I would join her for tea. Ma had told me that when I met her I should touch her feet, but as this was not the custom in Rajputana, I just folded my hands in the traditional *namaskar*. She must have been as nervous as I was, but with great poise she started to make small-talk, asking if my rooms were comfortable and whether I would like to drive with her to watch the polo the next day.

Eventually Jai came in from his game, cheerful as always and behaving in such a thoroughly ordinary and natural way that all the tensions seemed to fall away and we all had a drink together before going upstairs to change for dinner. Later Bhaiya dropped in, and his breezy manner and brotherly teasing made everything easier still. He, being now a member of the family, dined with Jai, the second Maharani, and me. During the meal we solved my immediate problem of what I was to call her by deciding on Didi, "elder sister." Jai always called her Jo because, just as his own name was simply the first syllable of his state, so Jo was an abbreviation of Jodhpur. In the end she became Jo Didi to me.

The next morning breakfast was brought up to our room, and with it came Jai's children. The room was suddenly filled with hooting, screaming, tumbling children, showing off wildly, demanding attention, and playing silly tricks. Bubbles, the eldest boy, kept trying to pick up little bits of butter while Jai tried without success to stop him. Bubbles was nine at that time, his sister, Mickey, was eleven, and after them came Jo Didi's two boys, Joey and Pat, then seven and five, respectively.

Our day-to-day life in Bangalore was, in a sense, much as it had been when I stayed there before. We went to the polo games and the races and saw many friends whom I had known since childhood. Besides Bhaiya, there were a number of people from other princely families with whom we played tennis almost every day, and, most important, my Baroda grandmother was also staying in Bangalore. I went to the polo with Jo Didi in a closed car, but those were the only occasions on which I observed purdah. There were, in any case, hardly any formal functions, and most of the entertaining was on a small and friendly scale. Whenever we went out to dinner, I accompanied Jai, and whenever we had a party, I was the one who acted as Jai's hostess. Although I felt that Jo Didi must resent my presence, she never showed it, and perhaps there wasn't so much to resent after all. Even before I married Jai, her life had always been lived in purdah. She didn't even go to the hairdresser; the hairdresser would come to her. Her life consisted of looking after the children, running the household, going for drives, watching the polo, and entertaining her women friends. All of that remained unchanged. She stayed in her own apartment as she had always done and led the same kind of life as she had always done. When there were only family present, we would all eat our meals together, but if we had guests, she would eat in her private dining-room.

I had one new restriction in Bangalore—a lady-in-waiting who now accompanied me everywhere except when I was with Jai. My Baroda grandmother eyed my lady-in-waiting beadily, longing to get me by myself. Finally she could wait no longer to cross-question me and sent instructions to Jai that I was to visit her without the lady-in-waiting. When we were alone she asked me how I was managing to cope with the unemancipated constrictions of my new life, and warned me that the rules would be even more rigid and confining after I went to live in Jaipur. She then gave me a long lecture on how to be a maharani. This entailed, among other things, never going to cocktail parties, never allowing anyone to call me by my first name in the undignified manner that my mother did, and never, as I had done, wearing emeralds with a green sari, as they looked much better with pink.

I was becoming more and more edgy about what the proper behaviour of a Jaipur maharani should be. For example, even when

Left to right, Joey, Mickey, and Bubbles.

Jai urged me to wear shorts for playing squash, I was so worried about what his servants would think at such a shameless baring of legs that I put on slacks over my shorts and took them off only when we were safely inside the court. But nothing, not my grandmother's advice nor my own timid guesses, really prepared me for my new life in Jaipur.

Jo Didi, with her kindness and tact, had made me feel that she was an ally, not a competitor, and she at least had instructed me in the ceremonies I would have to perform when I arrived. She was, as usual, to stay behind with the children in the good climate of Bangalore and to return with them to Jaipur only after the terrible heat of the summer there had abated.

On our train journey back, Jai and I changed trains at Sawai Madhopur, where he had a hunting-lodge, to the narrow-gauge line of the Jaipur State Railway, and travelled in a Jaipur State coach. As Jai pointed out landmarks, including Isarda, the village where he had been born, and as I gazed out at the countryside, a vivid green after the recent rains, both my excitement and my apprehensions rose. What would my everyday life be like? How often would I be with Jai? How would I get on with the Jaipur ladies and, in particular, with Jai's first wife? Who would tell me what was expected of me when Jai wasn't there? I knew that my marriage was not popular with Jai's relatives and the Jaipur nobility. The other two maharanis were related to most of the Rajput princely families, but I was a total outsider. Would this create tensions with the other Rajputana states?

The nearer we drew to Jaipur, the more terrified and unsure I became. I tried desperately not to show it, but Jai, I think, understood how I felt. As we entered the station, the servants pulled down the blinds around our carriage and very gently Jai told me to cover my face.

Chapter 10

Palace Life in Jaipur

ALTHOUGH my two previous visits to Jaipur had been private and informal, even then I couldn't help being struck by the ceremonial grandeur of Jai's court. But now I was to see it in all its full-blown splendour, as the palace prepared to receive me as the Maharaja's new bride. What's more, I would have to play a central part in all the palace festivities. I could only pray that Jai would stay protectively by my side.

Our coach, detached from the train, pulled up on a special siding which ran inside an enormous building made of carved and decorated Jaipur stone. This was Viman Bhawan, where members of the royal family and important guests could alight rather than use the public station. A comfortably furnished suite of rooms opened off the Viman Bhawan platform: a sitting-room and two bedrooms, with baths. There one could change and freshen up and appear properly dressed for the official reception outside.

Naturally, I hadn't taken all the clothes from my trousseau on my honeymoon; neither had Jai taken his formal dress clothes. They had all been sent to Jaipur from Cooch Behar, and my maids from Cooch Behar had come to Jaipur as well. They were waiting in Viman Bhawan, along with Jo Didi's maids, to help me dress in one of the unfamiliar Rajputana outfits that had been given to me as part of the Jaipur family's gifts to the bride.

As we stepped down to the Viman Bhawan platform, Jai's two married sisters, the Maharani of Panna and Rani Ajit Singh of Jodhpur, were waiting to receive us with a group of nobles' wives and daughters.

I had never met my sisters-in-law before. They hadn't attended our wedding because women don't go to the weddings of their male relatives. They perform the auspicious ceremonies before the bridegroom leaves and receive the bride when she returns with him.

Keeping my face carefully covered with the end of my sari, I paid my respects to my sisters-in-law and was then led to one of the bedrooms, where the maids helped me change, while Jai went to the other room, where his servants had laid out his formal clothes.

In Rajputana women don't wear saris, so I put on the full ankle-length skirt, the short bodice tied across the back with thin silk cords, and the over-jacket, and then the big shawl, used also as a veil, was draped over my head and tucked in at my waist. The jewellery to go with the outfit was traditional, too: a choker necklace which all married women have to wear; a round pendant on the forehead, consisting of a large diamond surrounded by small emeralds attached to a gold cord that follows the parting of the hair; earrings, anklets, the clip-on nose-ring that Ma had specially ordered for me in Cooch Behar, and, most essential for a bride, the ivory bangles that cover the forearms from wrist to elbow.

In Rajputana clothes always come in very bright colours. Mine, on that occasion, arriving as a bride, had to be red, and the whole outfit was embroidered with sequins and gold thread so that it glittered whenever I moved.

When I was dressed, we left Viman Bhawan and drove in a purdah car with curtained windows through streets I couldn't see but which, as I could tell from the noise, were crowded. We drove to the old capital, Amber, eight miles away, where Jai had taken me many years before. He told me that whenever he left the state for any length of time, the first thing he did on his return was to visit the temple of the goddess Shila Devi, the Jaipur family shrine. So we offered prayers there and asked the blessing of the deity before we drove back to Rambagh Palace, a huge white building set among gardens and Lalique fountains, outside the city walls.

At Rambagh, after another reception given by my sisters-in-law, who had invited the wives of the nobles and of the staff as well as

Doing a dance in the full-skirted Rajputani costume.

relatives to greet us, we had a moment of happy informality alone together while Jai showed me my apartments. They were far more modern and spacious than the rooms I had shared with Menaka at "Woodlands" or in Cooch Behar. They used to be Jai's own suite, but he had had them redecorated by a London firm for me. I was enchanted. There was a high-ceilinged, airy bedroom all in pink, with pale voile curtains, pastel divans, and chaises-longues; an oval bathroom with the bath set in an alcove; a panelled study; and a large sitting-room filled with objets d'art from the Jaipur collection. Small jewelled animals, rose quartz and jade, and curved daggers with white jade hilts carved to look like animal heads with jewels for eyes were displayed in glass cabinets. Jade boxes encrusted with semi-precious stones in floral designs held cigarettes, and heavy crystal bowls were filled with flowers. Jai had also remembered my love for the gramophone and had got me the latest kind, which could actually take several records at a time and turn them over.

Outside my rooms ran a marble veranda overlooking the central courtyard of the palace. There my four maids from Cooch Behar took turns to wait and answer any summons from me. On the other side, a small hallway separated me from Jai's apartments, which had also been completely renovated and were now filled with ultramodern furniture. I felt especially happy that Jai had given so much thought and attention to my needs and what would please me, even before our marriage had been definitely settled.

But there was little time to dawdle over the pleasures and comforts of my new home before the next engagement. My maids helped me change quickly into another skirt, bodice, and veil—still in the auspicious pinks, reds, and oranges—and to put on more jewellery, never forgetting the dozens of ivory bangles. As soon as I was ready, I was led, with my face once more veiled, to a garden courtyard in the zenana section of Rambagh, where Jai's oldest sister, the Maharani of Panna, was giving a party for us. There I was confronted by a seemingly endless succession of curious eyes trying to pierce through my veil to see what I looked like. I, in turn, kept my head bowed most of the time, as much out of embarrassment as out of the decorous modesty that I was supposed to display. The younger women, mostly daughters of the nobility, came up and spoke a few words to me, but, following their example, I kept apart from the elders—a relief to me, since I should certainly have been hopelessly tongue-tied in any conversation with them.

Only a few men were present, all close relatives, and they conversed exclusively with each other, except for Jai, who did come over to the ladies' side of the garden to talk and joke with his sisters and the rest of us. It was easy to see that they all adored him. Soon the court dancers and singers appeared, and while they entertained us glasses of sherbet and chilled champagne were handed around.

The next evening a similar party was given by Jai's other sister, Rani Ajit Singh of Jodhpur, and the next night another, and so on for eight or ten nights. The whole of that first period of my life in Jaipur had an unreal quality, and I found myself performing actions as if I were in a trance, changing my clothes over and over again, sitting dazedly in group after group of in-laws, acknowledging introduction after introduction to the wives and daughters of nobles and officials. Out of it all I remember only isolated incidents—how, for instance, removing the ivory bangles became increasingly painful, and how Jai, who was far gentler than any of my maids, would do it for me. I remember how oppressively hot the nights were in spite of the fact that the rains had already started. Like most north Indians we slept on the roof under the shelter of a cupola, on light wooden beds, and I lay awake for hours unable to sleep. One night I heard the faint tinkling of anklets in the distance and Jai told me it was a ghost, but it turned out to be only the pods of a flame-of-the-forest tree rattling in the night wind.

On a day declared auspicious by Jaipuri pundits, I was taken on the ten-minute drive to the immense City Palace, a bewildering complex of interconnecting courtyards, pavilions, secluded zenana quarters, men's apartments, audience halls, weapons-rooms, large and small sitting-rooms, dining-rooms, banqueting chambers, offices, and so on and on. It was the official home of the Maharaja of Jaipur, and I travelled there in a curtained purdah car escorted by Jai's personal bodyguard, the Bhoop Squadron of the Kachwaha Horse, mounted on superb matching black horses and dressed in white tunics, breeches, black boots, and turbans of blue and silver, with silver cockades. Again I could sense a surging mass of people on the streets all along the route from Rambagh, but as before I didn't dare peer through the curtains.

When we reached the outer gates of the City Palace, I was transferred into a palanquin and carried through a labyrinth of corridors and courtyards. Then I was set down and, as a new bride, had to perform a prayer ceremony at the threshold to mark my entry into my husband's home for the first time. After this there was a women's durbar, when one by one the ladies of the zenana and of the aristocratic families filed past me, parting my veil to look at the bride's face and, following the Rajputana custom, leaving a gift in my lap after their first glimpse of me. The senior nobles' wives mostly gave me jewellery, but from the younger officers' wives I received only *nazar*—a token present, usually a coin. The older ones made assorted comments, such as "What a lovely bride!" "How fair her skin is!" "She's got a small nose." "Let me look at your eyes," but the remarks weren't all complimentary. Fortunately Jo Didi had warned me that this would happen and had advised me to keep my eyes modestly and permanently cast down, resisting all temptations to stare back, even at the particularly inquisitive ones.

From the moment I entered the City Palace I was fascinated by it. Lying at the heart of the old walled city, it is almost a town in itself, with gardens, stables, and an elephant yard surrounding the many buildings and spreading over more than thirty acres. Like the town outside it, the City Palace was built in the first half of the eighteenth century in a blend of Hindu and Muslim architecture, with elegant scalloped arches on slender columns and latticed marble screens, with galleries and delicate wall-paintings. The whole place had a dreamlike feeling, each courtyard with its surrounding rooms producing another surprise.

Jai led me through the magnificent and imposing public courtyards and halls, which I would never have been allowed to see alone because they were all on the men's side of the palace. From the first courtyard, with its waiting hall enclosed by high yellow walls, we entered the council chamber with its own courtyard, coloured entirely in pink. From there brass relief doors, nineteen feet high, opened into the durbar hall. Another door from the durbar hall led to an audience pavilion, more like a huge veranda, where the decorative murals and the doors inlaid with ivory were masterpieces of local craftsmanship. This, in turn, overlooked the walled garden, in the middle of which the temple of Govind Devji, or Lord Krishna, stood. Jai told me that traditionally all the maharajas of Jaipur governed the state in his name. And so we wandered on, from courtyard to courtyard, from pavilion to gallery to chamber to hall to garden, until I could only think dizzily that this was all a setting for some fabulous and brilliantly imagined fairy-tale.

The zenana quarters were divided into a series of self-contained apartments. Mine, decorated in blues and greens, was much like the others, with a little square courtyard and a private durbar hall hung with blue glass lamps, and inner rooms opening off it. I later came to know it far more intimately, as we went there for every ceremonial occasion, sometimes staying as long as a fortnight. In the year of my marriage there were still about four hundred women living in the zenana. Among them were widowed relatives and their daughters as well as their servants and attendants; the Dowager Maharani and her retinue of laides-in-waiting, maids, cooks, and other servants; comparable retinues for each of Jai's three wives; and all the retainers of the late Maharaja's other wives, who could not be dismissed simply because their mistresses had died, and so remained the responsibility of the ruling family. Presiding over them was the only one of the late Maharaja's wives who was still alive. She was known to all of us as Maji Sahiba, or "Respected Mother," and we treated her with the greatest deference. As one of Jai's wives, I could almost never uncover my face in her presence and always had to be seated a few paces to her left.

Even though we remained on such formal terms, she showed me many kindnesses. One, in particular, touched me very much. She knew that I had been brought up partly in England and had led what to her was a highly emancipated Western life, and she was concerned that I might be bored and unhappy in the enclosed world of the zenana. She instructed her ladies to devise and act out plays

Above: The courtyard of the City Palace with Jai's personal guard.

Opposite top: Rambagh.

Opposite bottom: Elephants outside the City Palace on the holiday of Dasehra.

Below: View from the City Palace veranda of Govind Devji's temple.

for me to watch. During the war I remember struggling between giggles and tears of gratitude as the ladies, dressed up as soldiers, performed scenes in which Jai, victoriously and apparently single-handedly, triumphed over the German forces in the Middle East. Even apart from such naïve threatricals, Jai's activities were closely followed with extreme and affectionate attention in the zenana, and any achievement was promptly celebrated. When Jai's team won the All-India polo championship, for instance, skirts and shawls were embroidered with polo sticks; when he gained his flying license, the ladies, who never had—and were never likely to—set foot in a plane themselves, loyally decorated their clothes with aeroplane motifs.

During those early days, in the midst of all the parties and receptions for family, friends, nobles, ministers, and government officials and their wives, I thought I should never remember any names, never learn who everyone was at court. I wished so much for it all to be over, for Jai and me to be able to lead an ordinary life. The only family member I was not allowed to meet was Jai's father. It was not the custom in Rajputana for a wife to be presented to her husband's elder male relatives, and I only caught glimpses of him through a screen or at a distance. He was a wonderful-looking old man and always dressed in the traditional style: jodhpurs, a jacket fastened with gold buttons, a turban, heavy gold earrings, strings of pearls around his neck, and anklets on his feet. He had a town house in Jaipur and came quite often to Rambagh, but one of the ADCs always warned me whenever he arrived so that I could retire to the zenana. Jai's mother, of whom Jai was extremely fond, preferred to stay in Isarda. I met her only once and was much taken by her gentle personality. On that occasion she had wanted a gold coin to give to someone and, since she was carrying no money, asked me to get one. I remember feeling proud that she had singled me out to run her small errand, even though there were many other people present, including her own daughters.

At last the festivities and ceremonies connected with our wedding were over, and Jai and I could settle down to a more normal routine. It was only then that I had time enough to sort out my impressions a bit, to make contrasts and comparisons between the life and surroundings of my childhood and my new position as a married woman and a maharani of Jaipur. Right from the beginning a sense of spaciousness and of a grand design both in the palaces and in the city itself greatly impressed me. Of course Jaipur was a much bigger and more important state than Cooch Behar, but the feeling of size was somehow increased by the desert all around and the rocky hills on the horizon. Here and there were bursts of colour from the flowering trees—the scarlet of the flame-of-the-forest, the unearthly blue of the jacarandas, the brilliant yellows of the acacias—but the land was green for only a brief time after the rains. Cooch Behar, at the foothills of the Himalayas, was green all year round, even in the hot weather, because the climate was damp and the air humid, quite unlike the dry heat of Jaipur.

Another difference struck me from the very beginning of my new life. In Cooch Behar life was on a much smaller scale; for instance, many of the formal ceremonies and durbars were held right in the palace where we lived. In Jaipur, although we lived in Rambagh Palace and considered it our "real" home, all ceremonies and formal occasions took place in the City Palace, and tradition demanded that Jai worship outside the city at the Kali Temple in the palace of his ancestors, the kings of Amber, on certain specified occasions such as his arrival in Jaipur, after he had been away, or upon his departure on a trip. For me, Rambagh meant a pleasantly informal life where I was not expected to be in purdah although, as a married woman, I had to cover my head when I wore a sari. But when I went to the City Palace, I always rode in a purdah car, and there I had to behave like a queen. Every ceremony had to be meticulously performed, every formality observed, and I could not allow anything to go wrong. At the durbars I realized that my behaviour would be watched not only by the family and their retainers but also by the many ladies of the nobility. In Jaipur, unlike Cooch Behar, there were many aristocratic families, some with estates so large that they were considered minor princes. Altogether, those early days of my married life were a frightening time, and I was constantly worried that I might do something wrong. I couldn't have managed it all if Jai hadn't been there to encourage me, make fun of my doubts, laugh off my mistakes.

Gradually I began to learn new aspects of Jai and his world. Some of my discoveries were quite minor: for instance, his astonishing talent with animals. I had known that he understood and handled horses brilliantly, but now I saw that even birds of all sorts, ranging from sparrows to peacocks, had a mysterious confidence in him. When we had breakfast in the garden by the swimming-pool, he fed them and soon even the most timid would eat from his palm.

Some of Jai's other qualities reached me in oblique ways. I had wanted, early in our marriage, to learn Hindi and Urdu. I felt that this knowledge was essential for me to be able to communicate with even the limited circle of the zenana and whichever wives or daughters of nobles or government officials I was permitted to meet. Many of them spoke no English, and as my only Indian language was Bengali, I thought that surely it would be both less lonely and much more interesting if I learned some medium of conversation. Jai, very gently, refused to allow this. It was, he said, for my own protection. Still gently, so that I would not be frightened, but clearly, so that I should fully understand, he explained some of the difficulties I might encounter in the life of the two palaces where I should be living. He emphasized that everyone was watching me and my behaviour intently. If I appeared to have favourites—which might easily happen if, quite innocently, I enjoyed talking to one or several people more than others—then rumours and intrigues would start. People would try to set me against my "favourites," probably by telling me that the friends now currying favour with me had previously spoken against my marriage. Equally, there was a danger that anyone who had, for whatever reason, incurred Jo Didi's displeasure might try to get into my good graces and cause friction between us. And, also, there might be those who would try to hurt me, thinking I was too privileged and pampered, too close to Jai, or would try through flattery, or presents, or other blandishments to win Jai's favour through me.

I was very moved that Jai, knowing the simple family life I had always led, quite free of devious palace scheming, realized how vulnerable I was and did everything in his power to protect me. Whenever he was away from Jaipur, he left me in the special care of his two most trusted officials, telling them to be in touch with me every day and help me with any problems that might arise and deputing his brother, Bahadur Singh, to ride with me in the mornings.

There were, as well, very delicate relationships that could not be left to outsiders, however trustworthy. It is difficult to describe to Western readers the general attitude of many Hindu families to the idea of polygamy. Westerners are apt to assume that antagonism, hostility, or jealousy must, by the nature of the situation, exist between the wives of one man, and that an earlier wife is bound to feel humiliated or cast off when her husband marries again. In fact this is quite untrue, and from my own experience I know that a civilized and mannerly relationship can be cultivated between the wives of the same man, and that even a deep friendship can develop between them, as it did between Jo Didi and me.

It was in no way an unfamiliar situation for either of Jai's first wives. Both of them came from families in which the men had taken more than one wife. Indeed, polygamy was such a commonplace custom that even one's servants sometimes had two or three wives. In Jaipur it was accepted that the senior wife, First Her Highness, as she was called, would take precedence over Jo Didi and me on every formal occasion, just as Jo Didi would take precedence over me. Both of them, in their different ways, helped me. First Her Highness, small, reticent, with simple tastes, and much older than Jai, would tell me the correct and orthodox ways of conducting myself and of dressing—which colours, for instance, were appropriate for which occasion. I followed her advice, although I never understood why a particular colour was "right." I, in exchange, helped her draft her letters and telegrams.

First Her Highness spent much of her time with her family in Jodhpur, her home state, so Jo Didi, more modern, undertook the major part of the running of the zenana in the City Palace and spent much more time there than I did. I learned a great deal by watching and listening to Jo Didi. For example, a message would come from one of the secretaries that it was someone's birthday, and the astrologers had worked out precisely when the festivities should begin and when they should end, the exact time that the ladies' durbar should take place, and just how long it should last. Then Jo Didi would take over the organization of the affair: give the orders for the food, see that invitations were sent out to the right people, make sure that the proper presents were bought. Among her responsibilities was the distribution of the state jewellery to be worn by each of us on special occasions, and she had to make sure it was returned and locked away again afterwards.

Within Rambagh Palace, First Her Highness and Jo Didi had their own separate apartments, their own kitchens and housekeeping arrangements, their own staffs of servants and ladies-in-waiting. They lived in the zenana part of the palace, had their own gardens, and never ventured farther. I lived in Jai's old suite, which, as I have said, he had redecorated for me, and naturally that was outside the zenana. I was free to wander wherever I wished in the palace and in the gardens. My only restriction was that if I went outside the palace grounds I had to be accompanied.

My days in Jaipur fell into a pattern not too different from my life in Cooch Behar, except that everything was on a much grander scale and I had to get used to living within the peculiar conventions of being half in and half out of purdah. Every morning Jai and I went for a ride in the countryside and then returned to swim in the pool and have breakfast beside it. Usually Jai spent the rest of the morning in his office, conferring with his ministers and advisers and dealing with matters of state, leaving me to my own devices. Sometimes I met the ministers, if they stayed on to lunch with us, and asked them questions as I had seen Ma and my grandparents do. This amused the ministers enormously; one of them once nudged his colleague and said, "You'd better be careful. If you turn around for a moment she'll be taking your portfolio."

I began to see how much more complicated Jai's duties as a maharaja were than Bhaiya's. Cooch Behar was surrounded by British India, and consequently Bhaiya had to deal with only one government when a problem arose that might affect territory outside his state. Jaipur, however, had other Rajput states on every side, and so agreements about, for example, waterways involved rather delicate negotiations with other princes. Jaipur had its own railway system, and that too demanded acceptable arrangements about how it linked up with other systems of transport. Such matters, as well as the more familiar business of working out the state's budget and coping with requests for roads, schools, hospitals, post offices, and so on, occupied the major part of Jai's day. He was, at that time, an absolute ruler. He appointed his own ministers and there were no elections. Even the British-Indian Government could not interfere with his running of his state unless there was blatant evidence of misrule.

In those early months, in spite of the interests of my new life, I often had long stretches of loneliness. After being the fourth child in a large, casual, noisy, and carefree family in the freedom of Cooch Behar, I did sometimes find the atmosphere of palace life in Jaipur rather oppressively formal. I was treated with such respect and distance that natural conversation was impossible. I used to plead with the ladies in the zenana who spoke English to talk freely with me, to argue with me, even just to call me Ayesha in private. But they would smilingly, deferentially, ignore my requests. Once when Jai's younger sister ventured to disagree with me on some trivial point, she was given such a scolding by Jo Didi that afterwards she hardly dared to speak to me at all. I also realized that people looked upon me as more of a Westerner than an Indian—an impression I was helpless to correct, since Jai wouldn't let me learn Hindi properly.

Altogether it was not surprising that I often sought the company of Jo Didi, with whom I had more in common. Gradually, over the months of seeing each other every day, I got to know her better. She was only twenty-four when I came to Jaipur, just three years older than I was, and although her interests were wider than the other zenana women's—she was one of the few who had received a formal education—still, as I got to know her better, I realized how fundamentally different our lives, and the outlooks they fostered, had been. She had been brought up partly in the Jodhpur Fort and partly at Jamnagar with her uncle, the famous cricketer Ranjit Singh, protected in both places and confined by the customs of orthodox princely life.

When she first came to Jaipur her seclusion from men had been so rigid that when she was ill the doctor had to make his diagnosis from the passage outside her room, getting details of her symptoms—temperature and pulse—from her maids. (She soon learned the advantages of this system, and whenever she wanted to avoid a boring engagement, she would dip the thermometer in hot water and send her maid to show it to the doctor.) Another advantage which I sometimes shared with her was the comfort of going to the cinema in pyjamas and dressing-gown confident that nobody could see how we were dressed.

Although she had been betrothed to Jai since she was five years old, she had never met him to talk to until they were married. When he came on visits to Jodhpur, she told me, he would smuggle notes to her through one of his confidants, and at night they used to hold brief "conversations" with each other in Morse code, using torches to signal, with Jo Didi struggling to master Morse from a British Army code book. After they were married, the Jodhpur and Jamnagar families could always visit Jo Didi in the zenana, and so could more distant family connections, and later, my brothers, too, were welcomed. By the time I came to live in Jaipur many of the household officials and their wives were also invited to parties where Jo Didi was present. She was delighted at this widening of her circle. A naturally gregarious and warm-hearted woman, she loved to have her apartments filled with visitors.

She told me once, almost as a joke, that when Jai first broke the news to her that he was going to marry me, he gave a party for her on the same evening to cheer her up in case her feelings were hurt. I could only think that in similar circumstances the very last thing I would have wanted would have been some cheery party where I would have had to smile and chatter and be gay all evening. But she seemed to have been pleased and touched by the gesture.

Our life fell quite naturally into two divisions: the private and family life in which Jo Didi was included and the public life which, because she was in purdah, she couldn't share. Jai saw to it, after I had met all his immediate family and close relatives, that I should get to know his ADCs and their wives and that some of the younger ladies of the nobility should come with us on picnics and outings. I was pleased by his thoughtfulness but never really made friends with any of them. None of them played games, while I was very sports-minded; and in the end my social circle consisted largely of Jai's intimate friends, mostly fellow polo-players, and their wives, with whom we would spend cosy and easy evenings or stop in at one of their houses for tea after riding.

By Cooch Behar standards, even the small parties at which I was hostess had a certain formality and grandeur, and this began to affect my own behaviour. When Indrajit came to stay at Rambagh about a year after my marriage, he was stunned by the transformation and exclaimed, with characteristic brotherly directness, "Who the hell do you think you are, Queen Mary?"

Understandably, the pleasures and discoveries that I remember best from my early years in Jaipur were those I shared with Jai. Sometimes he took the day off from his duties as Maharaja, and then he would take me exploring on horseback or by car. He owned a number of forts in the country around Jaipur City, and we often went to one or another of them for a picnic. One trip I remember particularly vividly took us to an eighteenth-century fort built high on a hill overlooking the city which could be reached only after a long and tortuous climb. From there we rode along the crest of the rocky hills that surround Jaipur to another fort about five hundred feet above the Palace of Amber. It had a great watch-tower scanning the plains to the north, and it was here that the fabulous Jaipur Treasure was housed, closely guarded by one of the state's warlike tribes. Nobody but the Maharaja himself was allowed to enter the tower or to see the treasure. I waited outside the menacing walls while Jai went in. But true to tradition he never described to me what the treasure was like, and the only evidence I ever saw of its existence was the beautiful jewelled bird, with two large rubies for its eyes and an emerald hanging from its beak, which stood on the drawing-room mantelpiece at Rambagh.

From the verandas of Rambagh I had often admired another fort, called Moti Doongri, which was perched high on a rocky outcrop, its delicate crenellations scattered with bright bougainvillea. From a distance it looked like an exquisitely fashioned toy. One morning Jai took me up there, and when I told him how much I liked it, he simply said, "Then it's yours," and Moti Doongri became my own special possession. Jai had the interior renovated for me, and we often escaped there from the formality and panoply of Rambagh to have quiet lunches or dinners, often alone, sometimes with friends. I always associated it with a particular warmth and intimacy and relaxed pleasure.

Sometimes our outings were more complicated, involving large parties of guests and arrangements made weeks in advance. Usually these were the perfectly organized big-game shoots at Sawai Madhopur for which Jaipur was so well known. The first one after our marriage remains particularly clear in my memory. Jai had built a small shooting-lodge in the hills southwest of Jaipur, dominated by the famous fort of Ranthambhor, its battlements and walls spreading for miles across the countryside. While Jai and I, with our personal attendants, stayed in the shooting-lodge, our guests were accommodated in a camp even more elaborate than those I knew from my childhood, with tents fitted out with every comfort.

The shooting, too, was quite different from Cooch Behar. In Jaipur we didn't shoot from elephants but rather from raised platforms, *machans*. The game was just as plentiful, however: tiger, panther, bear, blue bull, sambar, and many sorts of deer. Much later we were to entertain Lord and Lady Mountbatten of Burma there, and the Queen and Prince Philip, too.

For more impromptu shoots or week-ends, we often went to another shooting-lodge that Jai had built on the edge of a lake about sixteen miles outside the city. It was rather like a comfortable French country house, and our life there was much simpler but just as active, for there, too, was an abundance of game, mostly black buck and wild boar.

And then, as a recurring theme in our lives, there was polo. As soon as the rains of high summer were over, polo began, and every other day there were practice games on the Jaipur polo-grounds, considered among the best in the world. Jai's obsession with polo had begun when he was a small boy and flourished when he went to Mayo College. His tutor once told me that Jai, even at the age of ten or eleven, would roll up his mattress to make a "horse" and, sit-

Moti Doongri.

ting astride it, with any ordinary stick in his hand, diligently practise his backhand and his forehand swings.

In Jaipur, our lives revolved around polo. In the late afternoons, after the heat of the middle of the day was over, I used to drive out to watch Jai playing or practising. I always took my knitting with me and sat in the front seat of my car, with the top down, gazing out at the polo-ground and the graceful wheeling of ponies and riders and keeping my hands busy with wool and needles in a feeble attempt to calm my nerves and anxieties at the danger of the game. Even through my tension, I couldn't help seeing—almost with renewed surprise each time—what a beautiful game it is, and how the elegance of the movements of horses and players, perfectly synchronized, raises the whole performance from a sport to an art.

On days when there was no polo we played tennis, and often we invited Jai's ministers to join us. Our lives outside of Jaipur were pretty much dictated by when and where the polo season arrived. We went to Calcutta for December and January, to Bombay or Delhi for special tournaments, to other princely states, and to England in the summer. In any of those places my own life as Jai's wife was filled with fun and excitement, with parties and excursions, and while I understood that there was good reason why so many people thought of him simply as a frivolous polo-playing glamour-boy, always seen with a beautiful woman on each arm—indeed, he *did* fit that picture to most outsiders—I also gradually began to learn that his real life was in Jaipur and that he cared most deeply about the welfare and just government of his subjects. Much of this was hidden under his light-hearted manner and characteristic easy friendliness. In Jaipur he spoke the local language and laughed and joked with anyone—farmers, shopkeepers, children on the street—and his attitude with all of them was startlingly different from the tenor of life in the palace. Once, I remember, I was driving with Jai in his jeep when we were stopped outside the gates of Rambagh by a group of young boys. One of them spoke up reproachfully to Jai. "You didn't come yesterday, and we were all late for school."

Jai apologized, but the boy persisted.

"But you didn't *come!* Will you be there tomorrow?"

"Yes, I promise I'll be there," Jai said reassuringly, and we drove on. In answer to my mystified questions, Jai explained that in the mornings when he went for his usual ride on the polo-grounds, these boys came and watched, and afterwards Jai would drop them off at their school, which was just opposite our gates. The previous day Jai hadn't gone riding, and the boys had waited and waited, certain that their Maharaja would give them a ride as usual, but he hadn't come and they had waited until they were all late for school.

On another occasion, I was driving my own car out of the palace gates when I heard an unusual uproar going on, with Jai in the middle of it. It was a few minutes before I could make out what had happened. Apparently a child had been chased by a monkey while Jai had been driving past, his dog as usual in the back seat. As he slowed down to help, the dog jumped out of the car and chased the monkey, which panicked and bit the child. Jai told me urgently to put the child in my car and drive him to the hospital. Only when I got there and saw the astonishment on the faces of the hospital staff did I realize what a strange picture I presented to them—their Maharani arriving in slacks, driving a sports-car with a small boy on the seat beside her. I took the child to the emergency ward, waited until he had been treated, all the while avoiding the stares of the doctors and nurses, and finally took the child home. To Jai there had never been the smallest question about which took priority, the needs of one of his subjects or the public decorum of his wife.

All the people in Jaipur seemed to feel a special and intimate kinship with their Maharaja. Jai never flew a flag on any of his cars, or used the red number-plates to which he was entitled, except on state occasions. But everyone in the city recognized his Bentley and his jeep and knew that they could stop him on the street, or the polo-grounds, or at the gates of the palace—anywhere—if they had a complaint, or wanted to bring some problem to his attention, or simply wished to ask after the welfare of his family and tell him about their own. It is a curious relationship—it was true in Cooch Behar too—this special blend of concern, intimacy, and respect that the people of the princely states felt for their rulers. Jai, like Bhaiya, was always called "Father" by his subjects, and he embodied for them the special qualities of affection, protectiveness, and benevolent justice that they associated with the ideal father. It is a relationship that exists nowhere in modern independent India.

There were established times when Jai was both a ruler and one of Jaipur's people. These were the festivals, the colourful pageants which Jai would lead, and in which all the townspeople and many of the villagers from the surrounding country would participate. Some were great religious feast-days, others formal state occasions. Jai and his nobles wore their finest jewels, their brocade jackets, their grand turbans, and their ceremonial swords. The women of the noble families dressed in their colourful Rajasthani costumes and their traditional jewels. There were parades and processions through the city streets, and celebrations and feasting inside the palaces. On such occasions the women would hold their own festivities in the zenana, quite separately from the men, but Jai himself always left his nobles and ministers and joined us there for part of the day. As these festivals unfolded in their age-old manner, we might well have been back in the eighteenth century, in the reign of the great Maharaja Jai Singh II, who built the modern city of Jaipur and who was famous for the splendour of his court and his wisdom in government.

The first festival I attended in Jaipur was Teej, celebrated in honour of the goddess Parvati, the beautiful and charming consort of the Lord Shiva. The festival was one of particular significance in the zenana because, in the stories of Hindu mythology, Parvati had meditated for years and years in order to win Lord Shiva as husband. Accordingly, the unmarried women prayed to Parvati to endow them with a husband as good as Shiva, while the married women begged that their husbands should be granted many more years of life so that they could "always be dressed in red"—rather than the unrelieved white clothes of widows. We three maharanis were supposed to perform the ceremonies of prayers and offerings in the shrine in the City Palace. But on that first occasion, Jai's other two wives were out of the state and I was told that I must enact each part of the ceremony three times, once for First Her Highness, once for Second Her Highness, and finally once for myself.

Mercifully Jo Didi, with her unfailing kindness, had briefed me when we met in Bangalore on what I should have to do and how I should conduct myself. To my great relief—this was the first important formal occasion at which I presided in Jaipur—the proceedings went off without any difficulty; I said the prayers and made the proper offerings to the deity.

After the prayers in the City Palace, the replica of the goddess was taken out of the zenana and carried in procession through the streets of the town. To watch this spectacle, the zenana ladies were led by the palace eunuchs through a labyrinth of dark tunnels and passages and up and down ramps to a gallery that overlooked the main street on the north-west side of the palace. We must have had to walk for over half a mile, twisting and turning behind the eunuchs through the half-lit maze. I lost all sense of time and direction and was conscious only of the rustling sound of silk and the tinkling of anklets as we hurried along. When we finally emerged, I saw Jai sitting in state in another pavilion, surrounded by his nobles. Through the lacy, carved marble screen of our own pavilion, perched like his on the top of the palace wall, we could get a clear view beneath us of a spacious arena made for elephant fights, a favourite sport of the old Rajput chiefs. This arena was being used by the townsfolk as a fair-ground and was thronged with sightseers, some of them city people but most of them peasants from the villages in the countryside surrounding Jaipur.

It was an exuberant and joyful sight. There were swings, merry-go-rounds, a big wheel, and endless rows of stalls selling trinkets, sweets, and little clay dolls, all mixed with the good-humoured jostling of an Indian crowd, everyone dressed in their best finery for their visit to the palace, children tearing about, yelling with excitement on this holiday. All of us gasped with admiration as on one side of the arena, the Jaipur cavalry gave a meticulous display of jumping and tent-pegging, while on the other a desert tribe of military ascetics performed a whirling sword dance of incredible dexterity. The elephants were lined up, their howdahs draped with sumptuous satins and velvets; the soldiers stood in perfect ranks, their silver trappings and uniforms brilliant in the sun; and all around them was the bustling mass of Jaipuris with their bright turbans and gaily multi-coloured dresses.

I watched enchanted for almost an hour. Then a signal was given, and reluctantly I rose with the others to be led back through the windowless passages into the zenana. Meanwhile the men, led by Jai, visited their own temple and later gathered in a pavilion in the City Palace gardens to enjoy their drinks and be entertained by musicians and dancers.

When the image of the goddess was finally returned to the palace to be enshrined for another year, I again performed the prayer ceremony. On that first day all the palace ladies, except the widows, had worn red. On the second day, when the parties and festivities continued, we all wore green. We spent hours peering through the screened galleries overlooking the streets to see the crowds and the gaiety. The pavement-merchants spread out their wares, especially little clay models of Shiva and Parvati that were in constant demand. Groups of women sang songs to entertain the passers-by, and one of the songs, I was told, praised the Maharaja's new bride, who had brought rains to the parched countryside. I was glad that at least one section of the public, for however unwarranted a reason, liked me.

The next big occasion, after the rains, was Jai's birthday. This followed, in general, the pattern I was accustomed to in Cooch Behar for Bhaiya's birthday. In the morning, a nineteen-gun salute was fired, the poor were fed, prisoners were released, and a public holiday was declared. The celebration differed, however, both in scope and detail. There were formal military parades, and elaborate prayers were offered up both inside and outside the zenana. Jai's first two wives always returned to Jaipur for the occasion and so did Jai himself, no matter where he might happen to be before it. In the zenana the Dowager Maharani presided over the ladies' durbar, and this was the only time when we, Jai's wives, were allowed to have our faces uncovered in her presence.

Jai held a separate, very grand ceremonial durbar in the audience hall of the City Palace, where he sat on the ancestral throne, his personal staff in attendance on each side, with the nobility, the state officials, and the military officers ranked beside them. Dancing girls and musicians performed at the end of the hall, facing the throne, while one by one, in order of seniority, the courtiers came up to Jai and presented tokens of their allegiance. The military officers drew their swords halfway out of the scabbards, and Jai touched the hilt in acknowledgement of their loyalty. Everything was done with a precision and panache that I had never seen before. Later, Jai came to the zenana for a separate durbar where he sat on a throne at the Dowager Maharani's left. No woman was expected to keep purdah before the Maharaja, though they might normally cover their faces as a mark of respect to the elder ladies, and while entertainers danced and sang Jai's praises, the ladies of the court, in their turn, presented tokens of their allegiance.

In all festivals the Maharaja played the central role. Along with the other ladies of the Jaipur court, I watched these ceremonies from behind windows of latticed stone and kept quiet about my great pride in the public figure that Jai presented. Dasehra, or Durgapuja as it was called in Cooch Behar, was the most important festival of the year. Jai led the worship of the arms and weapons of war, and afterwards rode in a golden carriage, drawn by six white horses, to a special palace three miles away, used only for the Dasehra durbar. The public ceremonies were perfectly organized, magnificent in appearance, and deeply, reassuringly impressive to Jai's subjects. The procession was led off by troops, cavalry, bullock-carts, and camels, all accompanied by military bands, followed by Jai's personal bodyguard riding their matched black horses preceding Jai's own carriage. Behind him came the nobility on horseback, wearing brocade costumes, their horses grandly caparisoned. (Some of them were not very good riders, and there was always a great deal of laughter and teasing among us zenana ladies as the procession passed our windows.) All along the royal route Jai received a tremendous ovation and people crowded every window, balcony, or look-out point to watch him and shout, "*Maharaja Man Singhji ki Jai!*" "Victory for Maharaja Man Singhji!" as he approached.

On the darkest night of the year, which falls, by the lunar calendar, late in October or early in November, Diwali, the Hindu New

Opposite: Jai going to the temple of Govind Devji on his birthday.

Below: Jai's birthday durbar later that day.

Year, is celebrated. It is a time when merchants and businessmen close their financial books for the past year and are ready for fresh expenditures and transactions. It is the only time when gambling is approved—even encouraged—and when everyone prays for a prosperous New Year to come. In Jaipur, as in Cooch Behar, the palace and the whole city were illuminated, looking like strange and beautiful fantasy buildings. But in Jaipur, the hilltop forts above the town were also lit up, and seemed to be magically suspended in mid-air. Beneath them, against the hills themselves, an outline of the goddess Lakshmi, the giver of wealth, was picked out in lamps, while in the city all the palaces, public buildings, and private homes were decorated. Rambagh and the City Palace blossomed with thousands of tiny lamps—clay pots holding oil and wicks—and, in the City Palace courtyard, dancing girls performed from morning to evening. Jai paid a ceremonial visit there, dressed in a black jacket and a black and gold turban, and, attended by his nobles, he offered prayers to Lakshmi while the dancing and singing continued, climaxed by an extravagant fireworks display.

Jai always invited many guests for the Diwali festivities and persuaded them to play games of bridge or roulette, or any form of gambling, to usher in the New Year. We ladies didn't join them. All of us, dressed in dark blue, the colour appropriate for Diwali, watched the fireworks from another terrace and later returned to Rambagh for a large family dinner followed by our own private display of fireworks.

A less grand ceremony, but to me the loveliest of all, is held a couple of weeks before Diwali, when the full moon is at its brightest and a durbar is held outdoors to celebrate the festival of Sharad Purnima. Nothing much happens, but at this durbar Jai and his courtiers would all dress in the palest pink, their swords and jewels glittering in the moonlight. To me it seemed an extraordinary, almost ethereal scene, engraved forever in my memory.

The basic pattern of festivals was similar to what I had known in Cooch Behar; still, some of them came as an uncomfortable revelation. Holi, which in Cooch Behar had been merely the expression of high-spirited delight in the arrival of spring, with people throwing red powder at each other, in Jaipur turned out to be both more ceremonial and less appealing. That first Holi, Jai rode through the streets on an elephant, as was customary, followed on this occasion by Bhaiya, who was visiting us. Holi was a free-for-all, with people throwing wax pellets the size of tennis-balls filled with coloured powder and water at one another. As they rode through the streets, Jai and Bhaiya were sitting targets for the townsfolk who crowded the rooftops, windows, and balconies. Bhaiya told me afterwards that it was the most painful experience he had ever suffered. Jai, ready for what he knew was coming, had equipped himself and Bhaiya with return ammunition and as an extra precaution had taken with him a water-hose with a compressor to shoot on the crowds and make them keep their distance. All the same, in spite of the ordeal they had shared, when Jai and Bhaiya returned from the streets to the City Palace they "played" Holi more gently around the fountain, with all the Jaipur nobles and officials dressed in court clothes.

In another part of the palace, in a courtyard off one of the apartments in the zenana quarters, Jo Didi and I also "played" Holi with the ladies, who were dressed in traditionally elaborate Rajputani costumes and, to my surprise, formally bejewelled. These ladies were expert players, and Jo Didi and I were the chief targets. Besides using the painful wax pellets, they threw coloured water with great force from silver and leather vessels, and we were soon drenched, painfully and colourfully, to the skin. To my dismay Jai, after playing with the men, joined us in the zenana, and the horrid game continued with renewed vigour.

In later years Holi became far less dangerous and distressing as we played in our own gardens, but the occasional accurate shot still hurt as much and the stains were just as permanent. I remember the embarrassing predicament of a friend of ours who had to leave immediately after Holi to return to her job in London. She arrived still covered with yellow dye, late for work and able to fend off her boss's wrath only by telling him that she was recovering from a bad case of jaundice that she had picked up in India.

With all its strangeness, its delights, its worries, its embarrassments, and its joys, those first months in Jaipur trained me for a kind of life I had never expected to experience. It taught me the duties and responsibilities, the pleasures and restrictions of being a maharani of an important state. It also showed me that it was possible to be lonely surrounded by people, yet happy even in the enveloping shroud of purdah life.

More simply, I suppose I was growing up. I might have muddled along for years, enjoying special occasions, often finding myself bored or at a loose end in my daily life, surrounded by luxury but with no interior furnishings for what I suppose I should call my soul, not seeing enough of Jai, fretting when I wasn't with him, making do with whatever company I could find in the zenana, unable to appreciate fully the deep satisfactions that such a life could offer.

But the war, once it got started in an active way, demanding the co-operation of the Commonwealth, changed my life as it changed so much more.

Chapter 11

Wartime

JAI WAS A very keen soldier—that was, after all, a crucial part of his Rajput heritage—and naturally wanted to see active service himself as soon as possible. But at first he was obliged to comply with the Viceroy's wish that the Indian princes should remain in India and lead the war effort in their states. Before the war broke out, before Jai and I were married, Jai had already reorganized the Jaipur state forces and had raised a special battalion, the Sawai Man Guards, training the officers himself. By the time the need came, two battalions of Jaipur forces were ready for active service. Soon, the First Jaipur Infantry left for the Middle East and the Guards were posted on the North-West Frontier, the border with Afghanistan made famous by Kipling and Yeats-Brown, where the warlike nomadic tribes had to be kept permanently in check by bribes or force or both, to keep them from raiding the Indian villages in the Himalayan valleys. The Guards, too, were later sent overseas.

India at this time was in the throes of a serious and complex political controversy. The Congress Party and its leaders—notably Mahatma Gandhi and Pandit Jawaharlal Nehru—were faced with a curious predicament. Gandhi's deep and far-spreading hold over the people of British India was incontrovertibly based on his belief, held with missionary zeal, in the principle of non-violence. It was on this platform that he had collected the support of millions of Indians and earned the despair of thousands of British officials, who could think of no way of controlling him except to put him in jail—which troubled him not at all and only seemed to increase his following among the people of India.

The war in Europe had to produce a new kind of response from Mahatma Gandhi and his followers in the Congress Party. He was absolutely clear about one point: He detested fascism and felt warmly in sympathy with those people who were fighting it. But, in his phrase, was it possible for slaves to come to the aid of their masters in a fight against tyranny? Where should India stand? Against fascism, certainly. But how should India show her stand? And should India pick this moment of Britain's weakness to force concessions?

No, Gandhi said. No, we must hold to our principles without embarrassing the British in their war effort. Certain chosen leaders of the Congress Party would go to jail for acts of civil disobedience, as a token of their resistance to the continuance of British rule in India, but the rest of the Indians should follow their conscience and keep in mind that none of us wished to impede the efforts of the British in a righteous war.

But more specific acts complicated the issue. The Congress Party felt that Lord Linlithgow, the British Viceroy of India, should have consulted Indian political opinion before involving the country in a foreign war. This had not been done, and the Congress members of the legislative assemblies across the country launched a campaign of nonco-operation with the British. A headline at the time told of Mahatma Gandhi's interview with the Viceroy in which he said that, though he deplored the Nazi aggression in Poland, he was powerless to move his party to assist the British in their stand.

In spite of all the political hazards and reluctances, India's contribution to the Allied war effort was magnificent. Two and a half million men and women enrolled in the armed forces and associated services, while several million others were engaged in war work. Indian troops played the predominant part in the victories of the South-East Asia Command, and the famous 14th Army was made up of nine Indian, three British, and three African divisions. The princely states, of course, backed the war effort in every way they could.

Eventually Jai was attached to the Thirteenth Lancers, who were at that time stationed in Risalpur near the North-West Frontier.

To my joy and relief, I was allowed to accompany him. Only then did I realize how burdensome I had found the trappings of rulership and the duties of being a maharani. It was bliss to live like any other army wife in a little bungalow in the cantonment, to run the house myself, and to be directly responsible for my husband's comforts—ordering menus, shopping for supplies, keeping accounts, typing Jai's letters. I got no special privileges or deference; I was just a captain's wife and, I should add, very much in awe of the colonel's wife.

Jai loved our army life quite as much as I did. When he was not on duty, we rode and played squash together, entertained other officers and their wives, and were asked out a lot ourselves. The club was the center of much congenial activity. Since the Thirteenth Lancers was a cavalry regiment, there was very good polo, and like the other cavalry officers Jai had brought his own horses to Risalpur. I attended and enjoyed the ladies' work-parties, and best of all there was the utter freedom of being one's unguarded self.

The crisp and cool air of this ruggedly beautiful countryside also contained a continual hint of danger which I found rather exciting. Jai never let me go out alone because the frontier tribesmen were always on the warpath, sweeping down from their mountain fastnesses to attack the unwary, hold up cars, and rob the occupants of their clothes and possessions. However, accompanied by Jai, I managed to see some of the famous sights around Risalpur: the magnificent fort of Attock; the Khyber Pass; Peshawar, the frontier town that guards the southern end of the pass; and Mardan, where the Guides Cavalry had a famous mess of which they were justly proud.

On ordinary days Jai came home in the evening to his wife, like any other husband, and recounted the events of his day. Some were amusing. For instance, the Thirteenth Lancers were taking a course in mechanization, but the cavalrymen were obviously much more at home on horses than in tanks, and Jai described how some of the less sophisticated of them tried, in an emergency, to stop their tanks by pulling hard on the steering wheel.

I, in turn, reading from my shorthand notes, gave him all the international news that had come in over the radio. For this, and in typing Jai's confidential letters, I found my training in the College of Secretaries very useful. The time I spent in Switzerland taking the domestic-science course turned out to be helpful, too. I knew what ingredients went into the food we ate and could see that only enough was bought to prevent waste. I knew how to order well-balanced meals and how to keep all my domestic accounts.

Like the other officers' families, we had a small (by Indian standards) staff of servants: a cook, a butler, a man to clean the house, a maid for me, a valet for Jai, and his army orderly. Of course there were, as well, grooms for Jai's eight polo ponies and for his other two horses.

I remember one embarrassing incident early in our stay when I had decided to take over the kitchen to make some fudge. I have never been a good cook—almost any dish I attempt seems to come out wrong—but this time the fudge came out perfectly, and I put some on the dinner-table for the small party of guests we were expecting that night. The fudge was a great success, and one of the officers' wives asked me where I had managed to find it. Rather proudly, I said that I had made it myself, and I couldn't understand why everyone's face dropped, or why all our guests avoided my eye. Afterwards, one of the younger women took me aside and said, "Don't you realize that sugar is rationed? All of us get only enough to put in our tea. How did you get enough to make fudge?"

Then I remembered that when I had gone into the kitchen to make the fudge I had found that there wasn't enough sugar and had asked the servant to go out and buy me some more. Obediently he had done as I asked, and must have bought the extra sugar on the black market. It was the first time I had come across anything like rationing, and after seeing those frozen faces around the dining-table I was extremely careful about the shopping lists I gave the cook or those I wrote out for myself.

We had taken only one car up to Risalpur, and even that was out of commission for a few days after our arrival. On our journey up, Jai had been very tired and had asked me to drive. He told me to hurry—he wanted a cold beer at Risalpur—so I hadn't taken the time to adjust the driver's seat from the far-back position that suited his long legs. I was doing all right on those twisting mountain roads and Jai was dozing in the seat beside me. Then, taking a turn more quickly than I should have, I ran the car into a whole herd of donkeys, one of which landed on the bonnet of the car. Jai opened his eyes to this astonishing sight and never stopped teasing me about it afterwards. The donkeys were uninjured, but the headlights of the car had to be replaced. I was the only one who was inconvenienced. Jai always rode to work on his bicycle, leaving the car for me to do the shopping and attend the various activities the officers' wives organized.

This happy domestic interlude came to an end all too soon. Just before Christmas of 1941 there was trouble with the Afghan tribesmen. The regiment was sent up to the border and the wives had to stay behind. Trying hard to keep the tears back, I stood with the other wives and waved good-bye as the regiment passed by. I wanted passionately to stay on in my little house in the cantonment, but Jai insisted that I go back to Jaipur, as he wasn't sure how long he'd be away and didn't want me to be all alone in that treacherous country.

It was my first Christmas in Jaipur. Jo Didi was there with all four children, and because of the English governess and nurses we had a full-fledged Western Christmas with all the proper trimmings, a huge tree, and presents for everyone, while outside the tropical sun blazed down, and in the evening, at the big children's party, Father Christmas arrived, amid howls of delight, on a state elephant.

I missed Jai terribly and constantly. But during that stay in Jaipur I had my first opportunity to make friends with his children. They were very responsive and took a great interest in me. Soon I found myself perpetually at their disposal, commandeered into bicycling with them, playing table-tennis, taking them out riding and shooting. They loved to come out with me in my car because they thought I drove so adventurously fast. So, as Ma had predicted, I did indeed spend a lot of time in the Jaipur nursery.

Mickey, First Her Highness's elder child and only daughter, was eleven at this time, just ten years younger than I was. She used to haunt my rooms, fascinated by my clothes, examining and touching everything from saris or slacks to nightgowns and underwear. She wanted to wear exactly what I wore, and pestered her governess to ask me where similar clothes could be bought in her size. Finally, I bought all Mickey's clothes myself. With Bubbles, her younger brother, she used to stand and stare at me when I was sitting at my dressing-table. I used hardly any make-up, and this struck Bubbles as a gripping eccentricity. "Why don't you put on lipstick?" he would ask. "Why don't you put on more and *more* lipstick?"

Joey, Jo Didi's elder son, was the most mischievous of the family, full of pranks and inquisitive questions and not at all shy. His younger brother, Pat, the same child who had cycled round and round the garden in Bangalore waiting to get a good look at me when I arrived from Ooty, was still too small to join in many of the games and activities of the other children.

My family were in Calcutta for the winter season, as usual, and Ma wrote to ask Jai's permission for me to join them. I timed my arrival at "Woodlands" for New Year's Day, 1942, because I didn't want to be there for the New Year's Eve festivities without Jai. It would have been too lonely and depressing. We always had a big New Year's Eve party, but this year Ma had written to tell me she was planning to mark the occasion with a particularly splendid fête at "Woodlands" to raise funds for the war effort. She turned the whole garden into a huge fair-ground and in a single night raised almost 100,000 rupees. When I arrived, everyone was still talking enthusiastically about Ma's fête, and I half wished that I had been there for it after all.

That season was as gay and busy as any I can remember. Perhaps we were all aware in some unexpressed way that, as the war intensified, our own social life would be sharply curtailed and might never resume in just the way we knew it. Throughout my stay in Calcutta I was very uncertain about precisely what my position as Jai's wife required of me, about what I could do and what I shouldn't.

I was not in purdah, yet purdah was very much the custom, not only in Rajputana but in most of the Indian states, and even in the rest of Indian society very few girls ever went out unaccompanied by some relative or otherwise chaperoned. My marriage to Jai had been widely talked about, and I was very much in the public eye. I had the feeling that I was continually being watched by not entirely charitable eyes to find some telltale sign in my behaviour that might show that our obvious happiness was not quite all it seemed. But I managed to survive and, much encouraged by Jai's letters urging me to enjoy myself, didn't put a foot wrong.

The last big celebration we ever held at "Woodlands" was on the occasion of Indrajit's engagement to the Princess of Pithapuram. With the fall of Singapore to the Japanese in February, the war suddenly moved much closer to India. "Woodlands" was converted into a hospital, and Ma and Bhaiya moved into the chauffeur's quarters when they were in Calcutta. But Bhaiya had to spend most of his time in Cooch Behar, as it was quite close to the war zone. A huge American army base had been installed there, and the famous Burma Road went through Cooch Behar; together they transformed the sleepy little town into a bustling international centre which came to be known as "the G.I.'s Shangri-la." After the war we thought we might move back to "Woodlands," but by then too much had changed and too much was happening in India. The country was on the verge of gaining its independence, the princely states were contemplating their merger with the Indian Union, and, more specifically, "Woodlands" was sadly run down. Bhaiya sold the land, and today there are many houses and a nursing home where we once used to live. Somehow it pleases me that the whole area is still known as Woodlands.

After a couple of months, Jai came back from the North-West Frontier in time to receive Indrajit and his bride when they returned to Cooch Behar after their wedding in her parents' home. Jai was restless and fretful, still very keen to go to the Middle East on active service, while the Viceroy was equally determined that the princes should remain in their states. Eventually Jai wrote to King George VI's Private Secretary to ask if he could join the Life Guards, to which he had been attached for a period in 1936, and at last permission was granted him.

Jai was ecstatic, but in Jaipur the news of his departure for the Middle East provoked worried opposition from his family and his ministers. He begged me to understand his feelings and to support him. He explained that it was the tradition of Rajputs to go to war, and against all their principles for the Maharaja to stay at home while his men fought. He reminded me that his direct ancestor, Raja Man Singh, had been the Emperor Akbar's greatest general.

He was so excited and so persuasive that I could hardly help coming to his defence whenever I heard the slightest criticism of his leaving his state and his duties at home. I packed his things myself, a skill of which I was inordinately proud, as I always managed to get twice as much into a case as any of his valets could. After a series of farewell parties in Jaipur, given by the family, the nobility, and the public, I accompanied Jai on a visit to my Baroda grandmother, for him to say good-bye to her. She was staying in a pleasant little resort in the hills behind Bombay, where she saw Mahatma Gandhi every morning on his daily walk. She didn't know that, although Jai had never met the Mahatma, he had once, in 1937, been urgently told by the British authorities to arrest the great leader when he was passing through Jaipur. There had been some muddle—the message didn't reach Jai in time, or the train didn't stop where the Mahatma was expected—anyway, nothing came of the whole affair. But Mahatma Gandhi now greeted Jai in a teasing voice with "Ah, so you're the naughty boy who tried to arrest me? I've met you at last."

My grandmother, who had been anxious that they should get on well together, was thrown into confusion by that first encounter, but neither Mahatma Gandhi nor Jai seemed to regard the conversation as anything but a joke.

On the ninth of May, our first wedding anniversary, Jai's ship sailed from Bombay. Ma and I went to see him off, and after that I left gloomily with Ma for Kodaikanal, a lovely hill-station in the south of India. Now that I was married, even my old family life was not the same. I was excluded from the excursions and parties organized by Menaka and Baby. I would have loved to go, but their friends considered me a married woman and too old to join in their activities. Instead I spent my days in endless solitary rounds of golf, looking after Jai's Alsatian, his favorite of the many dogs we had at Rambagh, and listening anxiously to the radio for any news of Jai's ship.

For my twenty-second birthday, Ma gave a party for me, but though, like all her parties, it was superbly organized, none of the guests was under fifty. All the young men we knew were away at the war, and most of the young women, if they weren't engaged in war work, were not spending their summers in the hills. Only the retired couples and Ma's older friends were available for parties, and at the club there was the depressing sight of women dancing with women.

My only consolation came when Jai's letters began to arrive. He wrote of his disappointment when he found that he had just missed his regiment, which had been sent out unexpectedly on a hurried expedition. He was sent to the Gaza area to join the Royal Scots Greys, among whom he found many polo-playing friends and shared a tent with a particularly famous one, Humphrey Guinness. Soon afterwards he was transferred to Cairo, and he wrote from there asking me to send him the Indian newspapers so that he could keep abreast of political developments at home. He was appointed the liaison officer for the Indian States Forces, a job he enjoyed although it brought him some moments of embarrassment; when he accompanied a general on a visit to an Indian State regiment, it would be Jai, not the general, who got the enthusiastic welcome.

I was delighted that he had been given this job, knowing how intimately involved he felt with the welfare of the Indian States Forces troops, but even more because it meant he would have to spend some time in India, mainly in New Delhi, but on each occasion with the possibility of a few days in Jaipur. His first return visit was early in September of 1942. Our private plane, a Dakota, was sent to meet him, and I decided to go with it, quite unaccompanied except for Jai's Alsatian. Jo Didi was full of warnings about the trouble I was certain to land in, because Jai was very strict about not allowing us to go anywhere alone. But to my relief, he seemed very pleased to see me. Even so, when we got back to Jaipur, the stern purdah ruling came into effect again, and I had to disembark at one end of the runway and be hustled into a purdah car while Jai taxied along the tarmac to the other end of the field to be received by his ministers, his nobles, his household staff, and half of Jaipur which had turned out to greet him.

While the war brought all kinds of restrictions to many people, to me, in Jaipur, it brought a certain measure of freedom. Jai encouraged me to work for the war effort, and I started at once by attending Red Cross work-parties at the Ladies' Club. I met all sorts of women there: teachers, doctors, and wives of government officials. Their company was far more stimulating than that of the purdah-ridden palace ladies, and besides I felt that, in however indirect a way, I was backing up the people closest to me who were taking an active part in the war—Jai, of course; Bhaiya, especially vulnerable now that the Japanese were advancing into Burma; and Indrajit, on active service abroad.

Jo Didi and I organized work-parties to knit and sew for the Red Cross at Rambagh for the more orthodox ladies, and I even managed to persuade some of the women in the City Palace that knitting prosaic things like socks and sweaters was not below their dignity because it was all helping their Maharaja. Besides this kind of sedentary work, I put much of my effort into raising money by organizing plays and fêtes at the Ladies' Club in order to buy all sorts of amenities for the Jaipur State Forces in the Middle East.

With energy still to spare, and with rather more confidence now that my war work seemed to be successful, both financially and socially, I started to take over the running of the household at Rambagh. It was Jai's suggestion, when his English comptroller left, that I should do so, and I realized that although I had lived mainly in Jaipur ever since my marriage, I hadn't concerned myself at all with how everything was managed but, like everyone else, had simply enjoyed the high standard of comfort provided. There were something over four hundred servants at Rambagh, and while Jai wanted to eliminate unnecessary extravagance, he had a military eye for detail and expected everything to be perfectly run. The guards at the nine gates, for example, were inspected at regular intervals. All the gardens had to be impeccably maintained. At various points throughout the palace, groups of boys were posted to prevent the many pigeons from settling or causing damage to the buildings.

The household and its running fell into two general departments. It was the function of the Comptroller to order the stores and maintain the store-rooms, make the menus, and issue the supplies to fulfil each day's needs. He was also in charge of the linen, including the uniforms of the staff. He acted as a sort of super-housekeeper, seeing to the general running of the palace. He had several people under him to handle such duties as attending to the laundry or collecting the vegetables, milk, and eggs from the farm that supplied the needs of Rambagh.

The other branch of the household was headed by the Military Secretary. It was his job to keep the building itself in perfect condition, see to any repairs that might be needed, and supervise the grounds and gardens, which had to be maintained in as flawless a condition as the building. He was in charge of cars for the constant flow of guests that we used to have in Rambagh, though he had an assistant to supervise the care of the garages and cars, just as another assistant was in charge of the day-to-day work in the gardens. Whenever we entertained—as we did a great deal—the Military Secretary would have to co-ordinate plans with the Comptroller in assigning rooms to the guests, seeing to meals and seating arrangements, and organizing activities for them. The ADCs also took their orders from the Military Secretary as to when they were on duty or which of them was assigned to attend a visiting nobleman or some other guest. Jai himself always had three ADCs on duty with him. Jo Didi and I each had one for the day and one at night. All these timings were worked out by the Military Secretary.

Finally, apart from the household itself, there were the people in charge of the shoots, who arranged for such things as providing bait for the tigers and getting the beaters ready in whichever area the shoot was to be held. Here, too, there were departments, and when I took over the managing of the Rambagh household I soon discovered that at least two of the departmental heads of the arrangements for shoots seemed to view themselves as running rival organizations. General Bhairon Singh, who looked after outdoor equipment like tents and camp furniture, and Colonel Kesri Singh, who was in charge of the guns and other shooting necessities, agreed on nothing and seemed almost to enjoy not co-operating with each other. I thought of a tactful scheme to resolve their differences and persuaded them to play a game of chess, the winner to have the final say in future arrangements for shoots and camps. I even had a special chess set made, with each of the kings carved to resemble one of the opponents and the other pieces representing members of their respective staffs. Colonel Kesri Singh won, but the game that was to have settled all their disagreements made not the smallest difference to the way they behaved on the very next shoot we organized.

What surprised me most, however, was the extravagance of the store-rooms in Rambagh itself. When I looked into them for the first time, I was flabbergasted. It was like some fantastic parody of Fortnum and Mason's. Everything was of the best quality and ordered not just by the crate but by the dozens of crates, "to make sure, Your Highness, that we don't run out," explained an attendant, seeing my amazement. There was enough to last us for years—wines, spirits, liqueurs, cigarettes, tea, biscuits, shampoo, Christmas crackers, toothpaste, lipsticks, face creams, toffees, chocolates, preserves, and so on and on—all beautifully arranged and labelled. Half of the things must have been there for years, and there was an appalling wastage of perishable articles.

When I asked for the names of the people who had access to the store-rooms, I found that there wasn't the least attempt to keep track of who helped himself to what. The palace had been supplying all the staff, the guests, the ADCs and their families, and anyone else who happened to want something. For Jai, when I told him, it was the end of at least one illusion. For years he had been touched by a small act of thoughtfulness at any party he attended in Jaipur—his hosts always provided his favourite brand of Egyptian cigarettes, by no means easy to obtain. He now learned, as a result of my researches, that the cigarettes came straight from his own store-rooms. Jo Didi, too, was shocked that the Evian water which she liked, and which was specially imported for her, was also regularly drunk by her maids and even by the governess's dogs.

The extravagance in the kitchen matched that in the store-rooms. The point at which the chef for Western food finally realized that I was serious about eliminating senseless waste and stopping the purloining of palace stores for private use came, ridiculously enough, over the recipe for *crème brûlée*. Jai had invited his new Minister for Education and his wife to lunch, and since it was to be a business occasion, in part, he wanted the meal to be a simple affair for just the four of us. Clearly, the second head chef didn't know that I had some education in domestic science and decided, apparently, that I would be easy to hoodwink. He ordered two pounds of cream for his *crème brûlée*. Horrified, I pointed out that so much cream would spoil the dish, but he replied grandly that for the Maharaja no amount of cream was too much. When I insisted, he reluctantly gave in, and from then on all our nine cooks—four for English food, five for Indian—paid proper attention to my orders.

Anyone who arrived at the palace, and that could mean dozens of people every day, was always offered a drink by the ADCs. In the hot summer months, iced coffee was the most popular choice. We had our own farm and dairy, but another of my maddening early discoveries was that our own milk was being watered down because there wasn't enough to meet the demands of the ADCs' room. When I insisted that such open-handed extravagance should stop because it was most unsuitable in wartime, I became, of course, highly unpopular. The servants took their revenge by purposely interpreting my orders overzealously. When the Home Minister arrived one day to see Jai and asked for a glass of iced coffee while he was waiting, he was pointedly informed that "Third Her Highness has forbidden visitors to be offered drinks with milk." Similarly, when the English governess asked for more lavatory paper, she was told she must wait until I returned from a shoot and could sign an order, as I had given instructions that no supplies of any kind should be given out without my consent. It was, however, some satisfaction to me that, in spite of all the resentment I caused, I managed in one year to cut down the expenses in Rambagh by at least half—and that without making any particular sacrifice in comfort or hospitality.

I knew that I was the object of a lot of criticism and that, after the old days of endless unchecked lavishness in the palace, many people resented my way of running things, but as long as Jai was pleased with me I didn't much care what the others thought. I hadn't realized, however, how much comment my activities both inside and outside the palace had caused among other Jaipuris until I read an article written years later by Mrs. Bhartiya, who had been the Inspectress of Schools in Jaipur at the time.

> The new Maharani was doing unimaginable things: she had started going to the kitchen and supervising it, she was on the fields playing badminton and tennis, she had bobbed her hair, wore slacks, drove the car, watched polo, and could be seen riding, not only in the Rambagh Palace grounds but also on the roads, alongside the Maharaja. It was reported that officers and employees of the Household were on tenter-hooks because of the watchful, though discerning, eyes of this impossible "She." She was taking a round, she was going to check accounts, she was going to get Rambagh Palace renovated, she was changing the arrangements in the rooms, she was ordering this, she was demolishing that. In short, "She" was a new phenomenon, who had emerged on the scene of placid unconcern, bringing about sweeping changes. Maharani Gayatri Devi, who was made differently, could not and would not accept a static state of affairs. Maharani Gayatri Devi started exploring possibilities and as a first step she started visiting the Ladies' Club and meeting on common ground ladies from all walks of life. Her example was soon emulated and, through her personal efforts and persuasion, the *Asurya Sparshas*—the *purdah*-ridden—condescended to come into the light of day. The blue-blooded Rajput ladies, the high-browed and commoners alike, started patronising the Ladies' Club. . . . Very soon the Ladies' Club became the hub of hectic activities and under its aegis, games, sports, socials, cultural activities, and fêtes were organized in which all participated with equal gusto.

efore our marriage Jai had told me that he hoped my example, owever modestly progressive, would encourage the women of Jaiur to come out of purdah to at least some small degree. We both new that the deep-rooted customs of centuries could not be erased vernight. I understood, too, that the public purdah that I had obrved in Jaipur was necessary if I was not to shock and alienate the adition-bound nobility. But Jai had often told me that he hoped ventually to break the purdah system in Jaipur—in fact, I dare say at one of the reasons, apart from being in love, that Jai had mared me was that a liberated and travelled maharani might set some rt of example for the orthodox ladies of Jaipur. He had tried ving parties for me to which he invited the state officials and minters, asking them to bring their wives, but very few of the women me. They maintained purdah quite as strictly as Jo Didi.

It occurred to me that perhaps one way of beginning the long sk of emancipation was to start a school for girls. This may seem, ow, an unambitious and straightforward task, but in the 1940s it prented endless problems and unexpected setbacks. I decided that the hool should be primarily for the daughters of the noble families nd the higher echelons of society, because it was their womenfolk ho observed the rules of purdah most strictly. Among the middle asses girls were already being educated, but the nobility had quite fferent ideas and were far more hidebound in their lives. Many of em owned enormous estates and lived in palaces that were almost princely as our own. Their women all lived in zenanas, and most their daughters received no education at all but simply waited to ow up and marry a suitable husband of their father's choice. Many them lived in outlying parts of the state and might never come the city, spending all their lives first in one zenana and then in other. If they came to my school, I thought, in ten years' time we ight see a break-through by them.

It is probably quite difficult for Westerners to understand why ost of these conservative women were perfectly content with what ems, from the outside, a hopelessly dull and claustrophobic existnce. In fact, their lives in purdah were much fuller and more active an one would imagine. Apart from running a large household, a oman with a wide circle of children, grandchildren, and relatives was the focal point of the whole family. As a girl in her own home she would have been taught the basic accomplishments consid ered necessary for any Hindu girl: cooking, sewing, and taking car of children. Later, as a young bride, she would learn the ways of he husband's family, and eventually, as a mother and grandmother her authority and her responsibilities would increase. Perhaps mos important of all, she would never be without companionship, an she would always be needed. Zenana life, with all its limitations, ha profound and solid compensations, too. Many of the women woul have been lost and threatened if they had been suddenly exposed t the outside world without the protection they had come to rely on

It was from these families that I hoped to draw my first pupil for the Maharani Gayatri Devi School, knowing that if I succeede with them the rest would follow. I managed to persuade a few of th nobles to enrol their daughters and then set about looking for a suit able person to run what was still only a proposal for a school. With the assistance of the Jaipur State Education Minister, we advertised t fill the post of principal, wrote to people who were recommended t us, and interviewed others. But as soon as we met Miss Lilian Donnithorne Lutter, we knew that she was the perfect person fo the job and that no one else would do.

Miss Lutter came from Edinburgh, originally, and before th war had taught for some years in Burma. When the Japanese troop moved in, she led her pupils, about eighty of them, on the long trek through the Burmese jungles to the Indian frontier without a single casualty en route. She was so obviously kind, sensible, an efficient that I had not a moment's doubt about appointing her t head my school and went off happily from our interview to tell Ja of our good fortune.

In 1943, the Maharani Gayatri Devi School opened in Jaipur with forty students. There were many misgivings on the part of thei families, and many doubts and second thoughts on my part. I ha little confidence that the school would run for more than its firs term. In those early days I used to go along to watch some of th classes. I remember in particular a gym lesson where I thought i would be impossible for anyone ever to discipline this group o giggling girls, all unsure of themselves, all unable to see the point of going through a series of exercises that must have seeemed to them both uncomfortable and immodest. But, with endless tact, patience, and perseverance, Miss Lutter guided the school through its first year and went on to build one of the finest institutions in India. To-day it draws students from all parts of the country and even from Indian communities overseas. It now sends girls out to become doctors, lawyers, and teachers, and to all the major universities of India.

All my expanding activities in Jaipur were interspersed with Jai's return visits to Jaipur and Delhi, when I would drop everything to spend as much time as possible with him. Delhi had, by 1943, become the centre of great military activity. The South-East Asia Command had made its headquarters there, and so had the Joint Intelligence, the U.S. Tactical Transport, the Delhi District, and the Indian Command. Our own residence in the capital, Jaipur House, had been given over to the WRENS. All over the city temporary structures had sprung up to accommodate the new personnel and transit camps for the military units passing through Delhi. They all obscured the beauty of Edwin Lutyens's design for the capital. Many of Jai's friends were on temporary duty in Delhi or were there for short spells on their way to various theatres of war. It was a hectic, unreal atmosphere. I remember in particular the officers of one regiment telling Jai that they were taking their polo equipment with them to the Far East. Two months later we learned that most of them had been captured by the Japanese and were now prisoners of war. I remember, too, that it was during that feverish time that I first met Lord and Lady Mountbatten, so striking in their good looks, so welcome in their reassuring air of confidence. He was then Commander in Chief of the Allied Forces in South-East Asia and after the war would become India's last Viceroy.

In spite of the duties that the war imposed on Jai, he managed, in his fleeting visits to Jaipur, to keep very much abreast of needs and developments there and to continue his long program of building and improvements in the state. Much of modern Jaipur is his creation: the Sawai Man Singh barracks, which today house the Secretariat; the Sawai Man Singh Hospital; the new buildings that were erected for the Maharaja's College and the Maharani's College; and much of the more recent residential area. He constantly sought the services of the most able administrators and in 1942 brought Sir Mirza Ismail to Jaipur to be his Prime Minister.

At that time the revenue of Jaipur State came mainly from agricultural taxes. These were levied in several different ways. In some cases the state dealt directly with a landlord, in others with tenant farmers through a landlord, in yet others with small independent farmers who gave the state a percentage of their produce or what they realized from their crops. There was no income tax, and all farmers were allowed to graze their herds on state land without payment. Also, the state railway brought in a certain amount of revenue, as did customs and excise taxes on imports. Of all this, about one eighth went into the Maharaja's privy purse, and the rest was deposited in the state treasury.

During the four years that he spent with us, Sir Mirza Ismail funnelled a large part of the state revenue into extensive programs for developing education and for improving the health services and other fields of administration. For all his reforms he had Jai's wholehearted co-operation, and when, years later, he came to write his memoirs, he commended Jai as "an enlightened ruler who, true to his promise, gave me his full support. What I liked best in Jaipur was freedom from intrigue. His Highness would not allow intrigue of any sort to raise its ugly head where he was concerned. He formed his own judgement, uninfluenced by busybodies, and acted on it."

Perhaps the most significant changes that Jai and Sir Mirza made during those unsettled years were in the field of constitutional reform. Up to that time, the government of the state had been carried out by the Maharaja himself, assisted by a council of ministers as advisers. Now, Jai agreed, it should be the Prime Minister, not the Maharaja, who should preside over these cabinet meetings, although the Maharaja was, of course, to be consulted before any important decisions were implemented. Even more crucial was the establishment, in 1944, of two elected bodies: a Legislative Council and a Representative Assembly. The Council was empowered to discuss and vote on the budget, to place questions before the government, and to pass on resolutions concerning law and order and other matters of public interest. The Assembly was a larger body designed to hear public grievances and to express views on matters put to it by the government.

These reforms were, perhaps, not very sweeping in themselves, and they did not reduce the importance of the Maharaja in the lives of his subjects, nor did they make him less accessible to his people. But they did, with Jai's full consent, begin to place him in somewhat the position of a constitutional monarch, and they did start what Sir Mirza described as a slow process of democratization, without violating tradition or endangering efficiency. The process continued right up to 1949, when Jaipur State was finally merged in the Rajasthan Union within independent India.

During the war years, my own interest and involvement in the affairs of Jaipur were increasing as my public life expanded. But very suddenly at Christmas in 1944 my responsibilities within the family deepened with the death of Jai's first wife. Jai was away from the state at the time, and I had taken the boys, Bubbles, Joey, and Pat, to a shooting-camp a hundred miles away. Before we left we had all gone to the City Palace to say good-bye to First Her Highness. We had climbed one of the narrow stairways in the zenana to her drawing-room, where arched French doors opened onto a veranda overlooking one of the courtyards, and from which there was a splendid view out to the hills behind Amber. Her Western furniture seemed quite in place, although the apartments were constructed in the traditional Jaipur style.

We knew that she had not been very well because of a recurrence of a long-standing liver ailment, but we found her dressed and sitting up on a sofa. She had talked to me while the boys ran around and played, as children will. When it was time for us to leave, she said to the boys, "Now be sure to shoot properly, and bring me back some partridges." I hadn't the slightest indication that she was so seriously ill. I was woken the next morning to the news that she had died, and with the urgent request from the boys' guardian that I should not breathe a word to them as yet.

I drove them back to Jaipur, making whatever flimsy excuse

came into my head, and immediately rang up Jo Didi, who was living at the City Palace at the time. I pleaded with her to come to Rambagh, but she refused as she had to attend to the death ceremonies, and so I was left to take care of the boys myself. Joey, who was always very gay and cheerful, remarked that it was a very dull Christmas Eve and asked whether we were going to have the usual parties and presents. Bubbles, I was sure, sensed something was desperately wrong, because he was so quiet and asked for no explanations at all. I felt I had to say something to him, and at last told him that we had come back to Jaipur because his mother was very ill and perhaps we would never see her again. Poor child, I think he already knew.

The next morning Bubbles and Joey were dressed in white jackets and khaki turbans and taken to the City Palace. Pat, the youngest, came to my room and said, in a puzzled voice, "I don't know what's happened, but Bubbles and Joey are wearing very funny clothes and they've gone off somewhere. They wouldn't take me with them."

As gently as I could, I tried to explain to Pat what had happened. He was too young to understand, and his only remark was an incredulous "You mean we'll never see her again?"

Bubbles, as the eldest son, had to perform the cremation ceremony, the lighting of the funeral pyre, a terrible task for a boy of thirteen. Then the boys came back from this grim duty and presented themselves in my room. Joey tried very hard to smile and even to make jokes, but Bubbles was silent. My heart went out to him in his shock and sadness, and I promised myself that whatever might happen in the future I would always look after him. Mickey, Bubbles's sister, returned from the shoot she had been on with some friends the day before Jai could get back to Rambagh. She spent that night in my room and kept asking me what dead people looked like. It was only when Jai returned and announced briskly that we would take all the children off to the shooting-lodge that we began to feel a little better and to realize that life would eventually resume its normal course.

The following year brought another family tragedy. I was staying in Darjeeling with Ma when she received a telegram saying that Ila was seriously ill with ptomaine poisoning. We had been expecting her to join us in Darjeeling, and I was looking forward especially to her arrival because life was much more amusing when she was around. We were naturally worried when we heard of her illness, but didn't realize how grave it was. Ma was planning to send our own doctor from Cooch Behar to attend her and to bring her to the hills when she was well. So it was with incredulity and numbing shock that we heard she had died.

This was the first death in our close family circle. Both my brothers, who were serving in the army, came to join us, Bhaiya from the Burma front, Indrajit from a staff job in south India. We all found it almost impossible to believe that Ila, who had had such vitality and such a zest for living, was actually dead. She was only thirty. Her three small children came to stay with us in Darjeeling. No one had had the heart to tell them what had happened, and neither did we. Later, I took the two older children with me to Jaipur and gradually, still without any direct information from me, they seemed to understand that their mother was gone forever.

In spite of personal tragedies and Jai's military duties during the war years, we kept up our contacts with other princely states. When he was in Jaipur, entertaining took up a good deal of our time, and the visit of a princely family still had to be conducted, as far as circumstances permitted, with a good deal of ceremony. Although I was beginning to go about Jaipur pretty freely on my own, on state occasions I still kept in the background unless the visiting ruler's maharani was not actually in purdah herself.

Jai received them at the airport or railway station, accompanied by his ministers and nobles, all in court dress. The Jaipur anthem and the visitor's anthem were played and a guard of honour inspected before the rulers drove to Rambagh together in an open car.

In those days no maharaja—unless he was a close relation on an informal visit—ever arrived with fewer than thirty attendants, and often there were many more. There was always at least one of the ministers of the state government, the head of His Highness's household, several nobles, ADCs, valets, ADCs' valets, and even valets' valets. Commodious as Rambagh was, there was often not enough room for everyone, and the lawns on each side of the palace were covered with tents to accommodate the visitors. During the Jaipur polo season, in March, the Rambagh grounds became a permanent camp, and the state guest-house, which had rooms for over two hundred people, was filled as well.

Jai and I, in return, paid formal visits to other states. Frequently we went to Jodhpur, the family home of both Jai's first two wives, where the Maharaja was extremely kind to me and accepted me as another daughter. Jai was very fond of him and called him "Monarch" with all the laughing affection in the world. He took me to watch the pig-sticking, the dangerous sport of spearing wild boar from horseback, for which Jodhpur was well known. Once we went out into the desert to shoot imperial grouse. I remember how pleased with myself I was for shooting thirty-five birds, only to learn later that no one else had got less than two hundred. But the Maharaja scolded Jai for equipping me with a sixteen-bore, which he said was too big for a bird shoot, and presented me, himself, with a splendid twenty-bore which I cherish to this day.

In 1943 we were invited, together with the Jodhpur royal family, to pay a formal visit to Udaipur, considered the foremost Rajput state, whose maharana (a variant of maharaja) takes precedence over all the other Rajput princes. It was the first time I had ever been there, and I was looking forward to seeing its historic sights, such as the Lake Palace, which is built in such a way that it appears to be floating on the water, or the great, fortified, ancient capital of Chitor. But I hadn't been prepared for the sternness of the purdah that all ladies were supposed to abide by in Udaipur. Jo Didi and I travelled down by train, in the Jaipur State Railway carriage, while Jai flew ahead.

When we arrived at Udaipur station, the railway carriage was shunted into a special purdah siding, where the Maharani was waiting to greet us. Immediately we were made aware of how completely we were to be sheltered from the public gaze. In Jaipur our purdah cars now merely had darkened glass in the windows, replacing the curtains of earlier years, but in Udaipur we discovered that we were expected to go about in a car with heavy wooden shutters, enclosing us in a blind, airless box.

When we went on a trip on the lake, our boat was tightly veiled with curtains, and the camera that I had brought with me turned out to be both useless and a source of some embarrassment. On the boat ride I had cautiously lifted a corner of the curtain and tried to take a picture. This rash act must have reached the ears of the Maharana, for later, on our departure, he pointedly presented me with an album of photographs. Even Jai was not prepared for the extreme formality of the official Udaipur receptions. When taking drinks, for example, everyone was supposed to follow the Maharana, sip by sip. Jai would certainly have disgraced us all if the Maharaja of Jodhpur, who knew this point of etiquette, had not nudged him and brought it to his attention. My own special ordeal came when the ladies were asked if they would care to have a shot at a wild boar. The Maharani of Jodhpur and Jo Didi wisely declined but hadn't time to signal me before I accepted with enthusiasm. They then told me that the honour of Jaipur would suffer dreadfully if I missed, and this seemed far from unlikely, since wherever we went we were surrounded by at least fifty women jostling and chattering. It all made for a ghastly period of suspense because I had to score the first time. Regardless of the dictates of politeness, I brazenly pushed myself well to the fore of our party and to my relief felled a heavy tusker with my first shot.

I remember those wartime state visits with particular clarity because, with the end of World War II, it became plain to us, to the Maharana of Udaipur, and to all the other princes of India that great changes were imminent for the whole of India, and for us especially. Indian independence was already taking shape, and we were gradually realizing that, in the new order, the princely states would no longer be able to retain their old identity.

Chapter 12

Independence

In March 1947, Lord Mountbatten came to India as Viceroy, carrying with him the British Government's mandate to bring about the independence of India as fast as possible. He began to work at top speed and even issued to all senior officials special calendars which read, "A hundred and fifty more days until Independence; a hundred and forty-nine more days . . ." and so on, in an effort to give them all his own sense of urgency.

It was an extraordinary time, and throughout India the atmosphere was tense with anticipation and speculation; after almost a century and a half, British rule was about to end. What sort of nation would now emerge? Jai and I looked forward enthusiastically to the independence of our country, and so did the other maharajas we knew, even though we could only guess at the changes it would make in our lives.

Ma, I remember, had always told us that India's future lay in all the small kingdoms merging their identity into one strong nation. Even as children in Cooch Behar we had supported the idea of independence, Mahatma Gandhi and Jawaharlal Nehru had been schoolroom heroes, and we often shouted Congress slogans about a free and united India. Following the teaching and example of Gandhi, we each had our own little spinning-wheel and dutifully spun our cotton yarn, without fully understanding what Gandhi had intended this to symbolize. When Bhaiya went to Harrow, we had all been thrilled that he inherited the room used by Jawaharlal Nehru, with the extra excitement of seeing the great leader's name carved on the bed.

India finally became an independent nation on 15 August 1947.

Although Jai and I were not together on that memorable day—Jai had left for London, taking Bubbles and Joey to school at Harrow—we both heard Pandit Nehru's moving and unforgettable words: "Long years ago we made a tryst with destiny and now the time comes when we shall redeem our pledge." From London, Jai sent this message to his people:

> An independent India will be called upon to shoulder great responsibilities; and I have every confidence that we, in Jaipur, will cheerfully assume our share of those responsibilities and assist, with the best that is in us, in the creation of an India which will take its rightful place among the free nations of the world.

For British India, that part of the country that had not been under princely rule, the transition to an independent government would have been a smooth handing over of the reins of power to the Congress ministries, headed by Pandit Nehru and supported by the superbly trained Indian Civil Service, had there not been, simultaneously with independence, the partition of the country into India and Pakistan. On the insistence of the Muslim League, and much to Mahatma Gandhi's sorrow, the division was made along religious lines. Those parts of the country—the far north-west and the extreme east—with a predominance of Muslims in their population became West and East Pakistan, while the whole central block of the subcontinent dividing the two Pakistans remained India and, more important, remained a secular state. To me, brought up in Cooch Behar where 40 percent of the inhabitants were Muslim, it seemed terrible to rend India apart in this way when we knew from long experience that it was perfectly possible for Hindus and Muslims to live peaceably side by side. Cooch Behar came to be bordered on three sides by East Pakistan (now Bangladesh). Amid terrible bloodshed and suffering, millions of refugees crossed the borders, panicked by the fear of persecution, and made the birth of a new India an agony as well as a triumph.

In the princely states, for both the rulers and the people, independence had a different and more complex meaning. The simplest way of putting it is perhaps this: If you had asked a resident of British India, before 1947, who ruled him, the answer would probably have been, simply, "The British." If you had asked someone from a princely state the same question, the answer would almost certainly have been "the Maharaja." To them, the presence of the British was represented only by the Resident, who acted as a liaison between the princely state and the government in Delhi and who impinged on their lives hardly at all.

For some years before Independence, the Congress had called for democratic rule and self-government throughout India, and it was partly in response to that political climate that Jai had encouraged his prime ministers, first Sir Mirza Ismail and then Sir V. T. Krishnamachari, to carry through their programs of constitutional reform in Jaipur. However, all along it was obvious that the princely states could not remain as they were once India became independent. Even the most conservative rulers recognized that, unless their states were integrated with the rest of the country, the new nation would be hopelessly broken up; there were, after all, more than six hundred princely states in India, some of them islands surrounded by British India, some of them linked by common boundaries, all together making up almost half of India's territory and population.

Although I accepted the idea that we would, in some way, be part of independent India, it never really occurred to me that our lives would change so radically once our states lost their special identities. Somehow I imagined that we would always maintain our particular relationship to the people of our states and would continue to have a public role to play.

In the weeks immediately preceding Independence Day, Sardar Patel, the Home Minister of the central government of India, had turned his attention to the intricate question of precisely what position the princely states should hold in the emerging country. A brilliant man, he argued both forcefully and tactfully for the integration of the princely states with the rest of India. At first the princes were asked to accede to the central government only in matters of national defence, foreign policy, and communications. But soon Sardar Patel persuaded many of the rulers to merge their states administratively, as well, with the new nation, giving at the same time a solemn undertaking, to be embodied in the constitution, to grant them privy purses and certain privileges of rank in perpetuity.

Every state had a slightly different agreement with the Indian government, but in general the privy purse would be about one tenth of the revenue in small states and one eighth in the larger ones.

I remember feeling sad as I read about these states being taken over, but I was far from politically minded and certainly did not understand the full implications. Jai, of course, was more personally involved. He himself signed the instrument of accession on 12 August 1947, attaching his state to the new India, but he still remained its ruler.

Apart from my own political vagueness, another factor kept me from imagining any great immediate change in our position among our people. Jai and Bhaiya had both become rulers of their states in 1922, and so they celebrated their Silver Jubilees within months of each other. In Jaipur the celebrations were held in December 1947, scarcely four months after Independence. The whole state was *en fête*; everywhere there were decorations and flags and bunting, and at night all the public buildings, the forts, and the palaces were illuminated. The festivities lasted for weeks because all the different sections of the public wanted to give receptions for their ruler. There were official functions and a military tattoo. Jai was publicly weighed against silver which had been budgeted for from the reserves of the Jaipur treasury, and which was then distributed to the poor. Jo Didi and I were also weighed against silver, but with only the ladies of the Jaipur court present, in their most ornate and colorful costumes.

Fourteen ruling princes, many with their maharanis, visited Jaipur for the jubilee, and all our guest-houses and the City and Rambagh palaces were full. Jai, Mickey, and I moved up to Moti Doongri, the fort Jai had remodelled as a little palace for me, while Jo Didi and many of our women relatives left for the City Palace so that Rambagh would be free to house the guests. Even the house where the British Resident used to live, which had been vacant since Independence Day, was converted into a guest-house. I had the tasks of rearranging and refurnishing rooms for our huge number of guests, and of helping Jo Didi to entertain the visiting maharanis and their entourages. The highlights of the celebrations were a state banquet at Rambagh, the long tables rich with Jaipur treasures, which Lord and Lady Mountbatten attended, and a specially grand durbar in the

Above: Jai with the Mountbattens on his Silver Jubilee, 1948.

Opposite top: The townspeople's Silver Jubilee reception for Jai.

Opposite bottom: Hazari Guard trumpeters at the City Palace during Jai's Silver Jubilee.

City Palace at which Lord Mountbatten invested Jai with the G.C.S.I. (Grand Commander of the Star of India).

Our days were filled with festivities and entertainments, with no time to discuss anything serious, but I noticed that often in the evenings groups of the men clustered together, talking in low, worried tones about the future or repeating radio accounts of the aftermath of Partition; the most appalling stories of carnage and butchery came from all over northern India as religious tension flared into violence in yet another area. Every day we read in the papers of new atrocities and new outbreaks of violence.

In Jaipur City, one third of the population was Muslim and we had many Muslims in our palace households, so the possibility of Hindu-Muslim antagonism was a very immediate one. It was quite natural for the Muslims to fear that the reprisals taken against minority communities in other parts of India might spread to Jaipur. But Jai was determined to protect his Muslim subjects and personally supervised their safety.

Every night after dinner he left the palace and patrolled the streets of the city in an open jeep, accompanied by the colonel of one of his regiments, a Muslim, assuring the Muslims of his protection and threatening the severest penalties to any Hindu who raised a finger against them. Once the colonel asked whether his presence was an embarrassment to Jai. "Don't be an idiot," Jai replied. "You prove my point that there is no difference to me between a Hindu and a Muslim."

Mahatma Gandhi, foreseeing the confusion and bloodshed that partition would unleash, had most strongly opposed Indian acceptance of independence if it meant the division of the country. On 2 January 1948 he was assassinated. Ironically, his murderer was a member of the extreme Hindu right wing who felt that Gandhi was betraying the cause of true Hinduism by being over-generous to the Muslims. But appropriately enough, the Mahatma died on his way to one of his famous prayer meetings which always mingled Hindu, Christian, Muslim, and Buddhist prayers, and his last words were "Ram, Ram," the name of the deity which every Hindu hopes to invoke on his death-bed, said in reverence to God and in forgiveness of his murderers.

In the shock of the tragedy and the deep sense of personal loss that all Indians felt, whether or not they had actually known him, there was only one slightly calming fact: at least his assassin was not a Muslim. There is no guessing what kind of savage and chaotic upheaval in India might have followed to make those months even more terrible than they were.

Soon we had to cope with the streams of Hindu refugees flooding in from the Sind and that part of the Punjab that had fallen within the boundaries of Pakistan. The government of Jaipur State had to start drawing up plans for the proper accommodation of this sudden influx of people.

Several weeks after Jai's Silver Jubilee, we both went to Cooch Behar to help Bhaiya celebrate his Silver Jubilee. There, too, behind the outward festivities there was always the dark menace of Hindu-Muslim trouble. There, too, a sizable part of the population was Muslim, and there was the added anxiety of Cooch Behar's being a border state. But Bhaiya, like Jai, had used his personal authority to guarantee the safety of the Muslim minority, and in Cooch Behar, too, there was no outbreak of Hindu-Muslim trouble. I remember that part of Bhaiya's Silver Jubilee celebration was one of the state's well-known tiger shoots. On our way, some of Bhaiya's Muslim subjects surrounded him and, with folded hands and tears in their eyes, asked what they should do: stay in Cooch Behar or leave for Pakistan. Bhaiya, looking very sad and grim, reassured them of their safety if they wished to stay and, suddenly overcome by the pathos of the encounter, quickly got back into his car and drove away.

My brother had wanted to mark the occasion of his Silver Jubilee by building an agricultural college which the state badly needed. Jai, with impressive solemnity, laid the foundation stone. It is still there, together with the skeleton of the college that was to rise above it. After Cooch Behar was merged with the state of West Bengal, the new government stopped work on the building, and in spite of the thirteen million rupees that Bhaiya left exclusively for the development of such projects in his state, it remains a roofless, useless shell of masonry.

Before these saddening events, before we began to see the gradual erosion of our way of life and the weakening of our identity with our state—and, indeed, the identity of the state itself—a couple of joyful occasions intervened. The first was Mickey's marriage to the Maharaj Kumar of Baria, a state in the province of Gujerat, in western India. As she was Jai's oldest child, his only daughter, and the first Jaipur princess to be married in more than a century, the wedding and the attendant processions, banquets, and entertainments were on a scale of unparalleled lavishness. It was perhaps the final grand display of the pageantry of princely India.

Since the Jaipur ruling family was related to all the big Rajput families, the guest list was staggeringly long. Headed by the relatives of First Her Highness and Jo Didi from Jodhpur and from Jamnagar, and including my Cooch Behar family, there were about eight hundred guests, counting the retinues, ADCs, ladies-in-waiting, personal servants, and dozens of others in the various entourages. Some of the princes arrived in private planes, others in their special railway carriages, others in fleets of motorcars. All of them were met either by Jai himself or, when two sets of arrivals conflicted, by some member of our family. Each party was allotted a car and had a Jaipur ADC in attendance, a job that was assigned to the sons of the state nobles.

All of us moved out of Rambagh to the City Palace, leaving accommodations there for about eighty guests, not counting their retinues. Tents had been pitched all over the gardens for the members of the entourages, and a special separate camp was set up for the bridegroom and his nearest male relatives. The logistics and the catering arrangements were prodigious. The book of instructions to our own staff and to all the young nobles who were helping us was about two inches thick, detailing every party, festivity, ceremony, and entertainment and containing programs for each group of guests and for their staffs. Even the menus for the servants and the vantage-points assigned to them for watching the processions had been carefully worked out.

The festivities lasted for two weeks. Every evening there were parties, usually held on the terrace of the City Palace, overlooking the gardens. The gardeners had been at work for months to be sure that there would be enough flowers for every guest-room, and even for decorating the railway carriage that would take the bride and groom away, without spoiling the colour and display of the gardens.

After drinks had been served, the male members of the immediate family would go down to join the other men for dinner. The ladies dined separately, as many of them were in purdah. It was the only time I saw the City Palace fully alive, bustling with people and parties, all the apartments of the zenana in use, and everywhere the vivid colours of the flowers and the women's Rajputani costumes, the sound of laughter and music and the jingling of the ladies' anklets. From the terraces we could see out across the city to the hills beyond, where each of the forts encircling Jaipur was picked out in lights.

For the wedding banquet itself, long tables were decorated with more flowers and, since the meal was entirely Indian, loaded with rich meat curries, several kinds of pilau, and sweets covered with gold leaf. All down the tables there was the bright gleam of gold and silver *thals*, bowls, and goblets. Throughout the meal, as *thals* were filled and refilled with fresh relays of dishes, the palace musicians played.

The job of collecting Mickey's trousseau fell to me, and what with supervising all the arrangements that were being made for the accommodation and entertaining of the ladies who would be our guests, I simply had not the time to go to Delhi and Bombay to shop. Instead, the best of the shops came to Jaipur with quantities of clothes and fabrics, linen and jewellery. I selected about two hundred saris for Mickey and the same number of Rajputani skirts, bodices, jackets, and veils. Besides, she had to be given several sets of traditional Jaipuri jewellery, the exquisite enamel-work and the beautiful delicate designs of precious stones set into contrasting precious stones both being special crafts of Jaipur. Jai's wedding present to Mickey was a complete set, consisting of diamond necklace, earrings, bracelets, rings, and anklets, while Jo Didi gave her a pearl set.

In the hurry and flurry of the whole affair, I quite forgot to buy my own present to Mickey. All her presents were laid out for display to the bridegroom's family, and a list was made up of who had given which particular item. To my embarrassment, I saw there was a gap opposite my name on the list, so I quickly wrote in "emerald set," as no one else seemed to have given her emeralds. When I met Mickey after the formal viewing of the presents, she was most distressed. "Do you know," she said, "when they read out that list it said that you had given me an emerald set. It's terrible; I couldn't find it. Could something have happened to it? I am very worried."

I had to explain what had happened, and promised that when I had time I would shop for something for her, but meanwhile I just wanted my name on the list with a gift beside it. In the end I gave her some pretty pearl drop earrings.

The marriage ceremony itself took place in the customary way, in the zenana of the City Palace. I will always remember that moment when the bridegroom, having left the party that had accompanied him to the palace, stood alone at the entrance to the zenana. I felt so sorry for him, a solitary figure coming in to get married. He looked so vulnerable standing there, all dressed up, nervous and speechless, when the curtain was drawn back to admit him.

Afterwards, of course, all was gaiety and celebration. The grand banquet was held; there was a magically exuberant display of fireworks; the poor and the Brahmins were fed; some prisoners were released. It was all done with truly royal generosity. The famous French photographer Henri Cartier-Bresson came to take pictures of the occasion, and the marriage celebrations made front-page news in much of the press. The *Guinness Book of World Records* mentioned it as "the most expensive wedding in the world."

After the wedding Jai and I went to England—my first visit since 1938, more than ten years earlier, and our first journey abroad together since our marriage. I was delighted to be back in London and spent most of my time window-shopping, for in spite of the astonished comments of my friends about austerity being even more severe during these post-war years than it had been during the war itself, still the London shops, compared with Indian ones, seemed a miracle of opulence. From England we went on to America, the first time that either of us had visited the United States. It was a marvellous experience, as everyone we met was so warm and welcoming and hospitable.

We travelled by the *Queen Elizabeth*, which was new then, and inevitably marvelled at the sight of the Statue of Liberty and the extraordinary skyline of Manhattan. Neither of us had ever seen skyscrapers before. As soon as the ship docked we were engulfed by newspaper reporters, another experience that we had never had before. They asked all kinds of questions, including how many wives Jai had. The first time Jai and I were rather amused, but as the same question came up virtually everywhere we went in America, it became quite tiresome.

Friends had arranged a house for us in New York and had even found a maid for me, but that first night I hardly slept at all because I could not keep away from the windows from which I could see the city all lit up. I was enormously impressed by the richness of everything—the food, the shops, the cars, the clothes people wore. And I was astonished at the efficiency of the telephone system and the politeness of the operators.

As we started to go about New York, I was charmed by the friendliness of everyone. I loved being called "Honey" or "Dear" by salesgirls. Once a taxi-driver asked me if I came from Puerto Rico, and when I said, "No, from India," he started to tell me all the things I could do and see in New York without spending any money. "It's free," he kept repeating as he listed Central Park and the zoo, various museums, and a number of other things. I suppose he assumed that anyone from India had to be poor. I wondered whether I looked like a refugee.

Jai found many of his polo friends, most of whom he had not seen since before the war, and they invited us to watch the polo at Meadowbrook on Long Island. Later we went to Washington, where we stayed at the Indian Embassy with our ambassador, Sir Benegal Rama Rau. Washington reminded me a little of New Delhi, but on a much bigger scale. Finally, like conventional tourists, we had to go to Hollywood to spend a week enjoying ourselves thoroughly and being suitably thrilled when we were introduced to a number of well-known film stars.

Soon after our return to India, Jai was plunged into negotiations that were to change our lives and the face of India ineradicably.

Chapter 13

The Rajpramukh of Rajasthan

THE LONG, ELABORATE TALKS that were to bring about the merger of most of the Rajput states into a new administrative grouping, the Greater Rajasthan Union, within the Republic of India, kept Jai exceedingly busy. In consultation with his Prime Minister, Sir V. T. Krishnamachari, he worked out the details of the merger of Jaipur. He proved so skilful that afterwards officials of the Indian Government often asked for his help and advice in their negotiations with other princes.

Although Jai had tried to convince me of the necessity of his actions, I really disliked the idea of his no longer being the ruler of Jaipur. When one of the chief representatives of the Government of India, in charge of making the new agreements with the princely states, came to visit us in Jaipur, as he frequently did, he confessed one evening that he was thoroughly tired of flying around on such political missions. I remember the moment particularly well because, unable to stop myself in time, I broke the code that demands courtesy at all times from princes and baldly asked him why, in that case, he didn't leave us alone and get some rest himself.

For Jai, of course, the merger of Jaipur into the Greater Rajasthan Union was politically wise and historically inevitable. He could never have sustained the position of being the only Rajput state to hold out—nor, in fact, did he want to. He hated giving up Jaipur and relinquishing his deeply felt personal responsibility for his people. But he was well aware that the interests of the country had to take priority over his own feelings.

Jai's troubles at this time were heightened by a serious flying accident which occurred right in the middle of his negotiations about the merging of Jaipur. He was due to fly to Delhi for further talks and had gone out to our airport early to inspect a plane which some American pilots had brought to show him. The special feature of this aircraft was that, although it had two engines, it could land or take off on only one. The pilots wanted to take Jai up on a demonstration flight. Jai's Prime Minister begged Jai not to go, and Jai had promised only to watch the performance from the ground. But, as anyone who knew Jai really well might have guessed, the temptation proved too much for him.

I was to fly with him to Delhi on that occasion, and I was mildly surprised, though not alarmed, to find not a sign of him at the airport when I arrived. Our own pilot told me that Jai had not been able to resist the invitation of the American pilots and had gone up in the plane with them. We both smiled, knowing Jai's passion for flying, when suddenly we heard the ringing of the crash alarm bell and saw smoke rising at a distance. Jai's pilot and I leapt into a jeep and sped towards the smouldering wreck. Jai was lying unconscious, his head resting in the lap of a villager, blood trickling from the corner of his mouth. Everybody was utterly distraught, and I could focus my mind on only one essential—he had to be moved away from the wreckage immediately. I asked for a cot, for anything we could use as a litter, from a nearby village hut. The farmer offered me one of the wooden frames webbed across with string which the villagers use as a bed, and on this we carried Jai away from the site of the crash.

We were only just in time. A minute later there was a shattering explosion, and the entire area surrounding the crashed plane burst into flames. I took Jai straight to the hospital and, leaving him in the care of the doctors, went myself to Amber. There, in the palace of the old capital, I prayed at the family temple for his recovery. Mercifully the American pilots were not badly hurt, but Jai's injuries were serious, and it was weeks before he could be moved even as far as Rambagh.

He was still convalescing when, in December 1948, the Indian National Congress, the party that had led the fight for Indian independence, held its annual session in Jaipur. It was, for the princely states, a particularly important session, because we were to discover there the overall design for the Indian Republic in which our states would have to take their place. Pandit Nehru and Mrs. Sarojini Naidu, a poet, an old friend and follower of Mahatma Gandhi, and an important Congress leader in her own right, were staying with us. I remember the incisive, analytical way Pandit Nehru spoke, asking simply by his tone of voice that we should be as roused by the challenge of building a new independent nation as he was. He told us that when he was asked what was the most exciting time of his life, he used to reply that it was the early days of the struggle for independence, the going to jail, the enthusiasm of being part of a great and just movement. Later he had thought it was the actual moment of independence, the moment when, at last, the movement had reached success, when for the first time the Indian tricolour was raised over the Red Fort in Delhi. But that time was marred by the bloody and agonized partition of India, and so soon after by the senseless assassination of the Mahatma. Now he felt that *this* was the most exciting time, *this* moment when we were all to take part in the most important and most thrilling task that justified all those years in jail, the meetings, the marches, the agitation, the speeches. Now we were all to share in fashioning a great, free, and moral country. "The Great Experiment," he called it.

In contrast, Mrs. Naidu was witty and irreverent, making us laugh with her absurd stories of other Congress leaders—she used to call Mahatma Gandhi "Mickey Mouse" because of his big protuberant ears—and teasing Pandit Nehru mercilessly about his looks and his vanity. But underneath all her chatter and gossip, she too was working seriously towards the success of "The Great Experiment." She left Jaipur early one morning, leaving behind a thank-you letter to me. It began, "Dear Little Queen of a fairy-tale land." After expressing her thanks, she told me about the affection she felt for my Baroda grandmother and for my mother, and that now it included me and Ila's two young children. She hoped I would give them a happy home, and she ended her letter with the wish that my "eyes would never be dimmed by sadness."

We began to see some facets of the new India in March of 1949, when the Rajput states of Jaisalmer, Jodhpur, Bikaner, and Jaipur were merged into the new Greater Rajasthan Union, itself one part of the Indian Union. Sadly I realized, at long last, that the identity of Jaipur as a separate state had really gone forever and that Jai had ceased to be responsible for the welfare of the people he loved and had been destined to rule. One honour, though hardly a compensation, was that Jai was named as Rajpramukh, or "Head of State," of the new Rajasthan Union for life. In this position he would have the overall supervision of the administration of the entire province.

The simple, sober ceremony inaugurating the Greater Rajasthan Union, and Jai as its Rajpramukh, was held at the City Palace in Jaipur on the thirtieth of March. Eight of the nineteen maharajas of the states that used to make up the old province of Rajputana attended the inauguration. We were somewhat worried about how the affair would go off, because a few days before a number of people had informed me that they were ready to create disturbances to prevent the ceremony from taking place, if Jai and I wanted them to. I gave them a horrified "No" as a reply but was interested that they, too, viewed the dissolution of Jaipur with angry misgivings. A further anxiety came on the day itself when, after an unnerving delay, we heard that the plane bringing the Home Minister, Sardar Patel, from Delhi, had made a forced landing forty miles from Jaipur City. But whatever these auguries may have suggested, the ceremony itself moved through the speeches and formalities without a hitch. I watched it all from behind a latticed screen, discovering only later that some of the eminent visitors interpreted this as a sign of my disapproval. The real reason, of course, was merely that in those days I never attended public functions.

Jaipur City was named the capital of the new union, which seemed only sensible because of its central position and its accessibility by air, rail, and road, and because of the many government buildings which had been erected under Jai's rule. To my private delight, this meant that we could continue to live at Rambagh, which was now designated the official residence of the Rajpramukh. In his new capacity, Jai was the Governor of the whole state of Rajasthan, but his duties were more ceremonial—almost nominal—and far less exacting than in what we had already started to call "the good old days.". He was expected to open the State Legislative Assembly sessions, to conduct the swearing-in of the ministers, and only if there was a political deadlock did he have the authority to try to resolve the difficulties or, with the approval of the Central Government, to call for new elections. For the rest, he had to perform many of the same social duties that he had carried out as ruler. The Maharaja of Kota was appointed Jai's deputy to act as Rajpramukh in Jai's absence, and the Maharana of Udaipur, as the most senior of the princes, was given the title of Maharajpramukh; he took precedence over Jai on all formal occasions but had no official functions to perform.

One of Jai's first duties was to preside over the disbanding of the Rajputana States Forces which, of course, included the Jaipur State Forces. The first of these ceremonies took place in front of the new Secretariat, the building that Jai had put up originally as a barracks for his troops. There was a huge open space in front of it that had been used in previous years as a military parade-ground. There the Jaipur infantry marched past in impeccable formation, and Jai took the salute and accepted the colours that were handed to him. Then the cavalry, their brave and historic names dating from centuries before the British Raj—the Kachwaha Horse, the Rajendra Hazari Guards, and some of the other states' cavalry—rode past and one by one presented their standards to Jai.

All of us, the spectators, could feel the tears pricking behind our eyes, but Jai, looking proud and sombre, gazed out at the perfect performance of his men, saluted the colours, and accepted them as the various officers handed them to him. Only Jai's favourite regiment, the Sawai Man Guards, which he had raised himself, retained their identity when they were incorporated into the Indian Army. They are still known as the 17th Rajputana Rifles (Sawai Man Guard). All the other Jaipur cavalry regiments and some of the other States Forces cavalry were amalgamated into the 61st Cavalry, now the only cavalry regiment left in India.

In the spring of 1949, as all these momentous changes were taking place in our lives, I had a private worry and hope that took priority over all the public events. The doctors had confirmed that I was pregnant and warned me to be extremely careful, as I had twice before lost the child I was carrying. That summer, with all the responsibilities of Jai's new position, there was no question of his going abroad. We spent most of our time in Jaipur, escaping to Kashmir for only a fortnight when Rajasthan was at its hottest.

Early in October I went to Bombay, where Ma had a flat, to await, in the conventional way, the birth of my child in my mother's home. My son was born two weeks prematurely, immediately before the festival of Diwali, the Indian New Year with its lights and fireworks. During the first few days of his life, his tiny body shook with fright every time a Diwali firecracker exploded in the street outside my windows.

I was scared stiff because my son seemed so very small, and I worried incessantly that something might happen to him. Ma noticed my anxiety and said, "What's the matter with you? You should be happy to have had a child, but you seem miserable."

When I explained my fears, she laughed and assured me that just because a child was small it didn't mean he was necessarily weak, and that my baby was quite normal and healthy. Bhaiya was particularly pleased about the baby's birth and came to Bombay specially to see his nephew.

Even though Jaipur no longer had an independent identity as a state, the people still thought of us as their ruling family. There was great public rejoicing at the birth of my son, and deep joy throughout the family. The Government of Rajasthan declared an official holiday in Jaipur City and fired a gun salute in honour of the boy, while the Chief Minister and other government officials came to Rambagh to congratulate Jai. It is the custom that the first person to inform the Maharaja of the birth of his son is handsomely rewarded. In Bombay, Baby and one of my ladies-in-waiting who were with me raced each other to the telephone, only to find that it was out of order. In Jaipur, it was one of our ADCs who first learned of the birth. He burst into Jai's room to give him the news, and later received a new car. My lady-in-waiting was the first to take the news to Ma, and she was rewarded with a pair of diamond and ruby

Jai speaking at the City Palace during the inauguration of the State of Rajasthan, March 30, 1949. Sardar Patel, Home Minister of India, is seated behind him.

Jai takes the salute at a march-past of the Jaipur State Forces before the Sawai Man Singh barracks.

ear clips. The pundit who cast our little son's horoscope told us that he should be given a name beginning with R or J. Jai decided to call him Jagat Singh, in honour of one of his famous ancestors.

Bubbles, as the eldest son, was of course the heir apparent. It is customary in such a situation for the ruler to give his other sons estates and titles. Both of Jo Didi's two boys, Pat and Joey, had been given their own lands and titles, and Jagat, too, was eventually provided for. Some years later Jai's older brother, Bahadur Singh, who had no son, "adopted" Jagat so that he would inherit the Isarda title of Raja and the estates.

This news appeared in the papers under the heading, "Maharani gives away her five-year-old son," and somehow Jagat came to hear about it from his nurse or from servants' gossip. For days he was worried and unhappy. I couldn't imagine what was the matter with him until, at last, he was persuaded to tell me the story and asked, "Are you and Daddy really going to give me away?" Furious with the staff for distressing him in that manner, I was finally able to reassure him that Mummy and Daddy had no thought whatever of "giving him away," that his uncle, who had no boys of his own, wanted to give him a big present when he was grown up, and that was all. He took some convincing, but in the end he did believe me.

During the two years following Jagat's birth, our life echoed something of its pre-war pattern. Polo was resumed and, although the disappearance of the princely states and the mechanization of the army's cavalry regiments had limited the game's scope and glamour, Jai was once again a popular hero on the polo-grounds. In 1950 the Argentine team came to play in India and we had three delightful, competitive months of the game in Bombay, Delhi, and Jaipur. Besides this, Jai soon started to play in England, where Prince Philip, recently back from Malta, was giving the game new life. We bought a farm near East Grinstead called "Saint Hill" and took a flat in Grosvenor Square in London. With Bubbles, Joey, and Pat all going to Harrow one after the other, England became our second home.

One appalling tragedy disrupted the even tenor of our lives. In 1951 Indrajit was burned to death when the house where he was staying in Darjeeling caught fire. We were stunned by the news, as were the people of Cooch Behar and even of the surrounding areas, some of which fell in East Pakistan. He had been much loved, and they, like the Cooch Beharis, voluntarily closed their shops and businesses as a sign of respect and affection.

I was deeply shocked and sorrowful, but when the mourning period was over I had to resume my day-to-day activities. I knew that there was nothing to do about a loss so great except to keep busy and allow time to blunt the edge of my sadness. In Jaipur this was not difficult.

In the early years of the decade Jai's position as Rajpramukh continued to involve us in a great deal of official entertaining, and I came to know a number of interesting and internationally famous personalities. Among the first of these were Lord and Lady Mountbatten. Lord Mountbatten knew Jai well from his polo-playing days in England. Jai had first met Lady Mountbatten on her visit to Jaipur in 1921 when Jai was still a boy, standing in for his adoptive father. She remembered him as a charming youngster and was always kind to him from that time onwards. Lady Mountbatten impressed me greatly with her warmth and interest in everything—and not a transitory interest, either. For example, when I was showing her around the Gayatri Devi School, she met Miss Lutter, who in the course of conversation casually mentioned that she was worried about an ex-pupil of hers in Burma. Within a week of leaving Jaipur, Lady Mountbatten had seen that inquiries were made and news of the student was sent to Miss Lutter.

Lord Mountbatten's successor as Governor-General of India, Chakravarty Rajagopalachari, also visited us, as did Dr. Rajendra Prasad, the first president when India opted to become a republic. Many other Indian dignitaries, and some foreign ones, came to Jaipur during that time, and my memory is studded with small incidents that touched or disconcerted or amused me. I remember that Dr. Ambedkar, the great leader of the Harijans, moved me greatly by recalling the debt he owed my Baroda grandfather, who had arranged for his education when he was a penniless boy and had given him his first start in public life.

Mrs. Eleanor Roosevelt's visit gave us some awkward moments, for she was due to arrive on the very day that the riotous festival of Holi was going to be celebrated in Jaipur. Jai asked the Central Government to change the date, explaining that the people of Jaipur "play" Holi with the greatest gusto and that it was more than possible that Mrs. Roosevelt would be peppered with wax pellets and spurted with coloured powder and water. But the Government of India couldn't change the date, and we waited for the arrival of Holi and Mrs. Roosevelt with misgivings. Jai decided that the only thing to do, as soon as she reached Jaipur, was to cover her cheeks with red powder so that anyone seeing her would assume that she had already had her share of Holi exuberance and would look for fresher prey. That, in fact, is exactly what happened. Mrs. Roosevelt arrived at Rambagh scarlet-cheeked and puzzled, but otherwise unharmed.

When Bulganin and Khrushchev came to Jaipur, we gave them a grand banquet at the City Palace. I remember Bulganin, when he saw the splendour of the setting, exclaimed with delight, "*C'est magnifique!*" Getting quite the wrong impression from this, I tried valiantly but briefly to converse with him directly in French, but to no avail, and I had to fall back on the interpreters through the rest of the meal.

All through the years of my marriage, Jai had never really told me much about his work and his official duties. Frankly, I never particularly wanted to know the intricate details of statecraft. Jai used to give me all his most confidential letters and reports to type, and although I was proud of this evidence of confidence, I was not too concerned with official matters.

Until Jai became Rajpramukh, I was not called upon to do anything official—even entertain. Sometimes I heard fragments of talk about various problems and was glad that I didn't have the job of coping with them. I could easily believe that Jai's unfathomed reserve of patience and tact would help him to smooth out interstate rivalries within the Rajasthan Union, or to deal with the knottier business of assigning responsibility. Pat often confirmed my faith in Jai's competence, saying, "He's the best politician of the whole lot." So it was not until 1952, when the first general elections were held in India, that politics began to assume a serious place in my life.

Part Three

Chapter 14

India's New Government

NATURALLY every Indian was interested in the general elections, this first national experiment with democracy, but we had a more personal concern because the young Maharaja of Jodhpur was standing for election to the Rajasthan State Legislative Assembly. He was Jo Didi's first cousin and was running from a constituency in his own state against the most powerful Congress Party leader in Jodhpur, Jai Narain Vyas. Obviously, our sympathies lay with the Maharaja, but we were not permitted to do or say anything that could appear to be backing or helping him. As Rajpramukh, Jai had to remain above party politics.

At that time there was really no political party in India capable of opposing the Congress Party, which claimed, with every reason, to be the party of "the people," the party that had led the successful struggle for independence. The Communists were no real threat, nor were the candidates of the extreme reactionary and orthodox Hindu Mahasabha. Anyone running against the Congress candidate was taking on a daunting opponent. Yet the Maharaja had the courage to stand himself, as an Independent with no organized party backing, and to set up other candidates to oppose the Congress Party in Rajasthan.

We had always known the Maharaja to be full of drive, enthusiastic about his ideas for reform, interested in public affairs and politics. He felt very strongly about fostering an influential opposition to the Congress Party in Rajasthan. The first step was to get as many Independents as possible into the State Assembly to act as a check and keep the Congress from having everything their own way.

Towards the end of January, while we were having a large dinner party at Rambagh, Jai was suddenly called away from the table. He did not come back, but instead sent a message to me to join him. He told me that he had received tragic news from Jodhpur. The young Maharaja had gone out flying in his plane to relax after the hard election campaign, and had crashed and been killed.

We were all profoundly shaken. Jai flew to Jodhpur the next morning, and the Maharaja's Congress opponent, Jai Narain Vyas, went with him. The palace in Jodhpur was teeming with people shattered by the death of their beloved ruler. Wild rumours were rife about the possibility of sabotage, and when the crowd saw Jai Narain Vyas, they became very threatening. They surged up behind him and tried to follow him into the palace, and it was only with great difficulty that he was able to escape ignominiously through the zenana and in a purdah car.

Two days later, when the results of the election were announced, the papers headlined the news that the Maharaja of Jodhpur had won by a majority of 10,000 votes. Jai Narain Vyas had fared so badly that he had forfeited his deposit. In surrounding constituencies, thirty-three out of thirty-five of the Maharaja's nominees had won their seats. It was with great sadness that we all wished he had lived to see the results of his hard work. But in the by-election that had to be held after his death, Jai Narain Vyas, with virtually no one to oppose him, was elected and became the Chief Minister of Rajasthan. With the death of the Maharaja there was nobody to lead the opposition.

It was the frightful, senseless death of the Maharaja of Jodhpur and the outcome of the subsequent by-election that made me examine why the people of his state had voted as they had. Whatever the situation might be in the rest of India, in former princely territories people voted, when they had the opportunity, from a sense of the age-old bond between an Indian ruler and his subjects. The actual political platform was a secondary consideration. The Congress leaders were well aware of these ties of ancient loyalty and had been active, before the elections, in soliciting princely support and asking members of the various royal families to stand for election as Congress candidates. They knew the response such candidates would get, but were nevertheless annoyed when princes who opposed the Congress Party were elected by large majorities. Their annoyance was severe enough to lead them to launch a virulent campaign alleging that the old princely states had suffered from gross misgovernment.

As a member of a ruling family myself, it is hard for me to refute these accusations without sounding either prejudiced or partisan. I, and most of the princes I know, would admit that the quality of the administration in the states varied greatly, and certainly there had been cases of misrule or exploitation. But for the most part, the princely rulers had done their best for their subjects, and in some states—Mysore, Gondal, and Baroda, for example—even the most dedicated Congress Party advocate would have to admit that the administration had been better than in the surrounding areas. Perhaps the fact that bewildered them, and was so clearly exposed in the general elections, was that the integral bond of mutual respect and affection that existed between most rulers and their subjects had certainly not ended when the princely states were merged with the rest of India.

In fact, elections aside, I do not think I have ever witnessed in Jaipur a more impressive and spontaneous demonstration of loyalty and warmth than on Jai's first birthday after the merger of the state. The people behaved exactly as if Jai were still their ruler, cheering him repeatedly whenever he appeared in public, showering him with messages of goodwill. Very possibly it was indications such as this that led to an increase of caution and distrust in the Government's attitude towards the princes over the next few years.

While some of these points lodged in my mind in a shadowy way, I was still too engaged in other activities to pay close attention to politics. I had just been elected president of the Badminton Association of India and took my duties very seriously, travelling to meetings all over India and even abroad. I was also vice-president of the Tennis Association of India, and that, too, demanded a lot of time and travel. Besides my sports activities, I was very much in terested in the All-India Women's Conference, India's largest women's organization, of which my Baroda grandmother had been president. It agitated for social and educational progress, and although its function was not really political, there were occasions—such as getting the vote for women—when its activities overlapped the political sphere. I remember well one particular meeting of the All-India Women's Conference at Delhi because it showed me so clearly and intimately the curious, uneven, lop-sided way the ideas of social change were coming to India. On that occasion the delegates, forceful, emancipated women, spoke out strongly against the repression of women under the old Hindu code. They demanded the right for Hindu women to inherit, for widows to remarry, and for women to be able to sue for divorce. It all sounded brave and admirable to me, but I was accompanied by one of my ladies-in-waiting, and she was most upset by all she heard. Why should the delegates wish to introduce divorce? she asked. Surely Indian women were much better off as they were. If they divorced their husbands, who would marry them? Who would give them clothes and food and a roof over their heads? What man would ever put up with such immodesty? It was the old argument for the zenana, and through her I could hear all the palace ladies protesting in the same way. And I wondered then at the odd mixture I had become, partly understanding and sympathizing with the zenana way of thinking, but still very much the product of Ma's cosmopolitan upbringing.

Whenever Jai and I went to Delhi, we stayed, of course, at Jaipur House. At one time all the land on which New Delhi is built belonged to the maharajas of Jaipur as their personal estate, but the property had been given to the government long ago, by Jai's adoptive father, for the building of the new capital, in exchange for some villages in the Punjab. (Now only the "Jaipur Column," a tall sandstone pillar which stands outside the President's Palace, remains as a monument to that old act of generosity.)

All around us in the Delhi of the fifties the social life was rapidly increasing in extent and animation as more and more new embassies were being accredited to the independent Indian Government. Jaipur House became the scene of constant activity, and as

Jai's hostess, I found my social responsibilities and the high standard of entertainment that he demanded a continual challenge and preoccupation. He encouraged me in some of my own projects: for instance, when I decided to hold an exhibition of Jaipur arts and crafts in Delhi. Nervously I asked him whether he thought that the Prime Minister, Pandit Jawaharlal Nehru, might be willing to open it. Jai replied briskly, "Well, you'll never know unless you try." To my surprise and relief, Pandit Nehru accepted the invitation, adding, to my delight, that he normally didn't do that sort of thing but would make an exception this once.

On the opening day I was in a dither, terrified by the number of people who had come and in a flat panic about what sort of speech I should make welcoming the Prime Minister and asking him to open the exhibition. When he arrived, I was standing jittering in the doorway, only just able to blurt out that I was pleased to see him and that it was really very good of him to take the time to come to my show. He nodded absently and asked me what he was supposed to do. I said, "Well . . . um, I should think—um, just declare the exhibition open. Do you think that would do?"

"Why not?" he said, and took the scissors I handed him, quickly snipped the ribbon across the main aisle, and announced, "I declare this exhibition open to the public."

It was all over in a moment, and amazingly I'd escaped without having to make a speech and could then enjoy showing the Prime Minister around to see the lovely work of the Jaipuri craftsmen, of which, on behalf of the state, I was genuinely proud. He was a marvellously appreciative guest, with great charm and an almost boyish enthusiasm. In those days Jai and I saw quite a lot of him, both at official receptions and on more informal occasions. He loved to watch the polo matches, which endeared him to Jai, and we both always had the warmest affection and respect for him.

In October of 1956, the Minister for Home Affairs in the Central Government, the Prime Minister, Pandit Nehru, and the President of India, Dr. Rajendra Prasad, all wrote to Jai informing him that, while they appreciated the way in which he had "discharged the onerous duties of his high office," the office of Rajpramukh itself was to come to an end. This news came entirely out of the blue. At no point had Jai been consulted or forewarned, and he was hurt and baffled. When he was first appointed Rajpramukh, Jai had been assured that he would retain that office for life, and he knew that the continuance of the office had been established in the Constitution of India.

In his letters of reply, Jai pointed all this out and added, "I find it most distressing that in spite of sincere cooperation and unflinching loyalty on my part throughout the seven years, my official connections with the administration of the State should cease so abruptly." He had, after all, trusted the Government to honour its part of the agreement.

I felt very deeply for Jai, though in spite of his profound hurt he never uttered a word of bitterness, even when Pandit Nehru wrote to him, replying to his letter with the bald comment that "the Constitution cannot be petrified." I began, then, to question the integrity of a government that could go back, so casually, on an agreement enshrined in the Constitution. Certainly, if it was necessary for the good of the country, changes should be made, but surely not without consulting all the parties involved.

At that time, our little son, Jagat, came home from school one day bewildered and upset. The other boys had told him that his father was no longer the most important man in Jaipur. We then had to explain to him the confusing business of how Daddy had been something called a Rajpramukh, more important than a Maharaja, but that now there was not going to be any more Rajpramukh, and there was a new Governor of Rajasthan, but Daddy's position among the people of Jaipur would remain unchanged. How much of all this he followed, I really don't know, but he understood immediately and practically the other changes that Jai was making. Jai had, for instance, decided that we must reduce our expenses and, as a first step, give up our private plane. Having had a plane at my disposal ever since I was twenty-one, I was rather spoilt. Jagat, aged about seven, comforted me. "Don't be unhappy, Mummy. You and Daddy will still be going everywhere. This will only affect Kismet and me." Kismet was Jai's Alsatian, the latest in a long series of Alsatians that

Jai kept. Jagat's common-sensical reasoning enchanted me, and I soon resigned myself to the idea that we would no longer have a private plane.

Jai, with his usual resilience, was soon absorbed in other matters. India had been invited to send a polo team to England to compete in a series of international matches to be held in the summer of 1957. It was Jai's task, as the president of the Indian Polo Association, to select the players and make all the necessary arrangements. This was the first time that a team representing all of India was going abroad—previously the teams had been drawn exclusively from one or another of the princely states—and the responsibility of picking the players and organizing such an expedition was time-consuming and complicated. People from all over India were most generous with their help and offered to lend their best ponies to the team, even if their own players were not represented on it. But just at this time the Suez Canal was closed, and this made it impossible for us to send any polo ponies from India. The highly trained ponies would never have survived the long sea voyage round the Cape of Good Hope, and besides they would not have reached England in time. So Jai would have to find mounts for his team in Europe.

It was while Jai was immersed in the details of arranging this important polo tournament that, quite unexpectedly, I received a request that I—of all people—should start to play a role in Indian politics. The Chief Minister of Rajasthan came to call on me one evening and asked me, as though it were the most ordinary thing, if I would consider standing as a Congress Party candidate from the Jaipur parliamentary constituency.

My first reaction was one of utter astonishment that anyone would imagine that I had the smallest intention of standing for Parliament. My second, equally instinctive, was that I should never know how to go out in public making speeches and campaigning. Although I was much less restricted in where I could go and what I could do than I had been when I first came to Jaipur, still that early training died hard. My third, after a little thought, was that I wasn't at all sure that I agreed with the policies of the Congress Party.

The Congress Party in many parts of the country was beginning

Above: A family portrait, 1951.
Left to right, Joey, Jai, Jagat, Pat, myself, and Bubbles.

Opposite: With Jagat at Rambagh, 1957.

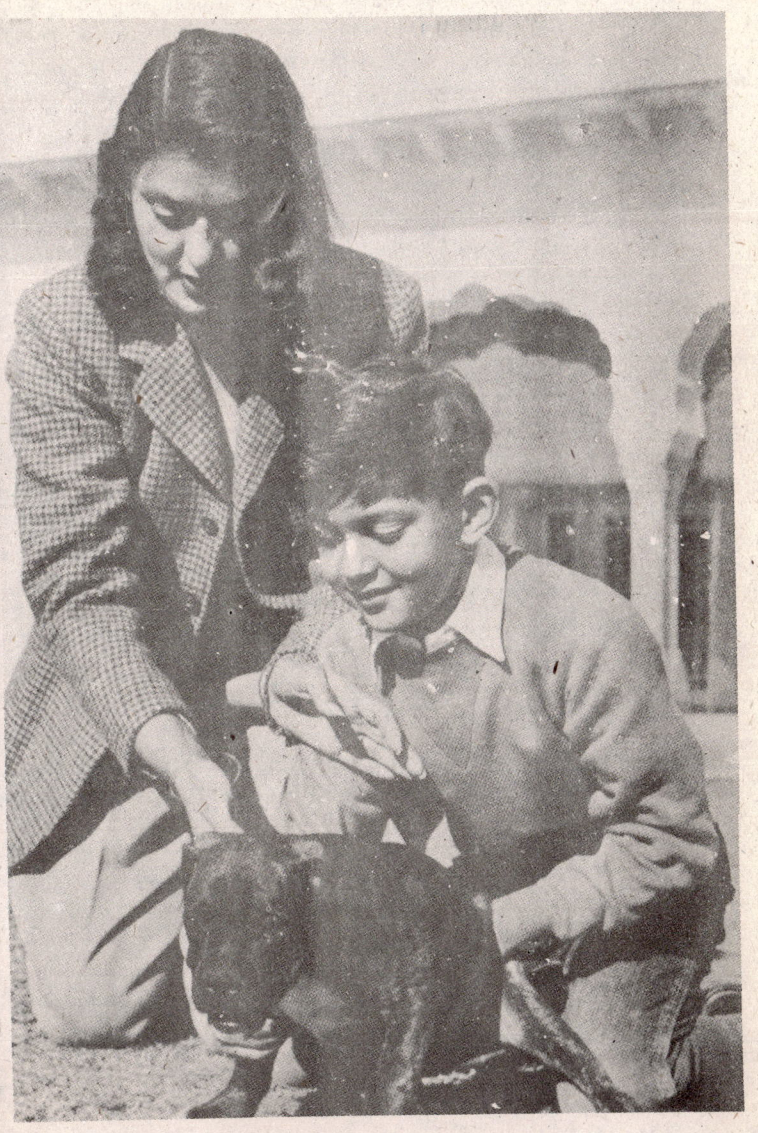

to acquire a reputation for corruption and nepotism. In Rajasthan, as in other places, the ministers put their protégés or people who had helped them in the elections in responsible government jobs which they had neither the education nor the experience to fill capably. It was rumoured that when government contracts were assigned to private companies, they were apt to go to whoever gave the minister concerned the most money under the table. We saw the effect of this practice in the ordinary things that any tax-payer comes across. The state of the roads, for instance, was deplorable. There were potholes everywhere, and in places the rains had washed out the roads entirely. Money had been allotted for repairs, but where it went we didn't know.

Jaipur State had been quite well known for its system of dams and irrigation works, built mainly in the time of Jai's adoptive grandfather. They had lasted excellently through floods and drought because they had been beautifully built to begin with and carefully maintained afterwards. When the Congress government took over, the maintenance of the dams was given out to new contractors, chosen for political reasons. Repairs were made from inferior materials and only the most cursory attention was given to the system. Once, after heavy rains, one of the dams broke—a calamity that could easily have been avoided by opening the sluice gates. The man in charge of the dam was in the cinema in Jaipur. Dozens of villages were flooded and the crops were ruined.

Even students applying for scholarships or admittance to college were chosen by political string-pulling. In Jaipur it was blatantly clear that a certain number of places were reserved for the relatives of the ministers. Jai had written to Pandit Nehru some time earlier telling him that corruption in the Congress government of the state was leading to a breakdown of the administration and of justice. But no action that we could see was taken as a result of his letter.

In any case, what I told the Chief Minister that evening was that I would have to consult my husband. He replied that there was no immediate hurry, that I should think it over and give him an answer in the next two or three days.

I rushed to Jai to tell him my astounding news, but he merely looked at me with an amused smile. Only then did it dawn on me that the Chief Minister would never have talked to me without consulting Jai first, and Jai must have told him to speak to me personally about his suggestion. It was typical of Jai's sense of humour not to warn me beforehand, and to enjoy the spectacle of my astonishment.

We debated the whole matter over and over again. In those talks I began to realize that, though I had given very little conscious thought to politics, somewhere in my mind ideas and opinions and arguments had been forming. Now, when Jai told me that he thought I might be able to do something useful for Jaipur if I joined the Congress Party, I felt that it would be dishonest to do so, since I did not fully believe in its policies and did not like the results of its administration. It had been great, I found myself arguing, when it had been led by Gandhi and when its followers had been idealists working towards the goal of independence. But now, I told Jai heatedly, just *look* at it! The Congress Party, with the achievement of power, had become the Establishment and, as far as I could see, was attracting people who were more concerned with a lucrative career than with achieving good for India. And what about all this austerity they were preaching, urging other people to tighten their belts? You didn't notice any of *them* tightening *their* belts. Certainly not. The Congress Party members seemed to regard themselves as a privileged class and were becoming more and more affluent every day. How Gandhi would have been saddened! He had always wanted the Congress Party to be disbanded once it had achieved independence, so that new parties could be formed. Instead, the Congress government remained a monolith, and now the most important thing we could do would be to help form a strong opposition, one that could effectively keep the Congress up to the mark.

I could hardly believe it, but I had, quite without meaning to, made a political speech. And Jai continued to sit there smiling at me. He prompted me to follow my arguments further, to express the feeling I had that it was becoming daily more apparent that the people were not happy, and to reach the point of saying, finally, that it was perhaps only by entering politics myself that I could be of any help in trying to put things right.

Over and over again groups that gathered at the gates of Rambagh, as they had always done, to catch Jai's attention, complained about the new taxes being imposed on them and the rising prices. They could barely make ends meet, and now there was nobody in the government who had time to listen to them, no one who felt it was his responsibility to help. While Jai had been Rajpramukh, he had been able to negotiate on behalf of his people with the government officials, but now he had no authority to interfere, and even when he tried it was almost impossible to pin down the right official, much less to get any action taken. Jai could do nothing but watch while things went from bad to worse in his beloved state. I suppose this was why Jai encouraged me to think things through for myself and hoped that I would conclude that I might indeed be able to do some good if I became a Member of Parliament.

The rumour that I might join the Congress Party spread rapidly throughout the state. A young man who had previously been an officer in Jai's personal bodyguard came to see me. He was one of the nobles of Jaipur State and had joined the opposition party to the Congress, along with the young Maharaja of Jodhpur, who had been killed so tragically. He explained that a new party had now been formed in Rajasthan, still in opposition to the ruling Congress. He said that if I joined the Congress, the new opposition party would find itself in a hopelessly weak position, and begged me to reconsider any such move. This brief interview was what made up my mind for me. If my principles meant anything at all, then I couldn't help to weaken an honest opposition party, even though I couldn't yet bring myself to join it. I gave the Chief Minister my answer that day. I could not accept his offer.

Jai, too, had been approached by opposition leaders and asked at least to speak out on their behalf, but he continued to feel that he himself should remain neutral, even though he was no longer Rajpramukh. So in 1957 no one from our family stood for election, and, leaving politics behind us for that summer, we went to England with the Indian polo team.

The polo-grounds at Cowdray Park had never looked so glamorous, with dashing gauchos from the Argentine competing with the

Indians in their brilliantly coloured turbans, all against the lovely setting of the English countryside. Our team had a series of accidents and didn't do as well as we had hoped, but after the English season the Indian polo team was invited to play at Deauville. There we stayed with Aly Khan, who talked about racing while Jai talked about polo, and both indulged their passion for horses. Deauville was refreshingly gay and carefree, with racing and polo all day and spectacular gala evenings at the casino, all climaxed by the Indian team winning the Gold Cup. It was easy to forget all that was happening in India.

We returned home in a triumphant mood. But almost immediately, my first clashes with the Government began—almost literally on our own doorstep. Both Jai and I were horrified to see that the beautiful old city walls and gates, built to protect Jaipur from invaders and deeply a part of its history, were being demolished. To me this was the ultimate act of vandalism—and of government-sponsored vandalism, at that.

Hardly any new buildings had been erected since Jai had handed over the administration of his state. (Even today most of the schools, colleges, hospitals, water reservoirs, and parks are the ones he built over twenty-five years ago.) The existing buildings were sadly neglected, and there seemed to be a total absence of any kind of sensible control or planning. Jai had forbidden any new building inside the city walls because the inner city was already crowded to capacity, and he had insisted that any expansion should take place in properly planned suburbs. All of this had been forgotten, just as the new government had ignored his projects for resettling and rehabilitating the hundreds of thousands of refugees who had poured in from Pakistan. Those refugees had been allowed to build shops and huts along the city walls, adding to the squalor of an already overcrowded area. Under the new state government, officials had been nominated who had little sense of social responsibility and no experience of town planning, and they were let loose to do exactly as they pleased.

Jaipur was Jai's home. He loved his beautiful capital and was justly proud of it. Under his rule everything had been properly maintained, the buildings had been regularly recoloured the characteristic Jaipuri pink, and nothing had been permitted to mar a style of architecture that had become traditional since the time of Maharaja Sawai Jai Singh, founder of the City of Jaipur. Each ruler had built to enhance the beauty of the capital, not to spoil it. And Jai, most of all, would never have allowed it to deteriorate in this shoddy, unthinking way.

Yet under the new government even the arcades which ran along the main streets, allowing pedestrians to walk in the shade, vanished as shopkeepers were permitted to enclose them for their own use. The balconies and terraces were starting to crumble, dirt collected in the gutters and lay in drifts against houses and sidewalks, the walls were defaced with crude and garish advertisements, and the new authorities were turning a blind eye to unauthorized constructions in open places—parks and commons. When visitors to present-day Jaipur think I am exaggerating the change that has taken place, I show them old photographs of the city so that they can see for themselves. I find it difficult to look at the photographs myself. They are too vivid a reminder of the loveliness that used to be Jaipur.

On that return from England, when we saw the pointless damage that was being done to the beautiful old city walls, I kept insisting that Jai should do something about this desecration. He protested that he was no longer in a position of authority, and that it would be very difficult to speak to people who obviously thought it necessary to knock down useless old walls. I tried, in desperation, to see the Chief Minister myself, but he was always busy and refused to see me.

I was miserable, but I knew that there was one person who would help: our Prime Minister, Pandit Nehru. He had a deep sense of history and our cultural heritage. I was sure that he would disapprove of what was being done in Jaipur. But at the same time, I knew he was a very busy man, and I hesitated to trouble him with what might seem like unimportant domestic affairs. I wrote him two letters and destroyed them both. Eventually, I wrote a third and sent it immediately, before I could have a chance to change my mind and tear that one up, too.

Within two days I received a reply:

Dear Ayesha,

I have received your letter. It is a sacrilege what they are doing to Jaipur. I am writing to the Chief Minister that this work should be stopped immediately.

Yours sincerely,
(Signed) Jawaharlal Nehru

After that the Government decided that nothing should be done to spoil the character of the city, and that if any changes were to be made, Jai would be consulted. If I had been more cynical, or possibly just more experienced, I might have known that this truce would last only a short time, that once again the deterioration would set in, and that we would, after all, have to watch Jaipur degenerate into a squalid and disfigured city. At the time I thought I had scored a wonderful victory for Jaipur.

Not long after, a dramatic change took place even closer to home—not merely on our doorstep. During the Delhi polo season that winter Bubbles and I went to a lunch party given by the Oberois, India's biggest hoteliers, and overheard talk of plans to convert Rambagh into a hotel. Neither Bubbles nor I had heard anything about this cataclysmic project before, and after quickly consulting each other, we excused ourselves and rushed back to tackle Jai with the news. We poured out the story to him, certain that it must be only some ridiculous rumour which he would soon dispel. Instead he simply smiled. I knew that smile. It meant the story was true, that he knew all about it. He had not wanted to tell us before everything was settled. He was afraid that we would be upset.

Upset! We were speechless. Jai patiently went on explaining to us that times had changed and that it was no longer possible to keep Rambagh in the way it had always been, and deserved to be, maintained. He also felt that now he was no longer Rajpramukh, or even the ruler of Jaipur, it was unnecessary for us to live in our previous style. If Rambagh was to be kept up in a proper way, it would have to be given up for a public cause. Jaipur badly needed a good hotel.

I was wretched, and so was Jo Didi when she heard the news. We had both come to Rambagh as brides. For nearly half my life—longer for Jo Didi—Rambagh had been the center of my activities and of my allegiance. It was my home. We both pleaded with Jai to change his mind, but he remained determined. Other maharajas were critical of Jai when they heard of the project. It seemed like such a concrete symbol of our vanishing way of life. Jai was the first of the princes to turn his palace into a hotel, but after a few years, others followed his example.

As it turned out, Jo Didi never had to leave Rambagh. That summer of 1958 Jai and I had entrusted Jagat to her care while we went to Delhi on our way to England. I knew that she had been suffering for some time with a disease of the gall-bladder, but when I went to say good-bye to her she seemed in excellent spirits and even joked about her illness, telling me that it was a wonderful way to lose weight but that she planned to go to Delhi for treatment.

Soon after our departure, she collapsed. She refused to see a doctor and sadly, infuriatingly, all her ladies-in-waiting were too obedient to her wishes to summon a doctor on their own initiative. Only Jagat, who was nine years old, kept asking for a doctor, but no one took any notice of a small boy's demands. Within a few hours Jo Didi was dead.

The news was telephoned to Bubbles, who was then the Adjutant in the President's Bodyguard in Delhi. He had to relay it to Jai, tracking him down, finally, at the airport. When I arrived a little later I found Jai stunned and speechless, and Bubbles whispered to me what had happened. Then we got back into the cars and drove the 200 miles to Jaipur. Joey and Pat, who were working in Calcutta, were sent for. It was an unhappy little group that gathered at Rambagh to live out the traditional thirteen days of mourning there, the last we were to spend in our old home. There was a lot of time to think when we went to the City Palace to receive the callers who came to condole, hours when my mind wandered back over the years I had known Jo Didi, remembering her when she was young and pretty and lively company.

I recalled ruefully how, when we were all together in Bangalore during Jai's and my honeymoon, someone had repeated to me a trivial remark overheard at the races. It had been a windy day and my hair and the end of my sari were flying about, as usual, rather uncontrolledly. Some race-goer, seeing me for the first time, had said, "Is *that* the new Maharani? Second Her Highness is much smarter." But most of all I thought how extraordinary it was that Jo Didi and I should have become so close, enjoying each other's company, entrusting each other with the children, laughing and gossiping together.

It seemed ironic that our last few days at Rambagh should have been so unhappy when I—and, I'm sure, Jai and the boys too—associated it with all the gaiety and good times of our life there together. My mind was full of memories of parties and joyful occasions of the old days, and of tiny details like the unearthly shrieking of the peacocks that used to wake me in the mornings in the hot weather, and the bird-songs at other times of the year. Even young Jagat caught the regretful, valedictory atmosphere. On our last night in Rambagh, he was in his room and his attendant told him to hurry up and get into bed because it was getting late. Jagat looked upwards and said, "I am just wondering whether I'll see this ceiling ever again and whether I'll ever drink milk in this room again."

Our new home was very close to Rambagh. It had been the old British Residency, which we had converted into a guest-house at the time of Mickey's wedding and now remodelled again for our own needs. It was much smaller than Rambagh, but when the workmen had finished it had charm and character and a pleasantly informal atmosphere. We renamed it Rajmahal—"Royal Residence"—and moved in at the end of the year. Soon after, Rambagh was opened as a luxury hotel.

For a long time I could not accustom myself to the idea that people could come and go as they pleased in our old home, and Jai used to complain, half amused and half irritated, that I treated the hotel guests as interlopers. On one occasion, before our swimming-pool at Rajmahal was ready, he came along to the Rambagh pool to discover one of my maids posted outside to keep the hotel guests away while I took my morning swim. After that, he insisted

Jai and I supervising the building of Rajmahal.

Jagat at eleven, with his first tiger.

that I really had to come to terms with the fact that, as long as the hotel guests paid their bills, they had as much right to be in the palace as I had.

One of the constructive results of our narrowed life was the starting of a museum in the City Palace. For a long time the treasures of the Jaipur family had been housed there, but although scholars had often been given permission to consult the ancient manuscripts and other people had come to see the buildings or the fabulous collection of carpets, the palace had not been open to the public. Now that Rambagh had become a hotel and we had also given up our house in Delhi, we had many things to store. We decided to empty the store-rooms in the City Palace to make room for the contents of Rambagh and Jaipur House.

The staff at the City Palace were instructed to take everything out of the store-rooms and assemble it all for auction, dividing it into small lots, each to be worth about four English pounds. There were countless items ranging from brassware and cooking utensils to old Rajputani costumes and shawls. Many of the things were of little interest or value, but some were marvellous antiques which should never have been separated from the Jaipur collection. Whenever I think of how carelessly such items were sold off, at no more than a fraction of their real value, I blame myself for having been so overpowered by the mass of things that was revealed that I didn't keep a proper check on it all. I watched the auctions, and there were many items that caught my fancy: enchanting little dolls' houses in the Indian style for which I couldn't think of any possible use and sadly let go, but some Mogul glasses which seemed to me pretty I kept aside, later to discover that they were very valuable.

When I saw items from the *pilkhanna* being sold, I objected strongly, partly from my sentimental feelings about elephants, but I was told that we had huge quantities of such stuff and must get rid of some of it. I took the matter to Jai and begged to be allowed to keep the elephant jewellery that bedecks the animals on ceremonial occasions and festivals, consisting of silver, gold, and jewelled anklets and plaques for their foreheads, together with the lovely brocades for their caparisons and howdahs. There were also the trappings for horses and camels and bullocks that draw the ceremonial carts. It wasn't that I personally resented all these things being undersold, but I felt strongly that their proper place was in the Jaipur collection where they could be seen, in a museum, in their proper historical setting. They formed part of the cultural heritage of all the people of Jaipur State and not just of the Jaipur ruling family. Jai agreed, and all the jewellery and decorations were stored away for eventual display to the public.

When arrangements for the City Palace Museum were complete, the whole Jaipur collection could be displayed to the public and to the growing number of tourists visiting the city. Today the museum has, besides its collection of carpets and old manuscripts, superb miniature paintings, traditionally carved and beautifully fashioned weapons, textiles ranging from the golden embroidery of Benares to the softest shawls of Kashmir. The maharajas of Jaipur had for centuries been patrons of the arts, and over the years their collections had been built up with connoisseurship and generosity.

In founding the museum, I came to learn more about these collections and to appreciate just how fine the new displays were. My favourites were the many Mogul and Rajput paintings executed on the finest rice-paper, the lines traced with a single-hair brush and the paints mixed with the costliest and most brilliant ingredients: ground rubies, lapis lazuli, gold. I spent hours examining these paintings, trying unsuccessfully to decide which I liked best. There were scenes from Hindu mythology, episodes from the lives of the great Moghul emperors, portraits of the old rulers of Jaipur, and, in contrast to the extreme delicacy of the miniatures, huge, vivid, exuberant paintings of love scenes between Lord Krishna and Radha.

We turned the main audience chamber, in which Jai had held his public durbars and other ceremonies, into an art gallery. Another hall became the royal library and now houses fifty thousand manuscripts, some dating back to the twelfth century. It is one of the most comprehensive private oriental libraries in the world. Almost every major language of India is represented—Sanskrit, Hindi, Urdu, Bengali, Marathi, Assamese, Oriya, Gujarati, Persian, Arabic—and the collection covers an enormous range of subjects, including

Sanskrit scriptures, history, philosophy, Tantrism, poetry, drama, lexicography, music, erotica, medicine, and veterinary science. In the gallery above another audience chamber we displayed the textiles, while yet another group of rooms became the armoury. This Jaipur armoury is known to be one of the finest in all India and contains almost every kind of ancient weapon imaginable, as well as such curiosities as guns designed specially to be fired from camel-back, and such exquisite objects as the ceremonial swords still carried by the nobles. Until I saw the Jaipur armoury I never realized that the weapons of war could be so beautiful. There were powder-horns carved from ivory, embellished with complicated designs, or delicately fashioned from the shells of sea-urchins; they say it takes a whole year for a master craftsman to make one of these. There were golden daggers with handles of wrought crystal, guns with barrels bound with gold and butts inlaid with ivory and mother-of-pearl, ceremonial swords encrusted with precious stones, and daggers with handles shaped to resemble animal heads.

Since we first opened it, the City Palace Museum has attracted a steady flow of visitors, including many people from overseas. And so, to the deep satisfaction I derived from helping to preserve the glorious things in the Jaipur collection has been added the delight of seeing its treasures admired and enjoyed both by the people of Jaipur and the public at large.

Meanwhile, the great complex of households that made up the City Palace has been disbanded. After the deaths of the Dowager Maharani, and then First Her Highness, and, most recently, Jo Didi, the zenana quarters gradually diminished. Many of the retainers were employed by the museum, and those for whom no jobs could be found, the very old servants and the eunuchs, all were given land or a pension by Jai. Now the museum staff and the temple priests live in the City Palace, and the bustle and feeling of life is provided by the tourists who throng the old courtyards.

Chapter 15

The Swatantra Party

IT WAS IN 1960 that I made my official entry into politics. The year before, when Jai and I had gone to Bombay to see Ma, we had heard our friends talk enthusiastically about a new party called the Swatantra ("Independent") Party. Now, at last, or so people were saying, there was some hope of effective opposition to the Congress Party, both in the country and in Parliament in New Delhi.

The leader of the new party was Chakravarty Rajagopalachari, a very eminent figure, the acknowledged elder statesman of India, who had been one of Mahatma Gandhi's close associates during the long struggle for independence and had subsequently been the overwhelming choice to succeed Lord Mountbatten as Governor-General of India. He had broken with the Congress Party the year before because, as he had often and trenchantly stated, he felt that Prime Minister Nehru's dreamy acceptance of socialist doctrine was quite out of keeping with the needs, wishes, and understanding of most Indians.

Specifically, the rift between Rajaji, as he was universally and respectfully called, and the Congress Party came over the issue of co-operative farming. The Congress high command and planners were trying to thrust the idea of co-operative farms and the economic benefits that they would bring on India's hundreds of millions of villagers. Rajaji thought it a ridiculous, expensive, and short-lived project to foster in a country so rooted in the idea and tradition of ancestral property, among people whose greatest security lay in working a plot of land, however small, that they knew to be *theirs*, that they had inherited from their fathers and would bequeath to their sons. Rajaji's differences with the Congress Party were much more varied than that, but perhaps that one was the deepest and most inclusive.

Rajaji soon found supporters and followers for his new Swatantra Party, many of them former members of the Congress Party who were now disillusioned by the behaviour of the party once it gained power. There were also many, like myself, who had never joined a political party before, and even if they had wanted to, couldn't have found one that expressed moderate and liberal views. They rejected the muddle-headed socialism of the Congress Party and the even more impractical schemes of the Socialists (of whom it was said at the time that "their minds are so open that their brains fall out"), and they couldn't subscribe to the extremism of Communists on the left, or the religiously oriented, orthodox Hindu Jana Sangh Party on the right.

Rajaji agreed with Gandhi's view that the best government is the one that interferes least with the lives of its citizens. For all of us, the Swatantra Party and Rajaji's wry, intelligent realism seemed like an island of sanity in the turbulent political seas around us.

I had first met Rajaji when he was Governor-General and had come to Jaipur on an official visit in 1949. He was an exceedingly thin, erect old man, dressed in the impeccable white, crisply starched, handspun cotton dhoti and shirt of his native Madras in south India. The eminence of his position and the pomp with which he was surrounded altered his habits not one whit. Like a true Tamil Brahmin he was a strict vegetarian, never drank alcohol or smoked, went to bed early, and rose before daybreak. Yet, dry and tiresomely pious as this sounds, this regime didn't interfere at all with the enjoyment he found in good talk and informed argument, nor does it give any idea of his charm, his wit, his love of south Indian classical music, his wisdom tempered with humour. He had a high bald head, a network of laughter lines around sharply observant eyes, and a wide, ironic smile, and he expressed himself in perfectly phrased, elegantly old-fashioned, literary English. He was an intellectual and a fine scholar, but he could still capture the imagination of a crowd at a political meeting. He went to jail for acts of civil disobedience to promote a national cause, yet he spent his spare time making brilliant translations of the great Hindu epics, the *Ramayana* and the *Mahabharata*, from Sanskrit into Tamil and into English. He held the country's most prestigious post as Governor-General and was acclaimed by all parties as the best man for the position, and was still able, half humorously, to warn Jai and me, in 1949, that the new government of India might not appreciate the need to preserve for posterity the many historically important buildings Jai had handed over to them. He included the palaces, the temples of the Jaipur rulers in Benares and Mathura, and the observatory in Delhi, but he expressed special concern for Amber, the wonderful old capital of Jaipur. How right he turned out to be!

It was many years before I saw him again, and in the meantime the whole country, and our personal lives with it, had changed beyond all imagining. His Swatantra Party attracted both Jai and me when we first heard about it. At last someone seemed to be saying that there must be an effective but reasonable opposition to the Congress Party if democracy were to survive in India—and was doing something about creating such an opposition. At last someone was speaking up against excessive state control and the disastrous results of the Congress Party's economic policies, and asking for a practical approach that wasn't shackled to visionary dogma. However, Jai still felt disinclined to enter party politics. He had always believed that in his position—and his position was an extraordinary one—he should remain neutral. I, as his wife, had accepted the idea that I should do the same. But now, for the first time, I was really tempted to join an opposition party. It was so clear that all around us our people were discontented and viewed the future with pessimism. In fact, the only section of society which seemed satisfied were those people closely associated with the Congress Party. There was little hope of remedying this situation unless some constructive action was taken to oppose the Congress Party in Parliament and in the state assemblies.

Not only had the ruling party failed to respect the agreement that made Jai Rajpramukh, it now seemed determined to isolate him. Since Jai had ceased to be Rajpramukh, we were seldom invited to official functions. It soon became apparent that the Rajasthan State Government members were envious and suspicious of Jai's undiminished popularity with the people of Jaipur, who would still greet him with enthusiasm whenever he appeared in public.

A typical incident took place shortly after he had recovered from an attack of measles. About sixteen miles outside Jaipur City is a temple where, in the month of March, those who have recently had measles, chicken-pox, or smallpox go to give thanks for their recovery to the goddess Sitla. Jai always observed these local customs, and he went to the temple unaccompanied, driving his own car. He was quite unprepared for the reaction of the crowd gathered there. When they recognized him, they surrounded his car and gave him the most tremendous welcome. This kind of spontaneous demonstration of the people's affection that none of the Congress members could command was not to the Government's liking.

Polo matches in Jaipur did nothing to ease the tension, for Jai would be mobbed when he appeared, while the Governor and other officials were ignored. On another occasion, a government minister invited Jai to an industrial exhibition that was being held in the city but asked if he would please come on the day before the exhibition was opened to the public. I was secretly delighted when I heard that the news of Jai's deliberately unpublicized visit had spread through the streets in less than half an hour and that crowds had rushed to welcome him, pushing the poor minister, unnoticed, into a corner.

If anyone had needed proof that the bond that existed between rulers and people in most of the princely states was deep and genuine, they had only to follow Jai around any day of the week in Jaipur. It was hardly surprising that as the Government imposed more and more taxes, and failed to cope with the rising cost of living, many people felt that they had been better off in the old days. Jai did nothing that could have been interpreted as disloyalty to the Government, but the officials, instead of enlisting his co-operation and making use of his great influence with the people, reacted by trying to cut him off from public life. Admittedly, after he ceased to be Rajpramukh, he was offered the post of Ambassador to the Argentine, but, as some people remarked, there could be ulterior motives which prompted an offer of such a remote posting. Jai's keen interest in polo might have tempted him, but he felt he couldn't go so far away while his own agreements with the Government of India at the time of the merger of Jaipur State remained so unsettled. I couldn't help sharing Jai's deep frustration, and this certainly played a part in my increasing dislike of the ruling party.

It was in this pent-up mood, and with the growing awareness of the dissatisfaction of the people around us, that, as time passed, I began to toy with the idea of finally getting down to action of some sort and joining the Swatantra Party. My intention after I joined was to canvass for its candidates, and perhaps raise funds and hold fêtes, just as I had seen British friends do in support of their political parties. I never dreamed of standing for Parliament or making politics a career. I had no personal ambitions and, in spite of my disappointment with the Government, felt no animosity to any individual.

I thought that the princes should find capable candidates, back them, and help in their election campaigns to Parliament in New Delhi and to the state legislative assemblies. In this way, I imagined, there would be a sensible, non-extremist opposition to the Congress Party. With these ideas in mind, and a rather inchoate wish to do something for the country, I finally took the step of joining the Swatantra. As it turned out, my timing almost made it a most embarrassing step.

The previous summer it had been announced that the Queen was going to visit India, and Jai, who had met her at a polo game in Windsor, asked her if she would do him the honour of visiting Jaipur. She replied that she would be pleased to accept if he would arrange the visit. He immediately got in touch with Sir Michael Adeane, the Queen's Private Secretary, and also with Mrs. Vijayalaxmi Pandit, the Indian High Commissioner in London. In due course, a visit to Jaipur was added to the Queen's itinerary. It was settled that she would come to Jaipur on 23 January 1961, two days after her arrival in New Delhi, and that her visit would be as informal as possible, allowing her plenty of time to rest before carrying on with her tour of India and Pakistan.

Such visits have to be worked out in great detail, and officials from Buckingham Palace, the British Foreign Office, and the Protocol Division in Delhi were soon busy ensuring that all the arrangements were in order and to everybody's satisfaction, and that substitute arrangements were understood in case anything unforeseen should require a change in plans. However, when, after a few weeks, it was announced that the Queen was going to a tiger shoot at one of our hunting-lodges, the Anti-Blood-Sports Group in England started to protest, and a little later the Indian newspapers picked up the cry. This worried Pandit Nehru, and he wrote to Jai asking him to be very sure that no live bait was to be used on this shoot.

At the same time, some of the Indian papers had published a program of the Queen's visit and had stated that Jai was planning to hold a durbar in the Queen's honour. Naturally, such a ceremony would offend the sensibilities of Indians, who were now independent of British rule. Again Pandit Nehru wrote to Jai, who replied that he was most upset that the Prime Minister should think him so irresponsible. It was perfectly clear from the wording of the invitation to the reception in honour of the Queen and the Duke of Edinburgh that there was no intention of holding a durbar. Jai was then asked why the guests had been asked to come in full dress and wearing their turbans. Jai replied that this was the traditional costume in Jaipur, and that the nobles always came to any ceremonial occasion dressed in their *achkans* and turbans and carrying swords. In fact, they had done so just before the Queen was to come to Jaipur, when Jai's son Pat got engaged to my sister Ila's daughter and they all attended the betrothal ceremony at the City Palace.

I don't know what prompted me to pick that particular day to take what was, for me, an extraordinary action. I remember waking up the morning of the betrothal ceremony and asking Jai if I could join the Swatantra Party. He was still rather sleepy, but he did say "Yes," and so, as I left Rajmahal to go out for my morning ride, I asked the ADC on duty to find out who was the local secretary of the Swatantra Party and to ask him to come and have breakfast with me.

When I returned from my ride, the man was waiting for me, and I inquired how one set about joining a political party. If he was surprised, he didn't show it and merely replied that it was quite simple; one paid a subscription and one filled in a form. I did both on the spot. Pat was sitting at the table with me and was the only witness to this scene. It was all over in a minute, and then Pat and I went on to the City Palace for the engagement ceremony.

Among the guests staying with us at the time was an old friend, the granddaughter of one of India's greatest Freedom Fighters, and as we were watching the betrothal I happened to mention to her that I had just come from joining the Swatantra Party. She stared at me, aghast, and said, "You must be mad."

"Why?" I asked. "You sympathize with the Swatantra, too."

"But the Queen is about to come and visit Jai!"

"What's that got to do with it?" I asked.

"Well, if you've just gone and joined an opposition party it will look like a deliberate insult to the Government, and you're bound to get an awful lot of comment and criticism about it. After all, the Queen *is* the guest of the Government of India."

"I can't believe my joining the Swatantra Party would be much of a scoop for the press," I said, beginning to feel more uncertain of my ground. "But for pity's sake, do keep quiet about it until after the visit."

When we got back to Rajmahal, I asked the ADC if there had been any calls.

"Yes, indeed," he replied. "The press have been ringing up all day to ask if you've joined the Swatantra Party."

Luckily, he didn't know I had, and so he had been strenuously denying the rumour. I told him to keep on. In fact, even Jai didn't know that I had acted so quickly, for, what with Pat's betrothal and all the ceremonies, he had been very busy that morning, and we didn't see each other until lunchtime. He was rather surprised by my hastiness and felt I should have discussed with him more thoroughly an action so potentially explosive. He entirely agreed that we should keep the news very quiet indeed, and it was not until a week or so after the Queen had left Jaipur that it became public knowledge.

The Queen's visit turned out to be a great success. The reception at the City Palace was really brilliant. As the Queen drove down the streets accompanied by Jai, while Prince Philip followed in the next car with Bubbles, the people of Jaipur came out in all their colourful finery to greet them. At the gates which are used for the official entrance of distinguished visitors to the City Palace, they left their cars and rode into the palace grounds on elephants. The pink courtyard of the City Palace was lined with elephants, camels, horses, and gorgeously decorated bullock-carts, and it was there, in the audience pavilion, that I received Her Majesty. I had seen many grand occasions at the City Palace, but this, I thought, was the most spectacular, with the brocaded costumes of the nobles and the gold and silver trappings of the elephants blazing under all the extra television lights. Then, as the Queen arrived, the official announcers cried out a warning to all people present to be ready to receive the most distinguished guest of the Maharaja, Her Majesty the Maharani Elizabeth of England.

The next part of the visit was much more informal. After dinner at Rajmahal, we all went by special train to our favourite shooting-lodge. We travelled down in a luxurious coach provided by the Government, taking no ADCs but only Jai's four sons and Colonel Kesri Singh, who was always in charge of our shooting equipment. Each compartment on the train had its own telephone extension, which delighted Jagat, while the relaxed informality of the whole trip delighted everyone else.

On the first day the Duke of Edinburgh bagged a large tiger with a beautiful shot, after which we had a picnic lunch and then drove through the jungle looking at wild game. The next day Sir Christopher Bonham-Carter shot a tiger, and then we all went up to visit the impregnable fort of Ranthambhor, sprawling across the hill-tops. The dinners at the shooting-lodge were marvellously easy and amusing, with Colonel Kesri Singh entertaining everyone with outlandish stories of shoots he had been on. He had insisted on wearing one of his most treasured possessions—a red velvet smoking-jacket made from a curtain said to have belonged to Queen Victoria, which he had bought at an auction in Bognor Regis. He was quite unable to resist the temptation of telling Her Majesty that he was wearing her great- great-grandmother's curtains.

The Queen's visit to Jaipur, 23 *January* 1961.

It seemed like all too short a time before the Queen and Prince Philip had to leave for the rest of their tour, and we returned to Jaipur. I wrote to Rajaji, telling him that I had joined his party, and received a reply thanking me and saying I was a brave lady. This rather puzzled me at first, for I saw nothing brave in joining an opposition political party in a democratic country. But I soon began to understand. In February the press carried the news that I had joined the Swatantra Party, and I was quite unprepared for either the public interest it aroused or the reaction of the Congress Party leaders in Rajasthan. The same Chief Minister who had asked me to join the Congress four years earlier angrily threatened in the State Assembly that princes who engaged in politics would forfeit their privy purses. He was somewhat sobered by the question of an independent member asking whether that principle would apply equally to former rulers who joined the Congress.

Then in April the leader of the Swatantra Party in Rajasthan invited Rajaji to come to Jaipur, and I learned to my consternation that I was expected to speak at a public meeting which he was going to address. Even though I had abandoned purdah some time earlier and drove my own open sports-car wherever I wanted, my formal appearances in public had been very rare. It would be quite a revolution in the history of Jaipur for a maharani to speak on a public platform. As always, I rushed to Jai to ask his advice. He pointed out that as I had joined the party, it was my duty to work for it, and he gave me his permission to appear at the public meeting. I had been hoping secretly that he would provide me with some sort of excuse so that I could avoid the whole thing. As it was, a large number of the people of Jaipur as well as my own family were uneasy about my doing any political work. Many simply didn't like the idea of their Maharani entering public life, while my own people were afraid that my action might expose our family to political retaliation of some sort.

However, there seemed to be no help for it. I couldn't think of any way to extricate myself from the situation I had encouraged, and now I had to accept the idea that I must appear at the huge open-air meeting that had been planned. My only duty was to introduce Rajaji. I had no more than four lines to say, and even those were written down for me. Still, I was overwhelmed with nervousness, and had a dry mouth and parched lips for days beforehand. At last it came, the day I had hoped would never arrive, and I shall never forget my string of anxieties. Would I stutter or forget my lines? Would I lose the piece of paper and be tongue-tied? Would the people be sympathetic? Would there, perhaps, be no gathering at all? One of the nobles and his wife accompanied me to the meeting, and when I confessed my fears that no one would bother to come, they burst out laughing and reminded me that Jaipur was a place where, if two monkeys danced, people would gather around them. I need hardly say that I didn't find this remark very reassuring.

Then, as we approached the grounds, we found that a huge crowd had assembled before the outdoor platform, and this made me even more terrified. But once my own small part in the performance was over, I enjoyed my first political meeting. Rajaji had been very kind to me before and seemed to understand why I was in such a dither. But once he started talking, I forgot my self-conscious worries and was enthralled by the clarity and logic and fearless good sense of his speech; I had never before heard anyone criticize the Government so openly and was pleased to see that the enormous crowd was equally impressed. It wasn't until later that I wondered at my own surprise. After all, isn't it one of the fundamental rights of people in a democracy to criticize their government as openly as they wish? Soon afterwards, Rajaji wrote an article in the party newspaper, which he edited, comparing me to the Rani of Jhansi. I found the comparison rather far-fetched. The Rani of Jhansi, a great Indian heroine, led her troops to battle against the British in the cause of freedom. All I had done was join a political party in a free and democratic country. It was only later that I discovered that to belong to an opposition party was not without its risks.

Chapter 16

Campaigning for Election

THE SUMMER of that year was peaceful. We went to England, as usual, for the season. News that I had joined a political party had travelled quickly among our friends, and Lord Mountbatten, who was very fond of Jai, said that it was most thoughtless of me, until I explained that I had joined the Swatantra Party which Rajaji, Lord Mountbatten's successor as Governor-General of India, had founded. But most of the time, far away from India, I forgot my possibly rash entry into politics and enjoyed the English summer. Jai played a great deal of polo, mainly at Windsor, Cowdray Park, and Cirencester, and I was kept busy settling into the new house we had bought near Ascot. It was smaller and more compact than "Saint Hill," as Jai felt that now the older boys were grown up and working in India we had no need for such a large house in England. Jagat, who had until then been at Mayo College in India, was enrolled at Ludgrove Preparatory School, which was near our house. I had wanted Jagat to stay at Mayo College because I felt that it would be of greater advantage to him to have a wholly Indian education and to grow up with Indian boys. Jai didn't agree, and I ended up, as usual, by giving in.

Soon after our return to India in the autumn of 1961, I received a letter from the General Secretary of the Swatantra Party, asking me whether I would like to contest the Jaipur parliamentary seat in the general elections the following year. I was appalled. It had honestly never occurred to me that I might be asked; I had only meant to help the party and campaign for its candidates. But Jai pointed out that it had been perfectly obvious from the beginning that this would happen. As Jai's wife, I would automatically have considerable popular appeal. There was no excuse I could think of beyond that I was frightened, so with Jai's consent I accepted. I think, though, that he was quite as anxious as I was about the outcome of this venture.

In 1962 the Swatantra Party was contesting elections for the first time. There was a meeting of some of its leaders and prominent party members in Jaipur, and there it was decided that besides contesting the Jaipur parliamentary seat myself, I should be responsible for securing the election of candidates for the whole area that had been the old state of Jaipur. This was a fearful responsibility for someone without political experience. Jaipur State covered about 16,000 square miles. It had five parliamentary seats, and forty seats in the State Legislative Assembly of Rajasthan. Finding suitable candidates immediately presented a great problem. The Swatantra was a new party, and, besides, many of the eminent citizens we approached refused to stand for an opposition party for fear of government pressure and reprisals. Businessmen were worried that their import permits might be cancelled or supplies of essential materials might be delayed. We did eventually manage to attract a number of good candidates, but through all the preliminary work I was continually confronted with evidences of my own ignorance of how much had to be done before a political campaign could be launched. I had never before heard of electoral rolls, did not know the names of the different constituencies, and did not realize that there were special seats reserved for the Harijans and the tribal people. I knew nothing about election agents, nominations, withdrawals, or parliamentary boards. Very fortunately, I had expert advisers and assistants from the party, and an election agent with a team of tireless workers who all performed magnificently—in educating me as much as in organizing the campaign.

As soon as it was known that I was actually running for Parliament, people from all sorts of different sections of society kept coming to Rajmahal to ask Jai and other members of our family to stand as candidates. Jai had made up his mind to stay out of politics and couldn't be persuaded to change it, but both Joey and Pat were roped in—Joey as a candidate for the State Legislative Assembly from a constituency where he would be opposing the Home Minister of Rajasthan, and Pat, at the last minute, as the parliamentary candidate from a constituency that held the first capital of Jai's ancestors.

This seat was to have been contested by the General Secretary of the Swatantra Party, but he decided that he would be more useful touring the country before the elections and entering Parliament later in a by-election. He left it to Jai to find a replacement. Jai went to the constituency, called a meeting, and asked the people whom they would like as a candidate. He suggested a number of possibilities—lawyers and eminent public men—but the people insisted that he should stand himself and, failing that, that he should propose a member of his own family. There was no question of Bubbles standing for election, as he was in the army. Joey was already committed, so there remained only Pat, who was in his late twenties and was working in Calcutta, in a business he had recently opened, manufacturing spare parts for agricultural machinery.

That morning I telephoned Pat to ask if he would agree to stand if Jai was unable to persuade the people to accept any other candidate. He was very reluctant about the whole thing, explaining that he would have no time to campaign and, even if he were elected, would hardly be able to fulfil his commitments to his constituents in Jaipur when his own work would keep him in Calcutta. I assured him that his father would not put forward his name unless it was absolutely necessary. We waited impatiently for Jai to come back; it was well past midnight when his cavalcade arrived. Exhausted and covered with dust, Jai came upstairs and said simply, "I'm afraid it's Pat."

We telephoned him again the next morning, and he was furious, saying that he couldn't possibly campaign for more than ten days. We tried to calm him down and urged him to come to Jaipur at once, because the nominations were to be closed at 3 P.M. three days later. Pat said he would fly to Delhi and motor from there, but by lunchtime on the last day he still hadn't arrived, and we were all waiting anxiously on the front terrace of Rajmahal. Telephones kept ringing as the press and well-wishers asked for news of his arrival. At 2:30 he drove up, scarcely said "hello" before he hurried to the Collectorate to file his nomination just before the books were closed, and then disappeared again, to return only for the last fortnight of the campaign.

Once we had managed to find candidates, however reluctant, for all the seats, the campaign began in earnest. To start off, Jai came with me to an area of the old Jaipur State which I had visited only once before, and then only for a day. It was a desert region, starved for water, where the very scanty irrigation enables the people, even in the best of times, to grow only one crop a year. Many of the sturdy men from the area are drawn to the army, and are known for their tough, disciplined efficiency as soldiers. It is also the home of many important businessmen, who may be engaged in commerce and industry almost anywhere in India but still maintain large ancestral estates in the region. Jai and I spent three days there; Jai met many ex-soldiers and discussed their problems with them while I was busy campaigning, learning painfully to overcome my timidity and beginning, for the first time, to feel the warm excitement of communicating with a sympathetic audience.

Jai and I drove to a number of different towns and villages, in a car where there was a road and by jeep where there were only country tracks. All the people had been alerted about our arrival and had put up welcoming arches over the roads. They crowded our route, called out to us, and often stopped the car or jeep to offer us fresh fruit and vegetables. Sometimes they sang for us and performed the local folk-dances. Always their speeches of welcome were in the most flowery language they could summon.

Gradually I got used to addressing large meetings, backing up the local candidates with a brief description of the new party we were starting and asking the villagers to help us by giving us their votes. Sometimes I quite forgot the crowds and hardly paid attention to the other speakers, gazing instead at the beautifully painted murals which decorate the houses in the towns of that desolate area. The doors were made of some kind of heavy silvery metal, carved and decorated, and one could see that although the land was poor agriculturally, still a lot of wealth made by merchants elsewhere in India was brought back to their home district and spent on schools and colleges, as well as the lovely façades of private homes.

During the next two months I covered thousands of miles, mostly by jeep, campaigning more for other candidates than for myself, and I discovered with wonderment that the mere hint of my arrival in the remotest sections of the state guaranteed a crowd beyond anything I had imagined. I generally started out at about six in the morning and returned to wherever I was staying at midnight or later. I slept under all kinds of conditions and in all sorts of places. I took my own bedding and can never forget the luxury of finding clean sheets and a soft pillow after the long, strenuous day. Bathrooms were something I couldn't arrange, and they turned out to be almost anything—a wooden stool and a bucket of water, mostly, sometimes not even that. I remember being intensely grateful when there happened to be a government rest-house in any village where I was to spend the night, or if there was a minor noble or big landowner in the vicinity, living in one of the many small forts that dot the Jaipur landscape. At least then I could be sure that my accommodations would be clean, however Spartan.

On these tours, my election team and I had to stop nearly every half hour in a village or small town, whether we had planned it or not, and we were often shockingly late for scheduled appearances. Astonishingly, the crowd never seemed to mind the long delays. In the manner of all Indian crowds, they managed to make an impromptu festival out of waiting for my arrival. Sweets stalls arose magically on the outskirts, children rushed about, the women in their festival clothes squatted in groups on the ground, gossiping and exchanging news, and village entertainers diverted the audience during the wait. It was all marvellously good-humoured and patient.

I thought it best to appear on these occasions dressed as simply as possible. So I wore my usual chiffon saris but without ostentatious jewellery—just a pearl necklace and glass bangles on my wrists. But I found that when the villagers gathered around to see their Maharani, they were disappointed; the women, particularly, were horrified that I was wearing virtually no jewellery, not even the anklets that the poorest woman among them would certainly own.

Added to the rigours of my touring—the heat, the dust, the long distances travelled in jolting jeeps over desert tracks and winding, unsurfaced village roads—was the problem of the speeches themselves. Although I had never learnt Hindi properly, I could read the phonetic Devanagari script. Consequently, I wrote all my speeches first in English, had them translated and written out for me ahead of time, and laboriously learnt them by heart. By the end of the campaign I had managed to understand enough to anticipate the most frequent questions and was even able to answer them in my broken Hindi, struggling and stuttering into the microphone, but managing without a script and with enough confidence to pass for spontaneity.

The whole campaign was, perhaps, the most extraordinary period of my life. Seeing and meeting the people of India, as I did then, I began to realize how little I really knew of the villagers' way of life. The world is too apt to think of India as covered by a blanket of poverty, without any variation except for the very rich. Contrary to this picture, I found that most villagers, despite the simplicity of their lives and the cruel experiences of famine and crop failure, possess a dignity and self-respect that are striking and have a deep security in an inclusive philosophy of life that made me feel both admiration and, in a way, almost envy. Their attitude was far removed from the cringing poverty and whining beggars of the urban slums of Delhi, Bombay, or Calcutta.

Hospitality is one of their great traditions; they would have offered it to any stranger in their village, even if he were merely passing through and had stopped only to ask directions to the next town. Wherever I and my election team went, we were given glasses of milk, tea, or precious water, had sweets and baskets of fresh fruit pressed on us, and were then offered fresh peas or whatever vegetables were in season, to take for sustenance on our further journey. I learnt immediately and vividly that water was the most important element in their lives. A good monsoon meant comparative wealth, perhaps a new bicycle or—luxury—a transistor radio. A failure of the rains meant hunger, dying livestock, and possibly death for the family, too. Drought is far from rare in Rajasthan, and in the old days the Rajput maharajas tried to make arrangements in advance, by seeing to it that water and grain were taken to railheads where villagers could collect them, and that camps provided with fodder were set up along the roads to receive migrating cattle. But after the merger of the states with the Indian Union, these measures no longer seemed urgent to the new government. Emergency measures were neglected when there was no longer a personal involvement of the authorities with the people, and the villagers of Rajasthan suffered more terribly than ever before.

That year, 1962, admittedly, more wells were being dug, but the water was far beneath the surface. Schemes for rural electrification which, ideally, could have solved the problem, were slow in developing, and even now have not reached more than an eighth of the state. As we drove along the narrow sandy tracks of the villages, past miles and miles of sun-baked earth, every now and again, with a sense of delighted surprise, we would pass splashes of brilliant green where the construction of a well had actually been successful and had created a thriving wheat or millet field in the middle of comparative desert. Often, as we travelled through the countryside, with only an occasional bullock-cart or camel in sight, it seemed unbelievable that all this brown emptiness should be part of one of the most densely populated countries in the world. Then, as we arrived in one of the villages tucked away behind mud walls, the men, women, and children would pour out of their houses and I would notice, with sadness, how the children far outnumbered the adults.

After such tours I would return to Rajmahal exhausted, dusty, wanting nothing so much as a civilized bath and sleep, to find guests—sometimes VIPs—assembled for a dinner-party. I was well past apologizing for my dishevelled appearance, and I sometimes had a bemused drink with them and then went up to bed, leaving Jai to cope with the rest of the evening. The only emotion I was capable of registering was relief to be in clean, comfortable surroundings. I was quite unable to conduct the ordinary small-talk that had been a requisite of so much of my social life. If anything, I kept thinking of how much I longed to take all our friends to *show* them this other life that I was discovering. Occasionally I tried to describe it—without too much success—and was met for the most part with blank or indulgent attitudes of incredulity that I was spending my time in such an eccentric way. Only Jai really understood, appreciated, and encouraged this odd adventure that I was immersed in.

Most of my meals were picnics, cold food taken with us and eaten indifferently at any convenient moment. For longer tours I took a cook along with me, to scrounge up whatever he could find by way of groceries while my political meetings were being held, and to provide us with a hot meal at the end of a wearing day, a meal eaten almost entirely in silence, where everyone was too tired to talk or even relive the events of the day. To begin with, my election agent had tried to arrange our program to allow for luncheon stops in the neighbourhood of one of the landlords who, of course, would invite all twenty or so of us to share a festive midday meal with his family. But I soon found that these occasions took up so much time—two hours or so, while the proper courtesies were being extended—that I ruled them out of our program. I may have offended some of the nobles, but to me it seemed much more important to spend that valuable time with the villagers, hearing their problems, answering their questions, and generally getting to approach some realistic acquaintance with the people of Jaipur. Sometimes one or another of the local landlords, hearing of our arrival, would set up a lavish banquet, with great *thals* of delicious food which we couldn't resist, but after a few times of having to struggle sleepily back into the jeep to get on to our next stop, I learned to refuse these invitations as graciously as I could manage. Such banquets included our drivers, elections workers, and all the retinue, but if they were disappointed at my cancelling of these delicious breaks in our gruelling routine, they never mentioned it to me.

I think the greatest surprise of the campaign was not the glimpse of "how the other half lived" but the astonishing fact that I was witnessing, and was a part of, what I can only describe as a campaign of love. Everywhere I went I was met with the traditional welcome arches, with groups of women singing songs of welcome, with decorations—all the signs of celebration. All these were offered not only to me but to Pat and Joey and to any connection of the Jaipur ruling family. It was intensely moving and, at the same time, alarming. It was only when I saw the jubilant, trusting reaction of the crowds—many of whom had walked as much as fifty miles to attend our meetings—that I began to grasp the full extent of the responsibilities we had all taken upon ourselves.

The one trap that I was determined to avoid was that of a politician's false promises. I was often urged to make a more effective speech, opening all kinds of attractive futures for the villagers if they would vote for us. But I replied that I couldn't. These were the people of Jaipur, and if I owed them nothing else, I certainly owed them the truth. For me, in any case, it was much simpler not to lie. I didn't have much of an idea of agriculture, or animal husbandry, or any of their problems in these areas, but at least I could listen and learn and, above all, not offer them impossible future wealth and freedom from hardship. I knew that in the old days, apart from a levy on produce, they had paid no taxes and had grazed their camels, bullocks, cows, and goats free on the common pastures, and I knew that now they had to pay a small sum to the Government for each animal—a sum that mounted oppressively by the end of every year. But I only became frighteningly aware of the dangers of our position when Pat, who was extremely level-headed and practical, said, early in the campaign, "Do you know one thing? These people are probably going to vote for us, and if we win, do you know what they expect? They expect that suddenly their taxes will vanish, prices will drop, water will miraculously appear in the wells, and everything will be wonderful. And then," he demanded, "what are you going to do?"

I knew that it wasn't much use trying to tell them that they were now living in a democracy, that the most we could do was to air their grievances and try to get some action from the Government, but that, unhappily, we could guarantee nothing. They couldn't believe these harsh truths. Their response was apt to be the traditional, almost feudal one of saying, in effect, *You* are responsible for us. *You* are our mother and our father. *You* will see that we are properly taken care of.

My decision to stand for Parliament had made a considerable impact both abroad and at home. It had attracted comment in the foreign press—"Maharani fights democratic election" and other such headlines—and often I was followed by television cameras when I was campaigning. Some of them picked up what was, to me, the most important facet of the campaign, the warm welcome I received from the villagers because they were sure that I genuinely wanted to help them. They knew that by standing for the Opposition I could benefit neither myself nor my family. As I look back on it, my most cherished memory is the conviction that the people had of our good intentions and the affection they expressed towards all of us.

On the evening before the campaign was to close, the Congress, the Jana Sangh (the extreme rightists), and the Swatantra each held a final meeting in Jaipur. The place chosen by the Swatantra Party was the ground behind the City Palace, where the festival processions took place. The area could hold about two hundred thousand people, about twenty times more than the squares chosen by the Congress and the Jana Sangh. I was worried that with the rival political parties holding their meetings at the same time, the area we had chosen might be too big. To my amazed pleasure, the ground was completely full.

We had invited Jai to speak, along with three lawyers who were standing for election from the city and myself. The Congress Party, in competition, had organized a procession of Indian film stars and had added a maharani—the Maharani of Patiala—to campaign for them. The Jana Sangh was more sober, relying on the attraction of their orthodox Hindu platform to draw an audience. Nevertheless, our meeting broke all records. The three lawyers were all good speakers, and they led off our meeting. I was determined to make the best speech of my life, but in the end I was so afraid and anxious that I think it was the worst one I ever gave.

Then Jai spoke. I was alarmed when he began by addressing the huge crowd by the familiar *tu* for I thought they might resent it. But he was speaking to them as he had always done in all his years as maharaja, accepting the traditional relationship as of a father to his children. "For generations," he said, "my family have ruled you, and we have built up many generations of affection. The new government has taken my state from me, but for all I care they can take the shirt off my back as long as I can keep that bond of trust and affection. They accuse me of putting up my wife and two of my sons for election. They say that if I had a hundred and seventy-six sons"—176 was the number of electoral seats in the Rajasthan Assembly—"that I would put them all up too. But they don't know, do they"—he made a disarming, confidential gesture to the crowd—"that I have far more than only one hundred and seventy-six sons?"

At this there was an enormous, swelling roar from the crowd. Then the people, in high excitement and joy, threw flowers at us, and we threw them back in a mood of spontaneous gaiety. That was the moment at which I knew that I would be elected.

At last the polling day arrived. Baby, Menaka, and other friends

Opposite: Campaigning for Parliament, 1962.

Below: Rajasthan voters during the 1962 elections.

who had come to be with me through the end of the campaign had often said, in a hopeless way, "But they don't know what they're *doing!*" as they helped me to explain the election procedure to groups of women. Since most of India is illiterate, at the polls people vote according to a visual symbol of their party. The Congress Party had two bullocks yoked together as a symbol of co-operative endeavor, the Socialists had a spreading banyan tree with its aerial roots to symbolize the spreading growth of socialism, the Communists had the familiar sickle with three stalks of wheat substituted for the hammer, and so on. The Swatantra Party had a star. Baby, all my other helpers, and I spent endless frustrating hours trying to instruct the women about voting for the star. On the ballot sheet, we said, over and over again, this is where the Maharani's name will appear, and next to it will be a star. But it was not as simple as that. They noticed a symbol showing a horse and a rider, agreed with each other that the Maharani rides so that must be her symbol. Repeatedly we said, "No, no, that's *not* the right one." Then they caught sight of the emblem of a flower. Ah, the flower of Jaipur—who else could it mean but the Maharani? "No, no, no, *not* the flower." All right, the star. Yes, that seems appropriate for the Maharani, but look, here is the sun. If the Maharani is a star, then the sun must certainly mean the Maharaja. We'll vote for both. Immediately the vote would have been invalidated. Even up to the final day, Baby and I were far from sure that we had managed to get our point across.

An Indian election is an uninhibited and joyful event. The women dress up and walk with their husbands and children to the polling booths, singing as they go. Villagers arrive in bullock-carts, the animals garlanded, the carts decorated with flowers and scraps of bright cloth, everybody on holiday, and, as always, entertainers, sweets-vendors, and storytellers set up their booths near the polling stands to amuse the crowds and make a little money. I drove about through my constituency, spending only a few moments in each place because election laws forbid campaigning twenty-four hours before the actual polling. Since crowds gathered wherever I went, I was afraid I would seem to be breaking the voting laws.

I was made doubly nervous by Jai's telling me that for the honour of the family I had to secure at least five thousand votes more than my nearest rival. And little Jagat sent me a cable from his school in England hoping that I would win by a thousand. That day I sat, unable to put my mind to anything else, simply waiting for news of the election results.

As returns started coming in, my election agent assured me that I was going to win by a tremendous majority and that we should plan a victory procession. Superstitiously, because so presumptuous an idea seemed to be tempting fate, I postponed thinking about it, and only after I learned that we had already won nineteen seats did I begin the arrangements for the procession. Pat and Joey had both won (Joey had defeated the incumbent Home Minister), and in all the Jaipur District only a single Congress Party man had been elected.

Finally the results of my election were announced. I had won by a majority of 175,000 votes over the runner-up, the Congress candidate. All my opponents had been forced to forfeit their deposits. The Jaipur family now appears in the *Guinness Book of World Records* for two wildly disparate events—Mickey's wedding, the most expensive in the world, and my election, the largest majority won by any candidate running for any election in any democratic country in the world. There is, perhaps, some ironic historical comment to be drawn from the juxtaposition of these two occasions, but I wasn't sure just what moral to look for and rested content with the thought that at least the people of Jaipur still trusted their ex-rulers.

Our procession that evening was made up of trucks and jeeps bearing the names of constituencies we had won. The people of Jaipur turned out in triumphant strength—even my Congress opponents were not going to miss the show and stood on the rooftops waving. I had never felt so greatly loved. I stood, touched and pleased at Jai's delight in my victory and his great generosity of spirit, and remembered how Ma had once said to me, "How lucky you are to have a husband who backs you up in everything. Can you believe that some men are jealous of their wives?"

But I knew that this was really Jai's victory. He stood with Menaka and other members of the family on one of the balconies of the City Palace and watched the procession drawing near. Then Jai threw gold pieces to the people as he used to in the days when he was still ruling Jaipur.

Chapter 17

Members of Parliament

After the excitement and elation of the elections were over, it was difficult not to feel a certain sense of anticlimax, but taking my seat in Parliament for the first time was an elating experience. Jai, Pat, and I went to Delhi together because Jai had his own post to take up; he had been elected to the Rajya Sabha, the Upper House, by the Rajasthan State Assembly. When the President appeared to open the new Parliament, there were four members of our family present in the Central Hall: Jai, Pat, and I, along with Bubbles, who came to attend the President as Adjutant of his bodyguard. (Joey was taking his own seat in the State Assembly.) Looking very dignified, Bubbles walked in behind the President, and though Pat tried to catch his eye, he never once glanced in our direction.

Like most of the official buildings in Delhi, the Lok Sabha, or Lower House of Parliament, was designed and built by Sir Edwin Lutyens. All of the 535 Members of Parliament sat in the great domed hall, on curved benches lining the walls in a semicircle, facing the Speaker in the center. The members of the ruling party, with almost 300 seats, were on his right, while we of the Opposition sat on his left. The biggest party in the Opposition was the Communist Party, so their members sat nearest the Speaker on the opposition benches. Next in size came the Swatantra Party, then the extreme right-wing Jana Sangh, the Socialists, and finally the Independents and the representatives of small local parties. Some time later, when the Communist Party split over the issue of the Chinese invasion of India, the Swatantra Party became the largest opposition party and we moved up to the Speaker's end of our benches. Indian parliamentary procedure was modelled on the Houses of Parliament in Westminster, except that we voted not by walking into lobbies but by pressing a button in front of our seats.

In the beginning Pat and I were very unsure of ourselves. Taking the oath of office had been a moving experience because it brought back to mind all that had preceded it, the campaign, the welcoming crowds, the ovations, the love and trust the people of Jaipur had expressed. My sister Menaka and her husband, the Maharaja of Dewas, were watching from the visitors' gallery, and later she told me that she had been nervous for Pat and me, worrying in case we stumbled over the words. We had scarcely recovered when I was told that I had to make my maiden speech. This was only three days after I had been sworn in and I was totally unprepared.

I was given only a few hours' notice, but since this was my maiden speech I was allowed to read it from a typescript. The speech was on the President's address to Parliament, typed for me by somebody else's secretary because I didn't even have my own secretary with me. I went into the House not knowing when my name would be called. One of my colleagues told me that it would be about two o'clock, but by that time I was in a panic because I had found, on reading through my speech, that the last two pages were missing.

I sat there, unable to leave, hoping that everyone else's speeches would be so long that there wouldn't be time for me. Miraculously, just before I heard my name called, one of the ushers came up to me with the missing pages.

Once I actually began to speak, I forgot all my nervousness and found that my voice was quite strong and carried well. In reply to the President's address, which was, as usual, a summary of events and developments in the country since the last parliamentary session, I suggested that he hadn't put enough emphasis on the fact that prices were rising and shortages of certain basic commodities were a special hardship for the poor.

Pat and I knew a few of the members in the Lok Sabha, but as our party was new, we hadn't really had a chance to get acquainted with our parliamentary leader, the Maharaja of Kalahandi, whose constituency was in Orissa, a state on the Bay of Bengal with many tribal areas that seemed to fit into no ordinary pigeon-hole of Indian life. He gathered us together and organized regular party meetings at which we were allocated special subjects on which to speak. Several other princely families were represented among the Swatantra members, and although most of the supporters had no connection with the old princely states, Pandit Nehru cunningly lumped us all together and dubbed us the "Party of the Princes." Unfortunately this misnomer stuck, even though the simplest tally would have shown that there were more princely families represented in the Congress Party than ever joined the Swatantra.

As we settled down into our new occupation, Pat and I found Parliament absolutely absorbing. We made a special point of attending when Pandit Nehru was speaking; he was in charge of the future of our country and of all of us. As Members of Parliament, we were entitled to the MP's accommodation in Delhi. Since Jai was a member of the Upper and I of the Lower House, instead of each of us being given a flat, we were allocated a house on a charming road in the residential section of New Delhi, while Pat was given a flat of his own. But just as we were beginning to settle into the new routine of our lives as MPs, our stay in New Delhi was cut short. We had to return to Jaipur to prepare for the visit of Mrs. Kennedy, the wife of the American President, who was due to stay with us for a few days as part of her trip to India.

Mrs. Kennedy's tour was only semi-official, but still the proposal that she should spend some time with us in Jaipur caused all kinds of complications. The Government of Rajasthan, as well as the American Ambassador, Mr. Galbraith, seemed to think, somewhat absurdly, that we were trying to reap some kind of political advantage from her stay. Mr. Galbraith even wrote to President Kennedy advising him to ask his wife not to come to Jaipur. The President replied that he never interfered with his wife's private arrangements.

As far as Jai and I were concerned, the visit was certainly meant to be a private, friendly, informal one. Earlier, when Lee Radziwill, Jackie Kennedy's sister, had told Jai that they were planning to come to India, he had invited them, quite spontaneously, to spend a few days in Jaipur. His spur-of-the-moment invitation had been accepted in the same casual, friendly spirit in which it had been offered. We had planned to entertain our guests with nothing more than some sightseeing, a polo match, relaxation around the swimming-pool, and, if they wanted, some riding.

Quite naturally, our sightseeing program for our guests included the City Palace. With Jackie's interest in the arts, it would have been ridiculous not to take her to see the Jaipur collection, and in any case Jai loved to show guests his ancestral home. I was, therefore, very surprised at Jackie's reaction when, on the second day of her visit, I told her that we would be going to see the City Palace. "But Ayesha," she said, "I've been told that I'm not allowed to go there."

In reply to my questions, she explained that she had been told that if she went to the City Palace with Jai it would appear that he was again trying to appear before the people as the ruler of Jaipur. The American Ambassador was concerned that such an excursion might offend the Congress government. It seemed too silly to believe, but all the same, Mr. Galbraith, who had accompanied Jackie to Jaipur, had to make a long telephone call to consult with Congress leaders in Delhi before Jackie was allowed to go to the City Palace and, even then, on condition that her visit attracted as little attention as possible—an absurd stipulation, since anything Jackie did was news. Petty as the restrictions seemed, we did our best to comply with them and arranged for Jackie to go to the City Palace at night so that no one would be aware that she was driving through the city with Jai. I went ahead, to receive her, and Jai and I were her only escorts on her tour of the palace.

In his book *An Ambassador's Journal*, Mr. Galbraith clearly indicated that he believed we were prompted by some kind of political motive, and it is useless to insist that he was quite mistaken. His views were perhaps influenced by the government officials, especially in Rajasthan, who always seemed rather unhappy when we had eminent guests, but as far as Jai and I were concerned, we enjoyed having Jackie to stay and felt that her visit cemented our friendship with a charming and attractive person, and with the greatest pleasure we accepted her return invitation to stay with her in Washington.

Aside from the demands of Parliament in New Delhi and the

entertaining of eminent visitors, my life in Jaipur had become busier than ever. My constituents would flock to Rajmahal, and as a conscientious Member of Parliament I would see them at whatever time they came. Most of their problems were disputes within their families about inheritances of land, or questions like "My mother-in-law is an awful tyrant; what should I do?" But so many people complained about harassment by government officials, some because they had been unwilling or unable to pay bribes, others merely because they were known to have voted for the opposition party, that eventually we had to hire a full-time lawyer to deal with the legal cases. Many of their requests were, as I was slowly discovering, the usual ones that any elected Member of Parliament must expect from constituents: grants for schools, roads, hospitals, electricity, and other amenities. Sometimes I was able to provide these by alerting local bodies to such needs. Other times, because the requests seemed so reasonable and so urgent, I donated my own money for such projects. I was greatly assisted by the charitable trust fund that Jai had started for the subjects of the old Jaipur State, naming it after his great ancestor, Maharaja Sawai Jai Singh, and providing for it an annual amount of 150,000 rupees from his privy purse (then about $30,000).

At one time I was strongly reminded of an occasion years before, in 1945, when the farmers in Cooch Behar flocked through the palace gates demanding to see their maharaja. They had just heard that they were prohibited from exporting their surplus rice for sale outside the state. It was up to Bhaiya to meet them and explain that the reason for the order was that there was a failure of crops in other parts of Bengal, which had already caused a food crisis. Famine had been predicted for the following year, so if they exported their surplus they would have nothing to eat. The villagers had enough trust in their ruler to return home satisfied with Bhaiya's explanation. If they needed proof of the vigilance of their state administration, it was abundantly provided the next year when over a million lives were lost in the great Bengal famine. In Cooch Behar not a single person died of starvation. In fact the state, small as it was, gave refuge to thousands of starving people from neighbouring areas.

My own experience was less dramatic, but for me it was both

With Jacqueline Kennedy during her visit to Jaipur.

novel and surprising. I found myself running a grain shop in Jaipur. In this at least I had a noble precedent. The previous Maharaja of Jaipur, Jai's adoptive father, was a devout man who made his morning offerings to the deity every day and asked for guidance in performing his duty to his subjects. After his prayers each morning one of his men would come to him, not with the public Jaipur news but with an account of what the word-of-mouth gossip was about, what complaints or satisfactions the ordinary people were expressing. On one occasion his reporter told him that the price of wheat, the staple grain of Rajputana, was at an all-time high. The Maharaja asked no further questions but left the table in the middle of his breakfast and walked, just as he was, in informal dress, with only a couple of attendants, to the grain market.

As he went, the people whispered among themselves, "What is the Maharaja doing, walking among us in these clothes?" They had always seen him in a horse-drawn carriage, his feet never touching the ground. He paid no attention to the muttering of the crowd but marched straight up to the leading grain merchant and demanded, "How much are you selling your wheat for?"

"Eighteen rupees a sack," came the timid reply.

"And what did you buy the wheat for?"

The merchant was so flustered that he blurted out the truth: "Ten rupees."

Then the Maharaja raised his hand for emphasis, though the merchant clearly expected a blow. He ducked, and his cap fell off, as the Maharaja thundered, "Then you *will sell it* for ten rupees! I won't have my people paying this outrageous price for their daily bread." He continued, more softly, to his Prime Minister, whom he had torn away from the breakfast table when he left the palace, "Send word to all the grain dealers in all sections of the city that the price of wheat is to be ten rupees a sack, and not an *anna* more. The government will subsidize the new price, and the merchants will not be deprived of their fair profit."

I did something very similar to this, but far less dramatic. I opened my own fair-price grain shop, for which the customers needed their government-issued ration cards. This served the basic needs of the poor, and the rest could, if they wished and if they could afford it, pay the higher prices. I found that without planning it I was learning to cope with the problems of the poor, the huge majority of my constituents.

With so much going on, and with my daily more intimate contacts with the people of Jaipur on the very level that meant the essentials of life to them, time passed quickly. I hardly noticed when April came and the weather started heating up to Rajasthan's terrible spring furnace, with the temperature hovering around 100 degrees Fahrenheit, and the dreaded Loo arrived, the searing wind from the desert which raises the mercury fifteen or twenty degrees and sweeps the surface soil into dust storms. The rivers dry up completely or shrink to thin, opaque trickles, and all farming comes to a standstill while the people wait for the monsoon rains.

Jai decided that we should leave, just as we usually did, for England, with its mild and lovely summer. But for the first time I felt I had to stay behind for a while and told him to go ahead without me. The reason was that I had promised to campaign for candidates in two important parliamentary by-elections.

One of the people standing for office had once been Secretary of the Congress Party, had broken away from it on ideological grounds, and was now an Independent. The other was the General Secretary of the Swatantra Party. One was running from a constituency in Uttar Pradesh, a very large state, home of the Nehrus, in north-central India, where in May the mercury soars to 116 or 118 degrees. The other was standing for election from a constituency in Gujerat, where the temperature can be even higher. In retrospect it seems astonishing that although I would have loved to be in England with Jai, and although the heat was overwhelmingly debilitating, I thoroughly enjoyed both campaigns; they rekindled the excitement and satisfaction of direct contact with our people that I had first felt in my own campaign.

Immediately afterwards I flew to Bombay, where I was to catch a plane for England. Just as I was leaving for the airport, news of the first victory reached me. I was wild with elation—it seemed to me more of a triumph than my own election because I had not been appealing to any ancient Jaipuri loyalties—and I insisted on having a party with Bhaiya and Joey, who were both in Bombay at the time.

In London a week later, Jai and I were at a dinner given by the Dutch Ambassador and his wife. Apologetically I kept disappearing into their library to telephone the press and India House, the office of the Indian High Commissioner, trying to find out if they had word of the results of the other by-election. Eventually I got the news, and however I may have annoyed my hosts, it was worth it; the Swatantra Party candidate had won. After that heartening bit of news, I was ready to relax and enjoy the season in England.

Soon afterwards I saw the leader of our party, Rajaji, in London. He was on his way back from the Nuclear Disarmament Conference in Washington, which, as India's first advocate of nuclear disarmament, he had been asked to attend by Pandit Nehru. It must have seemed odd to foreign observers, this easy exchange between members of opposing parties in India. It was part of Pandit Nehru's genius; when Rajaji had asked him why he was sending one of his severest critics to the conference, the Prime Minister, with the broad-mindedness that made him so unusual a political figure, had replied simply that Rajaji was the most appropriate person to represent India. Bound, in return, by honour, Rajaji couldn't say all the things he had wanted to and asked me to express his pacifist points without any obligations. But I declined. I knew I had too little political standing, but, more than that, I had no wish to embarrass Jai by carrying my politics abroad.

In October we left for America. We spent the first few days in New York and Virginia. While we were still in New York, the Cuban crisis broke out and the television, radio, and newspapers all gave instructions on what to do in the event of a nuclear attack. With some misgivings we stuck to our program and went, as planned, to Washington, where we were put up at Blair House, the presidential guest-house. Because of the crisis the Kennedys cancelled the dance that they were going to give for us and instead held a small dinner-party.

President Kennedy greeted me with a broad smile and the words, "Ah, I hear you are the Barry Goldwater of India."

I was a bit taken aback, though I realized that he was joking, so I reminded him that he had recently met the leader of the party which I represented in Parliament.

He then told me how impressed he had been with Rajaji. Expecting an old man dressed in white and talking pompous nonsense about the banning of nuclear arms, he had been bored by the very thought of an interview with Rajaji. But instead he had been so enthralled by Rajaji's wisdom and lucidity that his aides had had to drag him away for his next appointment.

I found John Kennedy an immensely attractive personality—boyish in looks and manner, and with such an infectious smile that I found it difficult to remember at times that he was the President of the United States. We didn't see very much of him, but the day after the dinner-party, when Jackie was taking us around the White House gardens, he called to us from his office window and asked me to come in.

There was an imposing group of Senators present, and to my confusion he insisted on introducing me to them as "the woman with the most staggering majority that anyone has ever earned in an election."

I greeted them as best I could and quickly retreated to the company of Jackie and Jai. She was a charming and thoughtful hostess, the best guide we could possibly have had to the White House, knowing and recounting to us the history of any portrait or piece of furniture that we admired. She made our visit to Washington an exceedingly enjoyable time.

All too soon it was over, and on our return to New York we heard the terrible news that war had broken out between China and India. It was 20 October 1962.

Already, according to the news reports, the Indian Army had suffered heavy casualties and were vastly outnumbered by the Chinese forces. I wanted to cancel the rest of our trip and go straight back to India, but for the first time my eagerness to be with our people was greater than Jai's. He pointed out, perfectly sensibly, that a change in our plans couldn't possibly make a difference to the situation in India. I understood his logic, but for once my sentiments were different. I wanted to be where any Jaipuri, for whatever reason, could reach me with any problem.

Still, I gave in, and we left for England to stay a few days, as we had planned. All the time I felt wretchedly unhappy and restless, not only because my constituents might be affected but also because Cooch Behar was so near the north-east border of India. What was happening there? How severely were Bhaiya and the people affected?

By the time we eventually reached Delhi, the Chinese had already crossed India's north-eastern frontier and had entered Assam to begin their southward drive. They had swept through the Indian defences without much difficulty because our troops were unprepared and ill equipped for high-altitude warfare in the daunting, treacherous terrain of the towering Himalayas. We had no roads on our side of the border, and our forces were crippled in their attempts to manoeuvre. The Chinese, having plotted their attack long before, had built roads right up to the frontier on their side and were equipped with modern semi-automatic weapons which our army did not possess.

In Parliament, when the debate about this unwarranted invasion began, for the first time we saw Pandit Nehru with head bowed, quite unlike his usual confident, casual self, helpless to explain our unpreparedness. A month later, on the twenty-first of November, the Chinese declared a cease-fire unilaterally but made it clear that they had no intention of returning to the positions they had held before the hostilities or of returning Indian territory to India.

Slowly, in Parliament, the truth came out. Since 1954 Pandit Nehru and his government had kept Chinese incursions into Indian territory secret and had done nothing more than counter their advance with mild protests. In 1960 he had disregarded the advice of the chiefs of the armed forces, who had argued that India had insufficient troops on our northern frontiers and that those troops we had were inadequately equipped. As a result, the vital funds for the training of our armed forces for high-altitude warfare had not been allocated, and the present disaster was directly attributable to that lack of foresight.

We were now being given evidence of the disasters that came of

Pandit Nehru's high-minded naïveté. He had believed that, despite their steady encroachments on Indian territory, the Chinese would never launch a serious attack on India. Indeed, he had led the Indian people to believe that the Chinese had nothing but fraternal feelings for them; his widely quoted slogan was *Hindi-Chini bhai bhai*, "Indians and Chinese are brothers." Our conflict with China exploded this myth and a few others, too, such as the idea that our only enemy was Pakistan, which had been separated from India in 1947 in circumstances of such bitterness and bloodshed that both countries were unable to overcome their suspicions and hostility.

In the Lok Sabha, the Lower House of Parliament, there was a lot of agitated activity. The Defence of India Act was passed with the primary intention of enabling the Government to detain fifth-columnists and other anti-national elements, but it soon became apparent that this Act was also being used as a blanket excuse to silence opposition critics of government policy. A Defence Fund was also started, to which contributions flowed in, many voluntary. Disgracefully, some were extracted under threats and pressure from officials. When my constituents brought this practice to my attention, I immediately wrote to the Prime Minister. He replied that forced contributions were entirely wrong and that all contributions to the Defence Fund must be voluntary. I asked his permission to publish his letter in the newspapers, explaining that an unequivocal assurance from the highest authority was necessary to give some courage to people who could ill afford to contribute but who were being harassed. Pandit Nehru granted permission and his letter was published. I don't believe it did much good.

As soon as the crisis was over, the Congress workers—even ministers—were sent around the country to call meetings and make speeches covering up the mistakes of their leaders, the gross and dangerous lack of ordinary caution and preparedness that had left us so vulnerable to the Chinese attack. Meanwhile, in Parliament, the Prime Minister tried to silence his opponents with blinding sarcasm. On one occasion, during a debate on the war with China, Pandit Nehru chose as his target the leader in Parliament of the Swatantra Party, Professor Ranga, replying to a critical speech with the remark,

"The Professor professes to know more than he does." The laughter of the back-benchers made this seem wittier than it was. That very morning the Professor had been telling me that we newcomers never understood the importance of backing up our leaders, unlike the government members, who at least encouraged their leaders by their laughter whenever the Opposition was being ridiculed. So when the Prime Minister picked on the Professor for his caustic comment, I automatically stood up, without thinking, and blurted out, "If you had known anything about anything, we wouldn't be in this mess today."

The Prime Minister, whose parliamentary manners were always perfect, had sat down as I rose to my feet. When he again stood up to resume his speech, he said that he had not heard what the honourable lady member had said. The Speaker said that my remark had been irrelevant and asked Pandit Nehru to continue. But the members of all the opposition parties sitting near me urged me to get up and repeat what I had said or it would not be recorded. Hot with embarrassment, I rose again and repeated my comment in more parliamentary language.

Pandit Nehru replied, "I will not bandy words with a lady," to which the opposition members called out, "Chivalry!" in mocking tones.

I sat down feeling crushed. I was surprised at myself and at my outburst, and so, I think, were many others. I didn't know whether I had done right to speak out so rudely, but when I reached home that evening, the Professor telephoned me to say how delighted he had been by what he called my "timely interjection." However, when I went to Parliament the next day, although many people congratulated me, others asked how I could have made such an unseemly remark to an elder. It didn't do much good to explain that I had the greatest respect for Pandit Nehru, but on that day I simply couldn't help myself. My only regret was that I hadn't couched what I said in better language.

The atmosphere in Parliament continued to be electric as people began to see how unsuccessful our foreign policy had been. We realized for the first time that none of the Communist countries whose friendship Pandit Nehru had tried to cultivate had come to

India's aid when our boundaries were crossed in an unprovoked aggression. Instead, it was the Western powers, whom he had rather cold-shouldered, that had been quick to offer and provide help.

In Parliament and throughout the country pressure mounted on Pandit Nehru to ask for the resignation of the Defence Minister, V. K. Krishna Menon. People felt that it was he who was mostly responsible for failing to equip the Indian Army adequately and for remaining unaware of Chinese intentions. The Prime Minister tried to protect him, but public opinion was too strong and in the end he gave in to it and asked Krishna Menon to go.

Like most people in India, Jai and I felt that the saddest part of the whole episode was the humiliation that the Indian armed forces had to weather. They were among the finest forces in the world and it wounded our pride—indeed, it enraged us—to think they had fared so badly because of the Government's naïve misjudgement of our relations with the Chinese and its lack of foresight that left our army hopelessly ill equipped to combat aggression. We were also unhappy at this proof that, despite the hopes that had been raised by Nehru's leadership, India had not become the most influential nation in Asia. Our failure in the war against China had been a devastating blow to our prestige, and we now ranked incalculably lower in the esteem of the surrounding smaller nations which had looked to us for help, guidance, and protection.

Even when there were not dramatic confrontations such as the Chinese invasion of India and the high-tempered debates about it in Parliament, I found that my time and my interests began to centre increasingly on my parliamentary duties and my new relationship with the people of Jaipur. I fought, alongside my Swatantra colleagues, such moves as the amendment of the Constitution to curtail the right to property, while at home I found it heartbreaking to have to repeat over and over again my refrain to my constituents: "I can't change the laws for you. I can't *make* the Government act to help you. I can only air your grievances and hope that they will be listened to."

In small things, however, I was able to do some good and solve some local problems, and I was astonished at how satisfying I found this. Among my constituents were two of Jaipur's tribes, the Meenas and the Gujars, who had an age-old tradition of feuds and rivalries. The tribesmen used to come to me with all kinds of complaints: a cow had been stolen, a wife had run away, a house had burned down—whatever the trouble might be, it was always the fault of some member of the other tribe. I was placed in an awkward position because usually both parties in the dispute had voted for me and both expected me to be on their side in the argument. I discovered in my new incarnation as a politician that I had an unsuspected and useful talent for arbitration. Other problems were more serious and less charged with emotion. A village wanted bus service, or a post office, or a school, or a train to stop in their vicinity. Where these demands were reasonable I was usually able to accomplish something by talking to the Central Government officials in charge of the appropriate departments.

In 1964, the country suffered a terrible loss which affected all Indians regardless of position, background, or party affiliation. Parliament had been prorogued, and there was to be a three-day break before it sat again. During the break Pandit Nehru went away from New Delhi for a rest, as he had not been in good health. The day we met again he was absent from the House, and by that time we had all begun to realize that he was critically ill. Before we could begin work on the issue before us, the news came that the Prime Minister was dead.

Pat, Professor Ranga, and I went at once to his house to pay our last respects to this truly great son of India. Later, at a meeting of all the Members of Parliament in the Central Hall, I was chosen to speak in appreciation of Pandit Nehru on behalf of the Swatantra Party. As always, I hated to speak in public, especially on such a moving occasion, even though I was told to "just say what you feel" by the Swatantra General Secretary. What I "felt" was that the most extraordinary thing about Pandit Nehru was his ability to be at home anywhere: in a palace, at a teen-agers' party with the rock-'n'-roll blaring, or in a village hut. But what I said was more conventional, that, like everybody present, I felt his loss deeply, that he had given up an easy life to work for the independence of his country, that people might have disagreed with some of his policies but no one could argue with the fact that he loved India and India loved him.

Chapter 18

Ambassador to Spain

WITH PANDIT NEHRU GONE, there arose the question of a successor. For a short period the Home Minister took over the duties of Prime Minister until the Congress Party elected Lal Bahadur Shastri to lead the Government. Shastri was a calm, competent, thoughtful Prime Minister, and if he lacked Pandit Nehru's charismatic flair, many people welcomed his moderation and his soundness of judgement. He was a small, gentle, plain-living man with a mild manner which belied the strength of his character. Without Nehru's panache and grandiose ideas, he quietly and efficiently turned the Government's attention to alleviating the country's economic situation. In an agricultural country, he insisted, it was only reasonable that agriculture be given precedence in the Government's five-year plan. The "green revolution" that was to do so much to improve the country's endemic shortages of food was largely the result of his intelligent foresight.

For us, the accession of Lal Bahadur Shastri made one enormous difference to our pattern of living. Jai had, for some time, been thinking of serving the country in a more specific fashion. When Lal Bahadur Shastri offered him an ambassadorship, giving him a choice of two or three countries, Jai decided to accept and, after much thought, chose Spain. There was a good deal of gossip and comment when his appointment was announced. Some people thought that he had been offered the job simply because the Government wanted him out of the country. Through Jai's influence his family had done so much damage to the Congress in Rajasthan that only when he was safely posted abroad (and me with him) could they hope to rally greater support. But whatever the Government's motives may have been, no one could deny that Jai had all the necessary qualities:

tact, experience, familiarity with foreign countries, and unswerving loyalty to India.

The family felt that his accepting the post was a good idea. However, while I was happy for Jai in his new appointment, I was in a quandary as to what I should do myself. I dearly wished to go to Spain with him and knew he would need me as a hostess for all the compulsory entertaining that an embassy demands. But I was now so deeply involved in parliamentary affairs and in my work at home that I would be badly torn between two jobs. Rajaji asked me to write an article about this peculiar dilemma and published it in the Swatantra Party paper. He was very much against the idea of Jai serving the Government but understood both points of view and was sympathetic when I told him that I should have to be at my husband's side as much as possible.

The question of how to be effectively in two places at once was not my only concern. I was worried that the Government might make things difficult for Jai as a result of my opposition stand in Parliament or of my Swatantra activities outside. Eventually I decided to go and speak to the Prime Minister himself. It was the first time that I had ever talked to Shastri alone, and I was impressed. Beneath his quiet, unassuming manner I sensed a strong and eminently practical personality whose greatest concern was for the good of India.

After the interview I felt reassured about my husband's future in his new job, at least as far as the Prime Minister was concerned. As I left, Shastri said to me, "Must you really be in the Opposition?"

At this I turned and answered, "Surely, in a democracy there must be some form of opposition?"

"Don't you think," he asked, "I have enough opposition already?"

I assumed he was referring to the self-servers in his own party who did so much to betray the brave Congress slogans. We both smiled, and I wished that other members of the Government could be like him.

In October Jai flew to Madrid to take up his new post, leaving me to follow in December when Parliament recessed. For the first few months he stayed in a hotel—India had never had an ambassador to Spain before, so there was no embassy residence—but after first I, and then Jagat, joined him, we moved into a flat.

We soon settled down to our life in Madrid and began to make new friends. Jai found many Spaniards as keen on horses, polo, and shooting as he was, while I was captivated by the warmth, hospitality, and helpfulness of the families we came to know. One occasion to which we were greatly looking forward was the marriage, in her ancestral home, of the daughter of the Spanish Ambassador in London, the Marqués de Santa Cruz. There were to be several celebration parties, and Jai and I had been invited to attend them. Just before we left for the wedding we received a message informing us that Lal Bahadur Shastri had died in Tashkent during the meetings that were to bring about an agreement between India and Pakistan. Coming so soon after Pandit Nehru's death, it was an especially cruel blow to India.

At the embassy we cancelled all our engagements and went into mourning. People streamed in to sign the condolence book. Soon afterwards Indira Gandhi became Prime Minister, and I remember how proud the ladies in the Indian Embassy were that a woman had reached this high office.

For me life continued to be uneasily divided between Spain and India. I often wished I could spend the whole time with Jai in Spain, because I hated being away from him. But then, when I was in India, I would become immersed in the affairs of my constituents and my parliamentary duties and left them only with reluctance. Still, I have many happy memories of the times I could spend in Spain. Madrid was a pleasant, easy-going city to live in, and we moved into a charming house in Amador de los Ríos. In many ways Spain reminded me of India, and sometimes when we drove into the villages I found it difficult to remember that we were not at home. The look of the countryside, the barren hills often topped with a fort or castle or the ruins of a crenellated wall, the harsh life of the villagers in districts where water was scarce—it could all, save for the looks and clothes of the people, have been Rajasthan. Even in the lazy summer we spent in the southern resort town of Marbella I was reminded of Rajmahal when, at night, the fragrance of jasmine pervaded the air.

We managed to see a great deal of Spain, sometimes staying with friends and sometimes in *paradores*—old palaces or monasteries converted into hotels. The Spanish government was very active in promoting tourism, and Jai and I were interested in seeing how many of their ideas we might be able to adapt for India. Once, when Zubin Mehta, the famous Indian conductor, came to the music festival in Granada, Jai couldn't leave Madrid so I went by myself to hear him. It was a superb concert and after it, Zubin, who was excellent and amusing company, made up a party and we all went to the local caves where the gipsies live to see them sing and dance flamenco. The sound of the castanets and the intricate rhythms they chattered out again reminded me of India and of certain styles of Indian music.

Diplomatic entertainments and duties took us to all sorts of occasions in different parts of the country. General Franco's annual reception for the diplomatic corps was held at La Granja, close to the ancient aqueduct of Segovia and a fairy-tale castle beautifully lit up at night. In Barcelona the annual Feria de Muestras was held, an exhibition of commercial products from different countries, at which Jai presided at the Día del India. We even visited the Balearic Islands, where there was a large Indian community—people who had been settled there as traders for a hundred years or so.

No sooner did I become absorbed in what Jai and I were seeing and doing in Spain than—so it seemed—it was time for me to fly home. Even in 1965, the year of our silver wedding anniversary, we were often apart. But the actual date itself, May ninth, I did manage to spend with Jai in, of all unexpected places, Cannes. Jai had been invited to help revive polo there, and some friends of ours had very kindly undertaken to give us a party at the casino. From Cannes I had to fly back to India, and I remember that flight particularly well because I spent the time, as I suppose anyone would on such an occasion, thinking back over my years of marriage to Jai—years he had joked about, saying, "Don't tell me I've actually managed to put up with you for twenty-five years!" I was no longer the shy little bride terribly, terribly in love and terribly, terribly in awe of her husband and his life, frightened that his family and the people of Jaipur didn't want her and wouldn't like her. What I had now become—a fairly independent, relatively active, and politically conscious woman—was, in great part, Jai's doing. Ma had always told me how lucky I was to have a husband who gave me so much freedom, who encouraged me in all my projects. If he stopped me from doing something (like learning Hindi), it was always for a good reason, though I didn't always see his logic immediately. If any of my endeavours went wrong, he was always there to advise me. Whatever successes I could count were always accomplished with his help and backing. Over the years we had evolved the same interests and the same ambitions—the good of Jaipur above all—and these, in turn, had made us friends and partners, trusting and loyal to each other. I wasn't the only one to feel that Jai was a pillar of strength. The whole family knew it and relied on it. He united me with his children and other members of his family, making us a close-knit group, deeply concerned with each other's welfare, and so we remain to this day. But the thing I remember best of all that went through my mind on that flight back from Cannes was what a precious and reassuring feeling it is to know that somebody is always on your side, no matter what.

Now, when I look back over the events of my life, I think of that year, highlighted by our silver wedding anniversary, as the last year of untrammelled happiness and success that I've known. Until then, except for the premature deaths of Ila and Indrajit, I had had to face no tragedies and had suffered no deprivations. These past several years have been, in contrast, the most taxing and the saddest I have ever known. I have wondered whether my participation in politics was worth-while—indeed, whether I had anything at all to offer people—but such questions did not bother me then. Somehow Jai, by his support, made it possible for me to go on, though I continued to be deeply disturbed by the feeling that I was failing to do justice to either my public or my personal life by trying to be in two places at once.

In 1966, Bubbles married the Princess Sirmur. I had come back to Jaipur ahead of Jai to make all the extensive and complicated arrangements, for the wedding was to be attended not only by members of the family but by many friends from abroad as well. In the middle of what should have been a happy and festive occasion, my beloved brother Bhaiya had a serious accident during a polo game that had been arranged as part of the celebration. The horse he was riding fell, bringing Bhaiya down too, and rolled over him. All of

Right: Jai and Bubbles, 1965.

Below: Prince Philip, Bubbles, myself, and Jai at a reception in H.R.H.'s honour at the City Palace, 1965.

Right: Bubbles arriving at his wedding.

Below: Jai and Prince Philip after polo in Jaipur. Joey is in the background, in a white shirt.

us were frantic, for Bhaiya was in critical condition for weeks. Jai had to fly back to Spain, but I stayed on until his life was out of danger. Even then it was difficult to rejoice at his "recovery." He never regained his health and remained what he hated most—a semi-invalid, in constant need of care and unable to engage in the sports he loved so much.

Later, when I had rejoined Jai in Spain, we were invited to stay with the Domecq family, the producers of the famous sherry. It was the time when the grape harvest was in and all of Jerez was celebrating. The fascinating *feria*, the superb horses, the thrill of bullfights, and the evenings of music and flamenco all should have made for the kind of time I love best. But I couldn't get the thought of Bhaiya and his senselessly cruel fate out of my head.

The next year, back in India, it was again time for general elections. Five years had elapsed since I won my seat in Parliament, and now I had to face the electorate again. A great deal had happened in those five years to change the political picture in India. Mrs. Gandhi, far from being a submissive woman, willing to take the advice of the Congress Party elders, had proved to have a strong mind of her own. With the growing support of the younger Congress members she was leading the party to a far more radical position in domestic policy. Meanwhile, in Rajasthan, the Swatantra Party's success in the last elections had made for all sorts of odd shifts and jockeying for positions in our own party and in other parties too. Among other things the Swatantra Party leaders thought that this time, by forming a coalition with the right-wing, orthodox Hindu Jana Sangh, we might win more seats for the Opposition in Parliament and the state assemblies.

It was clearly the correct thing to do to avoid splitting the opposition vote, but to me it seemed like little more than political suicide. I felt that one of the important aspects of the Swatantra was that its members were secular-minded, and I was particularly worried that an alliance with an avowedly Hindu party like the Jana Sangh would lose us our crucial Muslim vote. I knew that I had received many Muslim votes in the 1962 elections, thanks largely, I think, to Jai's decisive and reassuring action at the time of the partition of India and Pakistan. There had been some caution and nervousness, but no ill feeling between Hindus and Muslims in the old state of Jaipur. This situation would now be seriously threatened.

I wrote to Rajaji to tell him about my anxieties and my feelings, but party discipline prevailed. So, on the very day I arrived from Spain, I had to join other Swatantra Party representatives in Jaipur as, sitting around our dining-room table in the palace, we hammered out an electoral agreement. The meeting did nothing to alleviate my fears. The Jana Sangh kept demanding some of our most secure seats, and, in the end, worn down by their persistence, we had to concede a few. I got the impression, besides, that the Jana Sangh in Rajasthan resented the foundation of the Swatantra Party and felt—probably quite correctly—that we had captured many of their votes. Even in those early days I was afraid that the Jana Sangh would turn out to be competitors rather than allies and that we would have done much better to fight the elections alone. However, the pact was settled. And then another complication and, as I saw it, a further diluting of our strength appeared. The Congress Party in Rajasthan split, not on ideological grounds but because of dissatisfaction with the allotment of seats. They also wanted to reach an electoral agreement with us. Their argument was that unless all the opposition parties formed some kind of electoral alliance, their vote would be hopelessly divided and the Congress Party, even with a minority, would still be returned to power. So the breakaway section of the Congress also took over a number of seats the Swatantra had intended to contest.

That wasn't all. The boundaries of my own Jaipur parliamentary constituency had been gerrymandered so that, while in 1962 the whole of it had been in Jaipur District, it now extended to an area in what used to be the neighbouring state of Jodhpur. This meant that Jaipur City itself was only on the very edge of my constituency and, as a result, I had to do far more travelling and spend even more nights away from home. If, as before, I campaigned for other representatives as well as for myself, I should be covering most of Jaipur State and a good part of Jodhpur, too.

A further time-consuming business was finding suitable candidates for Pat's and Joey's constituencies. Both of them had become disillusioned with politics and had refused to stand for election again. It wasn't too difficult to find someone to take Pat's parliamentary seat, but Joey's State Assembly seat was another matter. Nobody was prepared to face his opponent, the formidable Home Minister of Rajasthan. Our party members insisted on having a strong candidate of our own because they wished to tie down the Minister to his constituency and so prevent him from travelling and campaigning elsewhere for other Congress candidates. Some candidates from our party actually threatened to withdraw unless I contested the seat myself. Time was running short, everyone seemed adamant in their stand, and when, finally, there seemed no alternative, I agreed. I knew from the beginning that it was a bad decision. I could spare very little time to concentrate on that particular seat. I had to campaign for several other candidates throughout Rajasthan and, most important, I had to cover my own parliamentary constituency.

Anyhow, I filed my nomination, prepared myself in my mind to lose that Assembly seat, and left it to our party workers to do most of the campaigning in that area. Because it was so late—the pre-election arguments, decisions, coalitions, and selection of candidates had taken so much time—I plunged desperately and unwisely into three hectic weeks of electioneering. Exhausted by all the travel, the speeches, and my other responsibilities, I fell ill with herpes and was confined to bed for the two most crucial weeks of the campaign.

All I could think about was how different all this was from the suspenseful exhilaration of my last campaign. I telephoned Jai in Madrid merely to hear the sound of his voice, although I didn't tell him how miserable I felt. But he knew me well enough to guess and offered to drop everything and come at once. Feeling better at the mere suggestion, I told him not to do this because he was, anyway, due to come to India in three weeks on leave. All the same, knowing how unhappy and lonely I was and understanding how horrid it was to have no one to come home to, he cabled Pat to send his wife (Ila's daughter), and their little son to stay with me in Jaipur, just for company. Once my fever was over, I started, more feebly, to campaign again.

The election results in Rajasthan were close. Of the 184 seats in the State Assembly, the Congress Party secured 89, while the opposition parties together won 95 seats, of which the Swatantra Party held 49, the Jana Sangh 22, the Independents 15, the Socialists 8, and the Communists, 1. The Home Minister defeated me for the Assembly seat I had contested, but I retained my seat in Parliament with a large majority, though not, this time, of any record-breaking proportions. In contrast to 1962, there were no victory celebrations, for we had hard and urgent work to do. Somehow we had to reconcile all the opposition members and form the necessary coalition, however uneasy, so that we could go to the Governor of Rajasthan and show that we had a majority in the State Assembly. It was the duty of the Governor to invite the majority party to form the state government.

When we presented our case to the Governor, he was noncommittal and we realized that he seemed to be delaying his decision. The regulation stated that the Assembly should be called within ten days of the announcement of the election results. Therefore his delay in inviting either the Congress leader or the Opposition leader to form a government made us rather suspicious. He certainly would not have equivocated in this manner on his own responsibility. We had reason to believe that he was continually receiving instructions from Delhi to try to retain Rajasthan for the ruling party, particularly since the Congress had already lost six states in the elections.

In Jaipur, political tension rose high. We knew that delay would benefit the Congress Party by giving them time to bribe away our slender majority. One of our members had already been persuaded to join the Congress immediately after he had won on an opposition ticket. We only had to lose three more and our fight to form the government would be destroyed. We knew we would have to act fast and decisively. We were determined not to give in and agreed that the safest thing to do would be to keep all our elected members together at the fort belonging to Colonel Kesri Singh's family, twelve miles outside Jaipur, safe from Congress blandishments, until the Governor gave his decision.

Soon we were indignant to hear that an anti-riot regulation banning gatherings of more than five persons had been imposed in the section of Jaipur where the Governor and the ministers had their residences. We quickly learned the reason for it. The very next day the Governor invited the leader of the Congress Party to form the government of Rajasthan.

Immediately we called a big protest meeting in the city proper, at which we introduced all the elected members of our new coalition party so that the people could see and count our majority for themselves. And the next day the leaders of the Opposition decided to break the Governor's ban by going in a body to his residence and asking him to reverse his decision.

Early in the morning we all met in the center of the city. Crowds of people were there before us, shouting anti-Congress slogans and yelling in unison that democracy was being murdered. As the leaders started their march towards the Governor's residence, the crowd followed. When they reached the area where the ban was in force, our leaders tried to persuade the massive crowd to turn back, but nobody would listen. Then I was asked, personally, to speak to them. The crowd gave me an overwhelming welcome but were in no mood to listen to any pleas that they should turn back. Instead they shouted over and over again that they would fight with me, that together we would keep democracy alive in India. I walked among the people and everywhere they courteously made a path for me, but they paid no attention to my advice and insisted on accompanying the leaders.

The moment they stepped into the residential area where the ban was in force the police, well prepared for their arrival, used tear gas on the crowd and beat the people back with baton charges. They never reached the Governor's house, and that day a twenty-four-hour curfew was imposed on Jaipur City. The busy daily life came to a standstill, no business was carried on, and everyone waited to see what would happen next. All the leaders except myself who took part in the procession were arrested.

Desperate to do something to avert a further eruption, when the crowd might well do more than just shout slogans, Jai and I flew to Delhi to see both the President, Dr. Radhakrishnan, and the Home Minister of the Central Government, Mr. Chavan. The Home Minister promised to lift the curfew. The President, too, was sympathetic and told me that we would have a chance to prove our majority when the State Assembly met. This we could do in the election of the Speaker. He made it sound easy. But I asked him to persuade the Government to advance the date of the opening of the

Assembly, pointing out that in other states the assemblies had already been convened, while in ours the opening was being delayed presumably to give the Congress leaders time to persuade the crucial three of our members to defect.

Jai and I were greatly reassured by our visit to New Delhi. That afternoon the radio announced that the curfew had been lifted in Jaipur. But then, as people started moving out of their houses and congregating as usual on the streets, the police opened fire on them. The first victim was a young boy, not more than fourteen years old. There were nine dead, forty-nine wounded, and no mention of the number missing. This ghastly news greeted us as we arrived at the Jaipur airport. Numb with horror, I wanted only to go straight to the city; Jai, however, persuaded me not to, reminding me that I would be a rallying point and that this might provoke the police to fire again. We then learned that police units from neighbouring states had been called in, because, I suppose, Rajasthan police might have been reluctant to fire on their own people in so brutal and cowardly a manner. This tense state of emergency lasted for days and I spent my time visiting hospitals, comforting the dying, and sympathizing with the wounded—I never saw a Congress member or government official visit the hospital.

The Assembly was to meet six days later. Our new coalition was still intact and so, with all our elected members in control, we gathered at Rajmahal to decide on our nomination for a Speaker. We intended to expose the Congress minority on the very first issue. We had just come to a decision when we heard the astounding news that President's Rule had been imposed on Rajasthan. This is a form of temporary government that is invoked when no party within a state is able to form a government or when conditions are so unsettled that the state is ruled by the Central Government until one party has a majority.

The excuse for President's Rule in Rajasthan was that the leader of the Congress Party felt that he couldn't form a government in the face of the people's outrage at so much bloodshed. Constitutionally, the Governor should then have asked the leader of the opposition coalition to form a government, but instead of doing this he called for President's Rule to avoid falling into disfavor with the powerful

Congress rulers in the Central Government in New Delhi. To counter this move, we took all the elected members of our party to New Delhi to have them, quite simply, counted by the President and the Home Minister. This time, however, they were non-committal. Though we knew that their attitude was, in a way, an admission of the Congress Party's defeat, still we realized that they were going to continue their delaying tactics until we lost our fragile majority. It was only a question of time. The Congress, with influential jobs and ministerial posts to offer, was bound to tempt away our less stalwart members. There seemed little point, now, in my remaining in India, so I joined Jai in Spain.

At that long distance I received the news that I had, discouragedly, expected: Some of our opposition members had defected. The Congress Party again had an absolute majority. President's Rule was removed and the Congress leader was invited to form a government. The whole affair was a bitter experience which did much to disillusion me with politics. The opportunism and the lack of principle displayed by our legislators amazed me. And later on I discovered that Rajasthan had the doubtful privilege of setting a style of political cynicism that other states were quick to copy. It was during times like this, when I was depressed and filled with a sense of futility, that I found Jai's support and the security of his presence most profoundly reassuring.

Even in Spain, without day-to-day news of events in India, we knew that yet another change was to be added to the long chain of revolutions that had taken place in our lives. Early in 1966 a resolution had been moved at the Congress Party convention seeking to abolish the princes' privy purses. Although there had not been a quorum at the convention for that particular resolution, the Home Minister in the Central Government, Mr. Chavan, had taken up the issue as part of the Congress program. Now, with the elections safely over, we were pretty certain that the Government would soon go back on the agreements that had been made with the princes when they ceded their states to the new Indian Union.

Jai believed that the assurances given by these agreements

would, in the not too distant future, prove worthless. The most radical members of the Congress Party, who called themselves the "Young Turks," were agitating more and more intensively for the total abolition of the privy purses. Their influence in the ruling party was growing, and Jai felt that the wisest thing the princes could do would be to reach some kind of compromise with the Government. Many of the other princes, however, felt that the Government was unjustified in reneging on their agreement and rejected Jai's more realistic view that it was not worth defending the privy purses as a point of privilege; it was more important to negotiate with the Government to protect the princes' families and many dependents who had no other source of income and for whom the privy purses were primarily intended. Jai had worked out a blueprint for a settlement of this sort, and when it came to the point of serious and constructive action, the Government seemed sympathetic and willing to find a compromise.

In September of 1968 Jai was to go to India to discuss the whole matter with the other princes, and I was eager to spend some time with Ma, whose health had been deteriorating with a variety of illnesses, the most severe of which was cardiac asthma. I left Spain a few days ahead of Jai and reached Delhi on the sixth of September. I immediately phoned Ma in Bombay. She was delighted to learn that I was in India and asked me to come to Bombay on the eleventh. She told me she had also asked my sister Menaka to be there on the same date. In spite of the series of ailments that had afflicted her, Ma had sounded well on the telephone and this reassured me. I made plans to fly to Bombay on the eleventh, as she had asked, but at the last moment I was detained by some urgent political work and postponed my departure by one day.

Early the next morning Menaka telephoned to say that Ma's condition had suddenly become much worse. My plane was due to leave only a few hours later, and I was watching the clock, paralysed by anxiety and childishly trying to will the hands to move faster. Just before I left for the airport I was informed that Ma had died. Menaka had been with her at the end.

Jai and I flew to Bombay as planned and were met by a pale,

stricken Menaka. Together we went back to Ma's flat, both of us unable to speak about her and both still unable to believe that Ma was not with us any more, would never again be with us. Soon after, Jai had to leave for Spain. I longed desperately to be with him, knowing that his presence alone could provide comfort.

Instead, Menaka and I began the long, heartbreaking job of settling Ma's affairs and disposing of her possessions in the manner she had wanted. Every room in the flat was still filled with her presence. The little gold box which held the specially scented areca nut she liked to chew after meals still stood on the small French table beside her favourite chair. The flowers with which she always surrounded herself were fading in the silver and crystal vases, and neither Menaka nor I had the heart to either throw them out or order fresh ones—Ma would never have tolerated wilting flowers.

Menaka and I packed and sorted and answered the telephone and talked about everything under the sun except Ma. For some hours every day we had to sit in the drawing-room and receive the callers who came to offer their condolences. That was the worst part. Both of us, as well as the visitors, I'm sure, could so easily imagine the room with Ma in it, the center of an endless stream of guests, filling the place with her easy warmth and fun. Even when she was ill, her involvement with life had been so intense it was impossible to grasp the fact that she was dead.

And all the time that Menaka and I sat exchanging platitudes with callers, the full-length, life-size portrait of Ma by László gazed dreamily down at us from the drawing-room wall. There was the tiny, fragile young woman, her diaphanous sky-blue sari drawn over her head to frame the exquisite face with its huge eyes and its odd, half-sad mouth. That was Ma at the moment when the whole world seem to be her domain and when all the men were in love with her and when she would—any minute now—smile her famous smile and make one of her unexpected remarks, outrageous or infinitely kind. She couldn't be dead.

Only when, from time to time, I caught Menaka's eye, did I remember with a sudden struggling sense of reality that she, Bhaiya, and I were the only ones now left alive to share the memories of those golden, carefree childhood days in Cooch Behar.

Chapter 19

Jai's Last Polo Game

WHEN I JOINED Jai in Spain a month after Ma's death I threw myself into activity of any sort, as I always do when I am deeply upset. The social life in Madrid, sporting events, entertaining—anything would do as long as it kept me fully occupied. For once I was relieved to be out of India, not only because I was away from continual reminders of Ma but also because further defections in our legislatures had increased my disillusionment with politics and I badly needed a change of atmosphere. Besides all this, I had begun to realize that my extensive engagement in politics had led me to neglect Jai and Jagat. I was now resolved to give them all my attention.

It wasn't long, however, before Jai told me that he was asking to be relieved of his ambassadorial post. He felt that events were moving so rapidly in India and the position of the princes was becoming so precarious that he really should be there to play whatever useful part he could in helping to direct the changes that were inevitable.

Enough time had elapsed since I had gone so gratefully to Spain for my deeper feelings about India and about Jaipur, in particular, to have risen again to the surface of my mind. I was glad to get home and to know that, once again, Jai and I could spend most of our time together. Jai had to be in New Delhi quite often to take part in the negotiations that were going on between the Government and the Concord of Princes, a body which had been set up when the idea of abolishing privy purses had first been raised and which sought to represent the interests of the former rulers.

As for myself, there was plenty of work to command my full attention in Rajasthan. The western part of the state had been badly hit by drought, and I went there to see for myself the condition of the people and what might be done to help them. The Government had organized famine relief work, but much of this was an exercise in futility. The roads that were being cleared would soon, with the strong, scorching winds, be covered again with sand. No rains would ever fill the tanks that were being dug. To me it was heartbreaking to see the proud and sturdy desert people doing this gruelling and pointless work in the dust and heat. No matter how much I and my fellow workers agitated, the State Government seemed more concerned with party politics and the juggling of power in the legislature than in pursuing a vigorous programme of rural electrification and irrigation which would help to solve the problem of drought on a long-range basis.

Jai was having his own difficulties with the State Government. For him the last straw was the extraordinary obstructionism displayed over what would appear to most people as an entirely nonpolitical issue. Jai had, largely with his own money and partly from public contributions, erected a marble statue of his ancestor, Maharaja Sawai Jai Singh, the founder of Jaipur City. He wanted the President of India to unveil this statue but ran into the most unreasonable delays and complications when he tried to place his request through the usual government channels. Eventually he approached President Zakir Hussein directly and found him delighted to come to Jaipur, and he did, in fact, unveil the statue in a simple but dignified ceremony.

If it hadn't been clear before, it was certainly quite plain now that the Government's attitude to the princes was far from friendly. Jai, with his usual practical equanimity, wasted no time on fruitless recriminations. Anticipating further changes in our circumstances, he planned to move us to a smaller house that was to be built on the grounds of Rambagh. He was concerned not only about the future of his immediate family but also for the future of his other relatives and the many people who depended on him for a livelihood. Some years before, when Rambagh became a hotel and when we set up the museum in the City Palace and opened it to the public, Jai's strong sense of justice had made him distribute his private lands to those who had served him for more than ten years. But there were still a large number of people for whose welfare he was responsible.

With all the arrangements for our future still in the planning stage, we left in May, as we normally did, for England, where Jai was to judge a horse show at Windsor. During that summer we travelled a lot, staying with Spanish friends in Marbella, going to the Argentine in the autumn, stopping in Venezuela and Brazil on the way, seeing some of the best polo in the world and as much else as we could possibly cram in. I don't really believe in premonitions, but that summer I was plagued by a haunting feeling that somehow our time was running out and we should do as much and see as much as we could reasonably manage.

When we returned to Delhi, Jai clearly felt unwell He looked extremely tired and had none of his usual energy, but we both thought that this was only fatigue after the long plane journey. He went on to Jaipur, apparently quite untroubled, while I stayed in Delhi to attend Parliament. In Jaipur, Jai unaccountably fainted. I learned about this only after I got there myself, the next day. I insisted on calling in an eminent heart specialist who happened to live in Jaipur. After examining Jai he advised a great deal of rest and ordered Jai to avoid exerting himself. Jai, of course, paid no attention to what he called "all this silly fuss about nothing," although he did confess that sometimes he felt very tired, and went cheerfully off to Calcutta to play in the polo tournaments for the 61st Cavalry Regiment. To our delight, they won the Indian Polo Association Cup, the highest award of its kind in India. But every time Jai played, I sat on the side-lines, even more anxious than usual. He, however, assured me gaily that he felt fitter with every game.

We stayed on in Calcutta to spend the New Year with Bhaiya, and that February Bhaiya spent a few days with us in Delhi—or, rather, he had intended to spend a few days, but the night he arrived he suffered a slight heart attack, was confined to hospital for almost four weeks, and returned to convalesce in our New Delhi home. I was, myself, unwell at the time, but still we both managed to stagger out to watch Jai playing on the Delhi polo-grounds.

Polo was not Jai's only concern in Delhi. It was more his relaxation from bouts of hard work attempting to negotiate some solution to the deadlock between the princes, determined to stand on their rights about their privy purses, and the Government, equally determined to abrogate those rights.

There was to be a further meeting of the princes at the end of the month in Bombay, and Jai and I travelled down together. While I was there, I consulted doctors, who told me that I should have a major operation as soon as possible. I went into hospital at once, and was still recovering from the operation when I heard that Bhaiya had become gravely ill after he returned to Calcutta. I was distressed that I was not well enough to be with him, but Jai and Menaka went to Calcutta and returned to report that he seemed a good deal better. In April, soon after I had returned to Jaipur, Pat's wife telephoned me to say that Bhaiya wanted to talk to me. I called him immediately and told him that I longed to come to see him but the doctors refused to let me travel until I was stronger. We agreed to meet in England in May.

On the eleventh of April the telephone rang. It was my niece, Indrajit's daughter, telling me that Bhaiya was dead. In tears I ran to Jai, who had heard the news earlier but had wished to spare my feelings until it was confirmed. I had lost the person who, after Jai, was dearest to me in all the world. Sadly, we flew to Calcutta and from there on to Cooch Behar.

Bhaiya had married an English girl sometime in the 1950s. They had no children. Even if they had had a son, he would not have been recognized by the people of Cooch Behar as their maharaja. Old customs die hard in India, especially in the princely states. So Indrajit's son was anointed by the Raj Guru, the chief palace priest, as the new Maharaja of Cooch Behar. After this, Bhaiya's body was carried from the durbar hall to be cremated. Following the custom, I remained behind with the women and watched the men escort the body as the cortège moved off into the distance, past all those places that Bhaiya had loved so well.

From Cooch Behar, Jai and I went to Delhi, where Jai had to spend an interminable amount of time persuading the Home Ministry to recognize Indrajit's son as the new Maharaja of Cooch Behar. This was far from easy, especially as the ruling party was about

Jai with 61st Cavalry, 1969, after winning major tournaments in Calcutta, Delhi, and Jaipur.

to introduce a bill into Parliament to abolish the princely order entirely. But eventually Jai was able to persuade them to recognize my nephew as the Maharaja of Cooch Behar.

In May the jacarandas came into bloom, turning the sunlight pale lavender as it filtered through their branches, and this was always a signal for Jai that it was time to leave for England. When he announced this, I tried to persuade him to stay on until our wedding anniversary. We bargained for a while, and finally he agreed to stay until the seventh of May, which by the lunar calendar was our Indian anniversary. Jagat, listening to this scene, was much amused. He remarked, "You have this same argument every year, and every year Daddy wins."

So Jai had his way and left for England. I very much wanted to accompany him, but felt I had to stay until the end of the parliamentary session. That year Bhaiya's death and my own illness had kept me from attending at all. But after Jai left I felt so miserable that I was determined to join him in time for my fifty-first birthday, the twenty-third of May, even though some of the princes thought it wrong of me to leave when the bill to abolish the privy purses was about to be introduced in Parliament.

I arrived in England the day before my birthday, but in spite of my great happiness at being back with Jai, I still carried about with me a lump of wretchedness that was the loss of Bhaiya. Jai, knowing me so very well, pushed me into countless parties and social activities and, of course, his polo events. One night at a ball at Apsley House, Jai complained that he felt tired. Two days later he had a bad fall while he was umpiring a polo game. I wondered uneasily whether we should cancel the cocktail party we gave every year after the finals of the Queen's Cup. It was usually attended by the Queen and Prince Philip, as well as all our polo-players and friends. This party was to be held three days after Jai's fall, but Jai insisted that he felt much better and that our arrangements should be allowed to stand.

During the party Jai seemed quite as well as he claimed he felt, and after it we went to a dinner given by friends, where the Queen, Prince Philip, and Lord Mountbatten were all present. I remember that Jai and Dicky Mountbatten talked for a long time about the situation in India. Jai told him how upset he was by the Government's apparent determination to abolish the princely order and by what he felt was an attempt to humiliate the former rulers. Dicky said that Jai was not the kind of person who could be humiliated, and they agreed to meet later and discuss the matter more fully. The princes' difficulties were very much on Jai's mind, and he longed to talk things over with someone like Dicky, who had experience and knowledge of India, followed events there with close concern, but still retained the necessary distance to keep a sense of proportion about it all and who could, therefore, make some wise judgements. I was the wrong person for Jai to talk to. I was still deeply affected by Bhaiya's death, and, knowing this, Jai tried to shield me from anything unpleasant.

Soon after, Ascot week began, with the British parliamentary elections adding to the excitement of racing and polo. Since his fall Jai had stopped playing polo, and instead he umpired during the Ascot week tournaments. I was surprised, but not unduly alarmed, when he announced that he was going to resume the game at Cirencester. The first game there was on the twenty-fourth of June.

It was a wet and windy day, and the play was slow and unexciting. At half-time, it was drizzling and I stayed in my car with Bubbles, who had come to watch his father play, instead of going over to talk to Jai as I usually did. I looked idly across the field to where he should be and suddenly saw him lying on the ground, surrounded by a crowd of people, among them a Red Cross nurse. Trembling, I leapt out of the car and ran over to him. I remember noticing in some part of my mind that someone had kicked his helmet out of the way and this, irrationally, angered me very much.

An ambulance arrived. Bubbles climbed in with me. Jai was still unconscious, and together we drove with him to the nearest hospital. There the doctor told me Jai was dead. Unable to believe it, I pleaded with him to do something, but he merely shook his head.

Feeling that I was caught in some hideous nightmare, I wanted only to take Jai away, to take him back to the reality of our home. But there were formalities to be gone through first, forms to be filled out, papers signed. Since nothing seemed real, I was able to go through all this with what must have appeared as extraordinary patience and calm. When we finally reached home, Jagat was there waiting for us.

The following day friends streamed into the house to say good-bye to Jai. Among the visitors was the Colonel of the Life Guards Brigade. He asked if we would like a memorial service at the Guards' Chapel. I said, "Yes," feeling vaguely that Jai would have wished for this. The flowers, the sad faces, the muted atmosphere—all seemed equally dreamlike. Even when Bubbles, Jagat, and I took Jai's body home to India I was still unable to grasp the thought that my loss was irrevocable.

Only when we reached Jaipur, the city that contained so much of our life together, did I truly realize that Jai had gone forever. The airport was crowded and the city was in mourning. His body was taken to the City Palace, and there, while the people of Jaipur filed past their Maharaja, his four sons kept a night-long vigil. I can't bring myself to describe that night, or attempt to recapture my feelings, but here is an account by someone who was there:

> As his body lay in state on the night of 26 June 1970, in the famous Chandra Mahal just opposite Govind Devji's temple, in full view of the deity he loved so well, the entire city turned out to pay homage to him throughout the night, in an unending stream of sorrowful men, women and children.

The funeral procession started at nine o'clock the next morning. As Jai's body was lowered onto a gun-carriage, the proper last conveyance for a soldier maharaja, a nineteen-gun salute was fired from Mahargarh Fort, high above the city. The procession, accompanied by men carrying lighted torches and a military escort of six hundred officers and men, was a mile long. At the forefront of the procession were richly caprisoned elephants with the chief mahout carrying the golden rod bestowed by the Mogul emperors on the rulers of Amber. Behind them came the decorated camels, the horses, the durbar, and the police bands.

Amongst the mourners were a dozen former rulers and princes; and the Chief Minister of Rajasthan, together with his two predecessors and the senior members of his cabinet, all walked in the procession. As it moved slowly through the streets of Jaipur to the sound of muffled drums, every terrace, balcony, and window was thronged with people, and still more clung precariously to trees and telegraph poles in an attempt to get a last glimpse of the ruler who had so identified himself with them and their welfare.

A crowd of more than half a million people lined the four-mile route to the cremation grounds of Gaitor. Many had started out from their remote villages the previous night, travelling as much as twenty miles by bicycle, bullock-cart, or on foot. As far as one could see, there was a surging mass of humanity come to pay homage to their beloved Maharaja, Sawai Man Singh.

At eleven o'clock the procession reached the Cenotaph of the Rulers of Amber at Gaitor. The horse riders beat their drums, announcing the last journey of the architect of modern Jaipur along the road that all his great ancestors had travelled. A crowd of about a hundred thousand had found places or vantage-points on the surrounding hills overlooking the cremation ground. The body of the Maharaja was placed on the pyre. The last rites were performed, and then the Maharaj Kumar Bhawani Singh, heir apparent, lit the pyre while the firing of the nineteen-gun salute echoed around the hills.

From my room in the City Palace I heard the sound of the guns as Bubbles set light to the funeral pyre. I could hear, too, the sound of the wailing, and grief seized me almost like a physical spasm.

For a month I remained inside Rajmahal. All the boys were with me, as were Jai's younger sister, Chand, and my own sister, Menaka. Then Jagat and I left for England to attend the memorial service in the Guards' Chapel, which was to take place on the twenty-fourth of July. My small group gathered in our London flat. Jagat and the Maharaja of Jodhpur wore their black *achkans* and their ceremonial turbans and carried swords. All our staff from our Ascot house joined us, all in suitably sombre clothes. At last Dicky Mountbatten arrived to accompany us. He had been ill and the doctors had advised complete rest, but he was determined to read the tribute to Jai at the service.

The chapel was filled with many friends, and the service, in its military simplicity, was deeply moving. In such an atmosphere it was almost impossible to be brave. Afterwards, Dicky Mountbatten came back to the flat with me. His words of comfort got through to me and gave me my first, though still tremulous, confidence about facing the future and living out the rest of my life without Jai.

Other friends, too, showed me great kindness and provided the sort of support for which it is impossible to thank people. But still, when they had left there remained the reality that Jai was gone forever. Since the age of twelve I had lived almost solely for him, and now I couldn't help feeling that there was nothing left to live for. Yet Jagat was still with me. He had known his father for such a pitifully short time and had lost him just when he most needed him. I tried to hold on to that fact and to my profound responsibility to my son to force myself to take an interest in life again.

In Jaipur, people were still shaken by Jai's death. Miss Lutter, the principal of the Maharani Gayatri Devi School, had decided to collect tributes to him from all sorts of different people who had known him and then have all the letters printed in a memorial album. The range of contributions was enormous. Here, in part, is what Prince Philip wrote:

Buckingham Palace

> I am not going to try to guess what Jai meant to other people or what sort of contribution he made to life. All I know is that I gained immeasurably from his friendship in all sorts of circumstances: in the things we did together, like playing polo or shooting or just sitting and chatting under the moon in Jaipur or in a country house in England.
>
> I suppose one is affected differently by different people, some annoy and irritate, some are stimulating, others again are happy and entertaining. To me Jai had a serene quality, a sort of cheerful calm, which may well have been exasperating for some but to me it was a most endearing and enjoyable characteristic. He combined with that a very rare quality in men, he was supremely civilized. Kind and modest, but with an unerring instinct for the highest standards of human ambition and behaviour.
>
> Perhaps this is a prejudiced view but then friendship is prejudice.
>
> (Signed) Philip

In this same volume, which was titled, *A Treasury of Tributes to the Late His Highness Saramad-I-Rajaha-I-Hindustan Raj Rajendra Maharaja Dhiraj, Lieutenant-General Sir Sawai Man Singhji Bahadur the Second, G.C.S.I., G.C.I.E., L.L.D., Maharaja of Jaipur*, giving Jai all his full titles and honours, there also appears a tribute from the man who took care of Jai's dogs. He couldn't speak any English, so his contribution is printed in Hindi.

> I served the late Maharaja Sahib for forty years. He was happy with me. Even if there was a fault he would never say a word. Maharaja Sahib used to go for a walk in the garden. I felt very happy in watching him do so. When he was at the swimming-pool, I used to take food for the dogs. He liked to feed them himself. I was very sad when he went to England. We were all very happy with the news of his coming back. I kept on looking for the aeroplane. Everybody was happy on his arrival at Rajmahal. He made me a Jagirdar [land-owner] before leaving for England, but how could I know that he would never return? Really, it was a great misfortune for us all. We could not see him again. I would have been the happiest man if Maharaja Sahib had returned. He always liked me. I will always remember him.
>
> Mangal Singh
> *In charge of Kennels*

One of Jai's gardeners, a Muslim, also wrote a tribute:

> His late Highness Maharaja Sawai Man Singh was born at Isarda in 1911. He was a great ruler. He was very fond of playing polo, and he was one of the famous players of the world. When there was a game of polo in Jaipur, people used to come in countless numbers to see the polo and to cheer him with shouts and slogans in his praise. He also loved his people very much. He considered it his duty to help people in trouble. He never differentiated between Hindus and Muslims. When some Muslims wanted to leave Jaipur during the communal disturbances, he stopped them and told them, "No Muslim should leave Jaipur and go. They are all like the hair of my chest." The Muslims of Jaipur will never forget this.
>
> I used to work in the gardens of this great Maharaja. The Maharani Sahiba got me admitted in the school and it is due to

her kindness that I am now studying in the 10th class. Every summer Maharaja Sahib used to spend in England. As usual summertime came and Maharaja Sahib went to England. Who could know that he will not return? He died on the polo field. The world was shocked with the news. When his body was brought to Jaipur, people thronged the route from the aerodrome to the City Palace in such a manner as if Maharaja Sahib would speak on seeing them. People were crying—if we had known that our Maharaja would not return, we would never have allowed him to go.

Mohammed Shamim

That same year—in fact, before I left England following the memorial service for Jai in the Guards' Chapel—I received news of yet more tragedies in our family. I remember so well how the litany of names used to roll out in my mind like some dreadful personal casualty list in an unexplained war: Ila. Indrajit. Ma. Bhaiya. Jai. And then the additions of Jai's daughter Mickey, still in her early forties, and my cousin Gautam, with whom I used to play in Cooch Behar in our childhood, and finally Jai's dearly loved older brother, Bahadur Singh, who had "adopted" Jagat, making him, now, the Raja of Isarda. All dead.

Jagat was, at the time, learning museology to help in our museum. He stayed on in England, and I returned alone to an empty Rajmahal.

Chapter 20

My Life Today

It is now five years since Jai's death—for me the most difficult and lonely of my life. Although I knew that Jai would not have wished me to retreat into stricken seclusion, overpowered by grief, that is precisely what I did. I don't know how long it might have been before I left the haven of my rooms in Rajmahal if political events had not forced me out to face the whole shoddy and meaningless world of public life again.

The bill to amend the Constitution to do away with the princes' privy purses was introduced in Parliament on 18 May 1970. This bill, the forerunner of yet more sweeping changes in the position of the princes, chilled all of us, not so much because of the personal monetary losses we might suffer but because of what it displayed of Mrs. Gandhi's government's view of history and of its own constitutional promises.

I may seem to be prejudiced—I probably am—so I will quote India's most eminent lawyer, N. A. Palkhivala, for the historical background against which this bill should be set. In an eloquent pamphlet titled, "The Privy Purse: Legal and Moral Aspects," he wrote:

> When the dawn of independence came for India in 1947 the biggest political question was whether the Rulers of the Indian States would make the supreme sacrifice and immolate their States at the altar of national unity. An India deprived of the Indian States would have lost all coherence, since the States formed a great cruciform barrier separating all four quarters of the country. The accession of the Indian States to the Dominion

of India was such a vital necessity that Coupland raised the rhetorical question, "India would live if its Moslem limbs in the North-West and North-East were amputated, but could it live without its heart?"

Mr. Palkhivala then went on to quote the White Paper on Indian States, published by the Government of India in March 1950:

> Moving voluntarily with the times, the Princes, big and small, co-operated in exploding the myth that India's independence would founder on the rock of Princely intransigence. The edifice of democratic India rises on the true foundation of the co-ordinated effort of the Princes and the people. . . . But for the patriotic co-operation of the Princes, the tremendous change that has come over India for the mutual benefit of the People and the Rulers would not have been possible. Traditionally habituated to an order of personal rule, the new order has involved a radical shift for them. They have given evidence of imagination, foresight and patriotism by accepting the change with a good grace. By their appreciation of the aspirations of the people they made integration of States and transfer of power to the people smooth and peaceful. They may well claim to be co-architects in building a free and democratic India in which the people of the Provinces and the people of the States will enjoy alike the full measure of freedom and march together as citizens of free India.

After all that, it may seem absurd that the Government was balking at paying what amounted to less than 50 million rupees—under 7 million dollars—for all the princely privy purses combined. The Maharaja of Mysore, of the two hundred and seventy-nine princes, got the most, 2,600,000 rupees, and the Ruler of Katodia, a tiny state in Saurashtra, got the least, 192 rupees each year. It may seem equally absurd that the princes should make a fuss about the whole question. But on both sides a matter of principle was involved: for the Government, the Socialist path they had chosen, and for us, a constitutional right.

In any case, the debate in Parliament over the privy purses was highly charged emotionally, but the bill was passed. It was then presented to the Rajya Sabha, the Upper House, without whose assent no bill could become law, and three days later it was defeated.

There was great dismay among the members of the ruling party, and the Union Cabinet met immediately. They decided that abolishing the privy purses was not enough; it should be merely a part of a much larger move to de-recognize the princes altogether. They advised the President of this decision. He happened, at the time, to be on tour in Hyderabad, in south-central India, but within twenty minutes of receiving the message about the Cabinet's decision, he signed the order de-recognizing the princes.

Naturally there were protests and action from the princes. They felt that the President had acted unconstitutionally and sought to deprive them of guaranteed rights and privileges. They were told that the President had exercised a non-judiciable political power. What he had done was in the nature of an "Act of State," permissible because, with the departure of the British, "paramountcy" had devolved on India as the "successor State."

The princes appealed to the courts, and this is the majority judgement of the Supreme Court of India:

> It is difficult to conceive of the Government of a Democratic Republic exercising against its citizens "paramountcy" claimed to be inherited from an imperial power. The power and authority which the Union may exercise against its citizens and even aliens spring from and are strictly circumscribed by the Constitution. . . . There can be no Act of State by a State against its own citizens. . . . The question whether the Rulers can be de-recognized by the President is of secondary importance. What is of utmost importance for the future of our democracy is whether the executive in this country can flout the mandates of the Constitution and set at naught legislative enactments at its discretion. If it is held that it can then our hitherto assumption that in this country we are ruled by laws and not by men and women must be given up as erroneous.

So, for a short time, the privy purses, the privileges, and the titles were all restored to the former maharajas.

Then the Prime Minister made an unexpected move. She dissolved Parliament and called for elections a year ahead of schedule. Many of us felt that February of 1971 was hardly the time to involve the country in the huge and time-consuming business of fresh elections. We were on the brink of a confrontation with Pakistan over the Bangladesh issue and what should be done about the refugees streaming into India for protection from the menace of West Pakistan's atrocities against its subjects in the East.

Still, once the elections were announced, political leaders again began to rally support, and in Rajasthan I was again approached to run for the Opposition from Jaipur and to help in campaigning for other parliamentary candidates. I was still in mourning and my heart seemed to have gone out of any public endeavour. I was very much in the mood to resign altogether from public life, but two letters persuaded me not to. One was from the grandmother of the present Maharaja of Jodhpur, and the other from the Dowager Maharani of Bikaner. Both ladies told me that while they sympathized with my feelings and quite understood that I did not wish to face the public in my sorrow, I must put my grief aside and continue to do my duty. It was imperative, they felt, for all of us to oppose the Congress Party. I had affection and great respect for both of them, and at their urging I filed my nomination.

For me, it was a terrible election. I had no sense of security without Jai. The Congress Party, with their new slogan, *Garibi hatao,* which means "Remove poverty," won with an overwhelming majority. The Swatantra seats in Parliament shrank from thirty-four to seven. I found that with only a half-hearted effort I still won my seat by over 50,000 more votes than my Congress opponent received, and reluctantly I at last came out of my retreat and went back to Parliament.

Once the elections were over, the Government had to give the major part of its attention to coping with the Bangladesh refugees. On a visit to Cooch Behar, now a border state, I had already seen the misery of the millions of people who had fled from their homes to take refuge in India. The tension between Pakistan and India was mounting, so the final act of the princely drama was played out against this background of gathering war clouds.

In August of 1971 the Twenty-sixth Amendment of the Constitution was introduced in Parliament. This sought to delete those provisions of the Constitution relating to the recognition of a ruler and to payment of the privy purses—in short, the de-recognition of the princes, unsuccessful before, was to be brought about by amending the Constitution. In the first week of December the bill was passed by both houses of Parliament. On the twenty-eighth of December the bill received the assent of the President. With that, the princes lost all that they were promised in the solemn agreements made when they merged their territories with the rest of India. Their privileges, their titles, and their privy purses were all abolished.

During the debate in Parliament, the Prime Minister, Mrs. Gandhi, declared that there was, in the country, a great levelling process, a process that was abolishing class division and class distinction. A great community of equals was being created, and she invited the princes to join it. "We may be depriving the princes of luxury," she said, "but we are giving them the opportunity to be men."

My nephew, the Maharaja of Baroda, replied, "Twenty-two years ago, on this floor, we were referred to as co-architects of Indian Independence. Today we are branded as an anachronism and, later, as reactionaries obstructing the path of building an egalitarian society."

In the blind drive to create men who are all equal in a Utopian society, the futility of legislating about the accident of birth seemed to have entirely escaped the great levellers of society. I couldn't help thinking how much more convincing the whole "levelling" process would have been if Mrs. Gandhi had introduced a bill in Parliament for the abolition of the caste system. This system, in spite of the efforts of reformers as revered as Mahatma Gandhi, still maintains its death grip on most of India. For centuries the caste system has rigidly divided Indian society.

Changes are, of course, inevitable. Not even the princes really believed that the agreements made with them by the Indian Government would last forever without, at some stage, being reviewed. But we had all hoped that the process would be one of mutual consent, rather than one of unilateral action on the part of the Government.

One small and entirely unimportant episode brought the change home to me. Soon after the bill de-recognizing the princes was passed, I had occasion to renew my passport. When it arrived, I saw that I was described as "Gayatri Devi of Jaipur (M.P.), Profession: Housewife/Member of Parliament," and "Holder's husband's name" was "Late Sawai Man Singhji of Jaipur."

I wrote to the passport office to insist that at the time Jai died he was still a maharaja. Whatever constitutional amendments may have been passed, however much those of us still alive had to relinquish our titles and rank, it could not affect the dead. Jai died, as he had lived, a prince.

The passport office made the alteration in my passport. "Holder's husband's name" now reads: "His late Highness Sawai Man Singh Bahadur, Maharaja of Jaipur."

Today my life is very different from what it was five years ago, mainly because Jai is no longer there, and also because the political and social climate is so different. When I am in Jaipur there are various projects that keep me occupied. There is, for instance, a good deal of work connected with the City Palace Museum and the Jaipur collection it houses. I am one of the trustees and have to meet with the other trustees regularly. We have appointed a new director, and I see him often to discuss the progress of the new hall we are building and the rearrangement of those parts of the collection that will be displayed in it. There is always some new problem to be solved and much planning for the future.

I continue my interest in my girls' school. Miss Lutter still runs it excellently, and the result is that more students than we can possibly take seek admission to the school. Like every educational institution we have constantly to expand to keep abreast with the times, and this, of course, needs funds. In India as in the rest of the world the cost of everything is soaring, and so we seem to be constantly trying to raise money. There are several other projects in which I am interested. One of them is a school of arts and crafts which I started some years back to ensure that the handicrafts of Jaipur would continue to flourish. More recently, with two young sons of the erstwhile nobility of Jaipur as partners, I have formed a company to export cotton rugs, or "durries" as they are called locally. I find this most satisfying as it gives employment to the weavers and also keeps this traditional craft alive. To begin with we had many difficulties, so when our first consignment was sent abroad we were so pleased that we gave a huge party to celebrate.

However, all that I endeavour to accomplish does not meet with such success. Before leaving Jaipur in May 1970 Jai had told me that he wished to make the area surrounding Moti Doongri, the little fort he had given me years ago, into a park for the public. He had taken the officials of the Urban Improvement Trust round the area and told them what he wanted done there, but still to this day I have not been given official sanction for this seemingly simple project.

And then there are my constituents to be considered. When the flag goes up over my house they know that I am in residence, and they come in to see me with their problems. The people in the urban areas want plots of land to build their own houses. Often the farmers will come with presents of fresh fruit and vegetables and will stay for a while to talk and tell me what the feelings of the villagers are about recent events. Last year they came in flocks from all the villages around, agitatedly asking me to intervene on their behalf to repeal the levy that had been imposed on grain produce. I tried to calm them down as best I could and told them that I would write letters to the ministers concerned, but that I couldn't guarantee that anything would come of my appeal on their behalf.

Apart from trying to help my constituents I do not take a very active part in politics. I go to Delhi when Parliament is in session. The Swatantra Party which I had joined with such high hopes and so much enthusiasm has been split up. Rajaji, its leader, is dead, and most of its members absorbed in a new political party. I sit with them but I remain an Independent member of Parliament.

It is not that I am not interested in politics, but I find that I have not been able to help the people of Jaipur as I would have liked—besides which, politics is a full-time job and with Jai gone and so many problems connected with his estate claiming my attention I just do not have the time. Bubbles has given up the army and now lives in Jaipur. He has a lot to keep him occupied, and I help him where I can. One of our major tasks is to make good public use of our properties. For instance, we are now transforming the huge garage that we had in Rambagh, which could accommodate sixty cars, into a motel for visitors who cannot afford the high charges of expensive hotels. The jungle around our shooting-lodge at Sawai Madhopur has been chosen as one of the nine preserves in India to protect the tiger. We have, therefore, opened the lodge to the public, and anyone wishing to see wild-life can stay there. There is still a lot more to be done, but I find that the boys do not share my sense of urgency. They are young and probably feel that they have plenty of time to pursue their projects. Joey and Pat have also made Jaipur their headquarters. Joey manages the Rambagh Palace Hotel and other family business, and Pat has a number of industries in which he is interested. Jagat spends half the year in Jaipur and the other half working in England. In the hills around Isarda which he inherited from Jai's older brother, Bahadur Singh, there is a certain kind of quartz that is used in making lenses. With Pat's help Jagat is planning to excavate this quartz and bring some industry to Isarda, as Jai had always hoped to do.

I moved out of Rajmahal about a year and a half ago and as my new house was not ready I went to Moti Doongri, set high on its hill. From there I could look down on the whole of Jaipur. I used to sit on the terrace and wonder what the future held for the city that Maharaja Sawai Jai Singh had planned with such meticulous care almost 250 years ago and which every ruler who succeeded him had enhanced—the last of them being Jai. From my vantage-point I could see how the city is expanding day by day, and I wondered whether it would one day become one of those anonymous characterless metropolises that could be anywhere in the world. No, that could not be possible; the hills crowned with forts that cradle Jaipur would always be there, and so would that clear blue sky. The air would always be pure—or would it? Jaipur has a westerly wind, and with a typical lack of foresight the town planning authorities have allotted land to the west of the city for industrial development. Factories are growing like mushrooms and soon the westerly wind will carry the smoke from their chimneys across the city and pollute the air. Businessmen and industrialists are agitating to bring a broad-gauge railway line to Jaipur. Mine seems to be the only voice of dissent to this scheme. We are well served by a narrow-gauge railway, good roads, and an airport. Forty miles to the west and thirty miles to the east of Jaipur there are two railway junctions on the broad-gauge line. This is where the railways could carry the heavy equipment needed for setting up factories, and this is where an industrial area is most needed to provide employment for the countless landless labourers. In this way the industrial development could expand without subjecting the city to the problems of environmental pollution which most other cities are facing. I can never understand why we cannot preserve the natural advantages that we have. Fortunately, the Government of Rajasthan has at last recognized that Jaipur's appeal to both domestic and foreign tourists lies in its walled city with its indigenous architecture coloured the famous Jaipur pink. Efforts are being made to preserve these, and much of the damage that was done almost two decades ago when I appealed to Pandit Nehru for help has been repaired.

I have now moved to the Lillypool, the house in the gardens of Rambagh that Jai had planned for us to live in. The house itself is not particularly grand or especially beautiful, but it stands in a lovely garden and all the rooms are bright and airy. I have my own lawn-tennis court and a swimming-pool, but what I like best about the house is the feeling of space. It is open all round and one has the feeling of living out of doors. All my life I have preferred the country to the constrictions of a town, so I am happy at the Lillypool. People wander in and out of the house—it has that sort of informal happy atmosphere. A group of young boys have made a habit of coming there, and they play cricket on my tennis-court and so there is always the sound of young voices and laughter.

Most of the ornaments, the jade, the rose quartz, the crystal that Jai had placed in my apartments when I came as a bride to Rambagh, are in storage at the moment, but I expect to bring them up to my new home to remind me of the happiness of those years. I would love to have Jai's many trophies—I have lived with them most of my life—but I think they should go, along with his polo helmets and sticks and other polo equipment, to the Memorabilia Room in the City Palace.

In the Lillypool, these days, I have far too large a staff for my needs, but it is difficult to dismiss people who have spent their lives in the service of the Jaipur ruling family. Sometimes I think of all the houses and palaces I have lived in over the years. Rambagh is now a hotel; Rajmahal, occupied at the moment by Bubbles, is soon to become one. The palace in Cooch Behar is fast disintegrating from neglect, but there are plans to remodel it as a medical school and teaching hospital. "Woodlands" remains only as a name in Calcutta, and I no longer have any occasion to visit "Colinton," our house in Darjeeling.

Recently I returned to Laxmi Vilas, my grandparents' palace in Baroda. As I walked through the main gate into the pre-monsoon brown and deadened garden, I half expected some ghostly trumpeter to strike up the Baroda anthem. I wandered through the undergrowth where the tennis-courts used to be, remembering the rather agonizing tennis tournaments, with all of us girls dressed in saris, when I partnered my cousins with such scrupulous politeness that the ball often shot between us, leaving us both courteously saying, "Yours."

Laxmi Vilas now contains a much less lavish life; the only things left unchanged are my grandfather's trained parrots. In the evening they were brought in to entertain me, and once again they fired their deafening salute on the little silver cannon.

Often I go in the evenings to the terrace at Moti Doongri and watch for the particular moment in Jaipur's twilight when the whole city glows with a warm rosy light. I can hear the temple bells announcing the evening *arti*, the prayers and offerings that accompany the presentation of the sacred fire to the deity. For a few minutes during that incredibly lovely time I can forget the changes that have come to the city and the people Jai loved and served so well. I can imagine that Jai will soon appear to have a picnic dinner with me, as he so often did in Moti Doongri, and that afterwards we will drive back to our home in Rambagh Palace.

Index